AWAKEN
YOUR CREATIVE
POTENTIAL
The Odyssey Begins

AWAKEN
YOUR CREATIVE
POTENTIAL
The Odyssey Begins

**Exploring A Heightened Order
Of Creative Functioning**

CONRAD SATALA,M.S.

with the assistance of
Joy Heinbaugh,M.S.

CLS press
**published in cooperation with
Knoll Publishing Company, Inc.**

I personally wish to thank
Joseph Laiacona
President of Knoll Publishing Co
for his guiding role in the
publication of this book

Published by **CLS press** in cooperation with Knoll Publishing
Company, Inc.
CLS press
305 West Washington Blvd., Fort Wayne, Indiana 46802.
Produced on a Macintosh SE and LaserWriter Plus using ITC
Bookman-10 point.

The author would like to thank the following publishers for
their permission to reprint:

Joy's Way by W. Brugh Joy, M.D. Copyright © 1979 by W.
Brugh Joy, M.D. Reprinted by permission of J.P. Tarcher, Inc.

The Possible Human by Jean Houston. Copyright © 1982 by
Jean Houston. Reprinted by permission of J.P. Tarcher, Inc.

The Body Quantum by Fred Alan Wolf. Copyright © 1986 by
Youniverse Seminars, Inc. Reprinted by permission of
MACMILLAN PUBLISHING COMPANY.

Library Of Congress Catalog No. 88-90616
ISBN: 0-940267-03-9 (paper)

10 9 8 7 6 5 4 3 2 1
First Edition

For those individuals who have chosen to awaken,
and the freedom I received from my parents
to actively explore life,
THANK-YOU!

CONTENTS

Cover Art:
Ilene Rush-Satala

Photography:
Jorge Ayala

FOREWORD

It is always exciting to experience another person's awakening into more expanded possibilities as a human being. In this book, Conrad Satala not only touches upon the best of contemporary vision regarding the process of significant changes in human consciousness, but adds his own creative experiences as well.

A personal transformation is always unique to the individual. The reader must be cautious and not expect to emulate identical paths of those who are clearly demonstrating these wonderful human potentials. Teachers like Conrad are capable of inducting major change in anyone who approaches either their writings and/or their class work because they manifest heightened states of awareness, and not because of a specific path of development. Therefore, the reader is encouraged to open to the *feelings* evoked by this material and not solely to concentrate on the concepts and instructions. It is the creative interaction between a heightened teacher/writer and the reader that inducts the reader into transformation.

You will find many of the techniques offered in this book so helpful to your unfoldment that you may think they were created just for you. But again, simply tuning to the energy behind this material offers, in my opinion, the greatest potential for personal transformation.

Often people approaching transformational process imagine expanded awareness to be solely psychic phenomena, such as out of body experiences, or states of bliss in which one is totally removed from the world. Conrad correctly presents the thrust of expanded awareness as representing a vastly enriched livingness, wherein the individual appreciates the fundamental interrelatedness of mind/body/spirit and the world at large.

The problem with many approaches to spiritual transforma tion is an escapist philosophy which tends to further divide the human psyche. In this book you are encouraged to renew your deeper appreciation of the physical form as a direct manifestation of your own spirit!

As you savor the richness of this book, I encourage you to evaluate the material through your own explorations. It is the fruit of your endeavor which should form the basis of evaluation, and not intellectual assessment. Although I have not personally tested the validity of many of Conrad's ideas, I can state that I feel the importance of Conrad's efforts as writer, teacher, and founder of a transformational organization lies in his living example, to which his many students can attest. Thus this book is a threshold to a personal living Presence, unique to you.

W. Brugh Joy, M.D.
    author of **Joy's Way**
        Lucerne Valley, California,

INTRODUCTION

THE NEW RENAISSANCE: SOUL AND BODY BECOME ONE

AWAKEN YOUR CREATIVE POTENTIAL is an odyssey into allowing you to understand a deeper part of yourself. In the course of your journey, you will learn how to shift your perceptions from an outer into an inner-awareness, altering your current perceptions about yourself and the ways you perceive and interact within the world around you. Rather than utilizing an intellectual process to understand these new concepts or ideas, this odyssey will awaken you into a direct exploration and a mapping out of your own inner realms, allowing you to experience a new and heightened order of creativity. This process will awaken an inner energy, a creative self-actualizing pulse within your heart, opening you into new explorations and inner dimensions of time and space. It is a journey that will guide you into your next level of human development, which I and others call the "post-biological phase."

This awakening begins an exploration into understanding yourself as an interacting human energy system, opening you into the inner dimensions of what it means to be human. You will directly experience the constant dance that occurs within yourself, with others, and with your environment, as all of life moves toward a greater unity and wholeness.

Such a quantum change is not new for human beings. Historically, the last time that a similar quantum shift took place was during the fourteenth century, when humanity moved from the medieval Dark Ages into the light of the Renaissance period. Suddenly people began to perceive their world through a new set of perceptions and subsequently began to live life differently. The transition period continued for nearly three hundred years, as a new cultural and creative revolution emerged. The way in which human beings perceived, sensed, and interacted with one another and with their world changed drastically. New perceptions of art, color, music, literature, science, and spirituality were brought forward. All of the perceptions that had existed during the medieval or Dark Ages became markedly altered. And today we question how civilization could possibly have existed without perceiving life from the viewpoint of these "new" perspectives.

For the first time in history, we are at a point of experiencing and understanding a quantum shift which can allow our inner consciousness to directly alter the outer perceptions of our world. Individuals can now choose to shift their outer perceptions into an inner-awareness, opening into a new way of perceiving and creating with life. We can assume that a similar unconscious process emerged at the onset of what we call the Renaissance, since individuals living prior to that time were not capable of perceiving many of the facets of life that we today take for granted.

At that time in history, I believe some inner guiding or self-actualizing force undoubtedly emerged which allowed man as a species to awaken and evolve into a new inner perceptual space, laying the foundation for our current theories of reality. Through this process, man learned to quantify, predict, and understand the objective world, thus moving mankind into a more complex form of synthesis in thinking. At the same time, mankind awakened into a new depth of outer sensations, which heightened his/her ability to perceive a new vividness and depth in color. All of these changes have since remained as the basis for man's outer understanding of reality.

At this time in our human development, humanity has once again begun to feel inadequate or incomplete in maintaining traditional structures as its current perceptions of outer reality. There exist a number of critical questions that have remained unanswered about the interaction and synthesis between man's brain, body, and inner consciousness. We have awakened to an inner world of perceptions, feelings, and sensations that are unexplained by our current theories of outer reality. I believe that we are once again within the process of a new evolutionary breakthrough that began in the late nineteenth century and that will probably continue for another several hundred years. During the next quarter of a century, we will be experiencing a major transitional period that will awaken humanity to a new level of inner exploration. A totally new perspective will emerge through an understanding of what our inner world is capable of performing and through an understanding of the laws that govern our outer constructs of reality. Through the emergence of inner explorations, mankind will begin to learn how to consciously direct the inner energies existing within the heart into a new order of creative functioning.

I believe that once the major transition period subsides, mankind will likely continue to explore these ideas for another one hundred years or more. This will then be followed by a much longer phase of exploration, during which time new depths will emerge in the ways in which man lives and creates from the new levels of inner perceptions, and this will continue to evolve during a cycle of several hundred years. This will be a process similar to, yet different than, that which occurred during the last Renaissance. This time man will be fully awake and will be aware of each of the choices as they are explored!

Throughout all of recorded history, there has been a simultaneous process of exciting civilizations evolving into new forms of creative expression and perceptual understanding, as other existing civilizations were on the decline. Some civilizations have lasted for longer periods of time than others. What we would call "modern civilization" occupies a rather short period of time in our understanding of what we perceive to be our current constructs of reality. As we enter this present twenty-five year transition period, we are existing at a point in history where no one civilization is at the focal point. Rather, we are in the midst of a Planet Earth Renaissance during which no particular civilization will emerge as a leader. We are moving toward an inner awakening that is infinitely more profound and perpetuates a deeper consequence of change than anything previously encountered in recorded history.

With the availability of rapid communication and travel, no one part of the planet can exist in isolation from its other parts. We have the capability to communicate information on a moment by moment basis. However, this new Renaissance is not going to witness a change merely in our outer perceptions or understanding. We are in the process of a quantum shift to understand and perceive both ourselves and our world from a totally new inner perspective. We are becoming one living unit with our planet and are moving toward a level of both perceiving and creating life in a very different way. We are face to face with the fundamental question humanity has pondered throughout the ages: "What is my true purpose for living? What is it I am meant to do?"

As our planet undergoes this next phase of its Renaissance, individuals will begin to shift their focus from one of gathering outer information into one of exploring inner consciousness. This shift is the underlying reason for today's seemingly continuous state of confusion, as well as for the acceleration in both the creation of vast amounts of outer information (doubling every six years) and in the awakening of individuals to an awareness of an inner consciousness (with the number of awakening individuals doubling every three to four years). This, I believe, is the direct result of the major transition period through which we are currently moving. Many individuals are already referring to this transition phase as "the time of chaos," because they find it difficult to accumulate, process, and assimilate all of the types and levels of information that are presently being generated. Everything that we thought we knew and understood no longer works in the same predictable way as before. Throughout the "information age," we will continue accumulating more and more data until we realize that whatever we believe our outer focus is capable of producing, can and will be proven through some form of scientific exploration. We will begin to understand some of the basic tenets of the quantum theory, such as "the observer effect" and the role it plays in the creation of our daily existence. As an outgrowth of this phase of confusion, we will begin to acknowledge the existence of another structure of reality that is actually more powerful and more vast than the structures we now call outer or consensus reality. We will come to realize that an infinitely deeper aspect unites and holds together what we now perceive as life.

As an increasing number of individuals awaken into an inner consciousness, humanity will shift into what some scientists and philosophers are calling the "age of consciousness." Only as we near the end of the twenty-five year transition period will the age of consciousness become a primary level of exploration for mankind as a whole. At that point we will be at a new beginning in our quest to live from the next phase of human development— the post-biological phase. The "age of consciousness" will allow us to explore depths of human potential that are now difficult for most to even imagine.

Due to the earlier Renaissance, man's intellect has evolved to the point that it is considered to be one of the most dynamic and important aspects of living. Individuals who possess "great minds" are admired by their fellow men. They are brought into positions of authority and are given the responsibility of creating laws and of governing others. As we enter the post-biological phase, the strong emphasis that we have placed upon outer awareness and intellectual understanding will no longer be of primary importance. It will become but a stepping-stone for us to deepen into our own inner-awareness, as we explore an inner understanding of our creative potential through the awakening of an inner self-actualizing energy, or what some refer to as an aspect of spiritual or inner guidance.

Although the intellect has served us well over the years, mankind is now in the midst of a new renaissance— one during which the focus will no longer be directed toward the development of the outer intellect and its perceptions of the outer world. We have neglected our inner emotional development for so long that current scientific researchers view man's human emotional condition as being very primitive or "animal like." We have currently placed so much emphasis on our verbal intellectual abilities, that we have ignored a more powerful inner emotional force, a feeling state of unconditional love that extends beyond our primitive human emotions. As we awaken into the awareness of an inner consciousness, we will begin an exploration of reeducation, whereby our intellect and our emotions will evolve into a new order of functioning. We will evolve into a realization that every human being maintains an inner world that is actually more organized, more loving and gentle, and infinitely vaster, than that of the outer intellect. This awareness is capable of moving us into realms which the outer intellect cannot even begin to comprehend.

We have been mistaken in our earlier perceptions that the inner world is one of chaos, disruption, and confusion. The inner feelings of our most primitive human emotions are the only emotions that we have as yet learned to develop. Up to now they have emerged only as feedback for us to understand the intellect, which has operated independently of our inner awareness, or inner self-actualizing path. But when the intellect at last moves into balance with the inner creative force, our outer emotions will also shift into a totally different level of sensations, feelings, and perceptions, thus allowing us to experience our outer world differently.

During our new Renaissance, we will explore the vast and changing areas of science and gain a deeper understanding of the human brain and nervous system. As we begin to directly experience the awakening of our inner energies, we will learn to channel the inner creative self-actualizing energies into our new human potential— our post-biological phase of development. Through the activation of this creative inner pulse, we will move into an awakening of both our inner and outer sensations, which will then transform our current beliefs, attitudes, and perceptions into a much larger gestalt or global perspective.

As we awaken into the post-biological phase of development, we will begin to explore the vast resources of our own "inner space" and will then open into a new understanding of "inner timing." As we allow these levels to emerge, we will begin to awaken a powerful loving force of energy. And as this level of energy emerges, it initiates the process of self-actualization of our own unique inner blueprint. This inner self-actualizing energy is one of the strongest and most powerful of human resources. Its awakening releases within each of our hearts a new understanding of ourselves and of others. As we allow the inner energies to merge with the physical body, we will begin to live under the guidance of our inner spiritual self. I believe this will become the next level of human development and the beginning stages of living in the next Renaissance

The inner shift of one's consciousness will allow us as human beings to be fully conscious and alert to our own inner-directed nature, which in turn will open us into a new depth of awareness and into new levels of human functioning. It will free us from the limited and primitive emotional ways of the present, bringing to us the opportunity to create with life, rather than reacting to it. The movement into our post-biological development will free us from being held prisoner by the limited concepts of what we perceive we can or cannot do. We will awaken into new awarenesses of both outer and inner sensations. Through the new levels of inner sensation will emerge a profound level of inner silence and peace, opening us to understanding new psychological and emotional constructs of ourselves as humans. We will awaken into a spiritual understanding that will allow our current states of meditation or prayer to deepen, opening our awareness into the inner realms of transpersonal or mystical experiences. Through such an inner spiritual emergence, all previously held perceptions will be altered and brought into a new inner perspective of unity. This becomes the actual awakening into our next level of human development— the merging of the inner spiritual self and the physical self.

New potentials and vistas will subsequently emerge regarding what human beings are physically, emotionally, intellectually, and spiritually capable of becoming. Our world view will also change, as we will no longer be focused merely upon ourselves and our immediate world. We will inherently desire to explore new ways of interacting with one another.

As we deepen further into the inner self-actualizing energies, we will automatically move into and create a new level of relationships with our inner self, our loved ones, friends, workers, and humanity in general. Our understanding of our collective heritage will become more complete. As a result, we will move into the unique position of awakening our own individual potential while simultaneously awakening new levels of cooperative ventures with others. For the first time in recorded history, mankind will be able to develop both the individual potential and the collective potential, without the need to eliminate one in order that the other might thrive. Humanity will learn to explore ways whereby both individuals and nations may "win" simultaneously. We will at last begin to encompass an understanding of the personal and planetary role in our own solar system and in the vast universe that extends beyond it.

A new form of psychology will emerge that will no longer be based upon limited or negative aspects of self. Those in the helping professions will no longer aid individuals in adapting to a system that is, in truth, calling out to the individual for change. There will evolve an understanding that each individual has his/her own very unique journey on the earth, and that it is important not to "normalize" any human being into a particular mold. Instead, we will create a new set of perceptions, attitudes, and beliefs regarding who we are and what we are becoming. The feedback of this direction will become apparent as we explore the evolving phase of post-biological development and allow the inner self-actualizing force to emerge. The process of learning will be totally new and different, unlike the traditional years of scholarly instruction that most individuals attempt, only to find that they still feel inadequate in their understanding of basic human values, of their world, and of themselves.

In both Eastern and Western civilizations, we have focused our awareness for the center point of physical balance and gravity of the body at a point an inch or two below the navel. Some cultures have called this point the "Hara Center." This focal point has allowed individuals to harness an inner bodily strength and has become the focus for their inner consciousness. As we move into our post-biological development, the focal point of awareness for both our physical body and our inner consciousness will shift into the heart chakra, which is located at the center of the chest cavity. This will allow humanity to awaken and create from a totally new foundation. A heart-centered focus will allow us to move into our own inner self-actualizing energy, which will guide our physiological and psychological processes into the direction of unity.

Initially this may all sound quite complex to you and may seem to be a great deal to cover in a single book. In one respect it is! And yet, once an individual begins the inner awakening into his/her own inner guidance, it moves very quickly. In fact, some individuals feel that the process actually moves too quickly, and they would prefer to slow it down. But once you begin your own journey, you will experience for yourself the natural ascent into becoming YOU!

If I were to discuss each one of the aforementioned ideas in a linear fashion, it would take volumes of information to bring forward even a minimal level of understanding; and many readers undoubtedly would still not understand how to apply the ideas in their own lives. However, I am not going to be talking about this information, nor am I going to be trying to help you to intellectually understand it. Instead, I will be guiding you through a series of EXPLORATIONS, allowing you to experience for yourself the inner spaces and creative potentials. Once you have begun to open to your own inner self-actualizing energy and can allow this level of the Divine or spirit to emerge, you will easily open into your own level of inner knowing. It will ignite YOU, just as it has ignited me and the others who have preceded you in this odyssey.

This odyssey is a synthesis of information ranging from that of the ancient mystics to a blending of the current ideas of scientific exploration. I follow no outer specific formal school of thought. This odyssey has evolved as a result of my own personal awakening, my inner synthesizing of the resulting information, and the processes through which I have learned to bring this into a living structure. Thousands of individuals have awakened into their own odyssey, learning to leave behind old habits, perceptions, beliefs, feelings, sensations, and body structures (anything that limited them) and have learned to awaken to a process of "getting out of their own way."

I have found this process to be an exciting and safe way to peel back layer upon layer of man's traditional outer focus, thereby allowing a deeper layer of inner creative self-actualizing energy (or the Divine Essence) to emerge. With this emergence, our lives, perceptions, and the quality of interactions change drastically, allowing us to move into our own levels of inner perceptions and creative expression.

The journey of allowing myself to change and of watching other individuals experience and understand similar events in their own lives has been very fulfilling to me. For me, understanding how each individual can be guided into his/her own inner purpose, and yet simultaneously be synchronized in a "dance" with humanity, is a profound experience. **AWAKEN YOUR CREATIVE POTEN-TIAL** will guide you into unknown parts of yourself. As you open into your own inner creative self-actualizing source, you will be released into the "Divine Essence from within your heart" and will explore ways of allowing this essence to emerge into all aspects of living. This is the ultimate realization of one's human potential.

I begin all individual and group sessions with an exploration of centering into one's inner self-actualizing awareness. This shifts one's focus from the perspective of the outer mind and its everyday concerns into the "observer state," allowing the heightened ener-gies of the inner-directed guidance to emerge. The process of cen-tering will change throughout our explorations, as it will be based upon the level of inner awareness which we are exploring at any given time.

If you have a tape recorder nearby, allow yourself at this time to play the commercial edition of EXPLORATION #1: BASIC CEN-TERING. If a recorder is not available, or if you have not purchased the accompanying tapes, read through the following exploration and follow this basic centering process to shift your awareness into the observer state. If you prefer, you yourself can prepare a tape (or tapes) by reading and recording this and subsequent exercises. The *** indicates a pause to allow for your inner movement. When multiple groups of *** *** appear, allow accordingly for longer periods of time.

"Close your eyes *** allow the focus of your inner-awareness to shift into the center of your inner screen *** allow that awareness to shift into the center of your chest *** ask to feel and sense a radiance of emerald green light slowly pulsating from the center of your chest *** allow the waves of this pulsation to slowly deepen into the center of your chest and to spread throughout your physical body*** allow it to move to the tips of your fingers and toes *** if you wish, ask the pulsation of emerald green light to deepen, and then just let it happen, for it knows what to do *** ask it to move beyond the limits of your body *** ask that light to become brighter, and to release pulsation after pulsation of waves of emerald green light *** *** *** allow your awareness to remain within this inner focus, continuing to release these waves even after your eyes are open *** open your eyes when you are ready."

Begin exploring your own creative potential by reading this book from the observer state. You will begin to recognize when you are within this state, because you will continue to feel the subtle movements of the inner pulsations at the heart chakra moving through you. If you shift out of this awareness, allow yourself the time to focus back into the observer state.

I would like to close this introduction with a statement concerning my present understanding of my own PURPOSE OF BEING HUMAN:

"In exploring this odyssey through life,

I am to awaken to my inner heritage of being a creative human being;

I am to open to all of life that manifests this DIVINE ESSENCE;

I am to create and live from this union of the Divine with my physical body, allowing the focus of my awareness to be within the rhythm of my inner heart, from which each thought, feeling, and image emerges.

Through the inner awakening of my self-actualizing energy, my own livingness will emerge into a heightened order of creativity.

And thus evolves the next evolutionary leap into our human potential!"

CHAPTER ONE

OUR PURPOSE OF
BEING HUMAN

In early December of 1981, as I returned to my office following a well-deserved vacation, I experienced an overwhelming desire to enter into meditation. Stretching out on the floor, I felt a spiral of powerful energy move through me as I simultaneously opened into a profound feeling of inner ecstasy. Within this space I felt nurtured, loved, and secure. A new level of inner silence emerged that allowed me to directly feel the presence of my own inner guidance or creative self-actualizing energy. Although similar experiences had been rather common for me since 1977, this one felt very different.

During the meditative experience I was shown a letter bearing that very day's date at the top. It was a letter of resignation from my position in the Department of Consultation and Education at the Mental Health Center in Fort Wayne. I was next shown an image of myself opening a center in downtown Fort Wayne, where I would conduct a series of explorations called "The Human Energy System and Transformation." I then saw a list of individuals to contact who would help me to organize a series of free lectures that I was to conduct at the downtown public library during the second week of January 1982, a mere six weeks hence. I received information concerning a meeting room at a local church where I would hold the initial eight-week exploration entitled "Exploring The Human Energy System and Transformation," and I was informed that by the time the last meeting of this series took place a facility would become available for the center that I would be establishing.

Every possible objection that my outer mind could bring forward emerged simultaneously—money, bills, work, feeling responsible to my family and friends, and a host of other legitimate outer objections. However, as long as the powerful self-actualizing energy was flowing through me, none of the objections seemed to hold any weight or validity, and I was shown how to move easily and quickly through them. The final piece of information which I received focused upon my readiness to explore the next phase of my post-biological development as a human being. Whatever that might mean!

Over an hour had passed since I had first been drawn into the meditation, and when I got up I felt stunned. I sat down at my desk and stared out the window wondering, "Am I really ready, today, to embark upon this next phase— not in a year or two, but now?" The mere presence of that one doubting question brought forth a massive anxiety attack. However, I instantly felt an energy move and quicken within me, propelling me back into my previous level of profound inner silence and peace. As a result of this experience I understood what I needed to do, and I knew that my reply to the previous self-inquiry was an unequivocal, "YES! YES! NOW!"

Writing **AWAKEN YOUR CREATIVE POTENTIAL: THE ODYSSEY BEGINS** allows me to summarize and share with you my personal transformative experiences covering the years of my life from 1970 to the end of 1987. I now realize that this period of my life can be broken down into four distinct phases. Each one of these phases encompassed a particular level of understanding for me in relationship to how and what I perceived the construction of my outer reality to be in each respective phase. I was thus able to open into and explore a certain level of "inner knowing" through my own inner guidance during each phase.

While engrossed in the process of living within a particular phase, I would continually think to myself "What more could possibly exist beyond this point of awareness?" I now realize that these inner questionings and feelings were my first indication that something new and profound was about to begin. Such thoughts were always followed by drastic changes in my meditations. What seemed to be naturally coming forward for me no longer was effective. I would also begin to feel an inner restlessness and would feel uncomfortable exploring the inner states. At the same time, however, I was able to maintain and live an outer awareness that was more stable and profound than I had ever before thought possible. I soon realized that these times were not the same as those when both my outer and inner-awareness felt unstable, restless, and disruptive, indicating that I was avoiding something in my life. This form of inner restlessness with outer stability seems yet today to always precede an inner shift in my awareness.

I now realize that each one of my four major phases contained four sublevels. The way I interacted and communicated with my inner guidance always changed, opening me into a new awareness of inner spiritual understanding. My physical body would begin to change both its physical shape and its flexibility in movement. My emotional awareness deepened, while I continued to explore and directly feel levels of human emotion that I had never realized were possible. At the same time my intellectual and verbal processing of information, as well as my perceptions of my outer environment, would be altered. This change somehow allowed me to inwardly understand new levels of information, and to be able at the same time to communicate the information to others.

Although individually the four sublevels of change were not as dramatic as the composite restructuring of each major phase, they did collectively blend together to create a new inner dynamic. Change within one level automatically precipitated a change in another. Not until I had moved through the inner experiences would I realize that something new and profound had just occurred. As I explored the sublevels, I began to feel excited and secure about the ways in which I was going to be changing. This also paved the way for the emergence of a major transformative energy that would then restructure quite easily and quickly the ways in which I perceived, interacted, and communicated with my inner guidance and my outer world.

Each awakening experience began with a quickening of a self-actualizing energy within my body. As a result, every perception that I maintained of a well-defined, structured, solid world began to change. My physical body subsequently changed in ways that made no sense to my outer intellectual mind. I found myself in the process of exploring a new level of inner development, where shifts in my consciousness would bring me into contact with a world and a body that was very fluid and unrestricted. By exploring these inner spaces, or transpersonal realms of human nature, I could see beyond the linear, logical, objective structures of reality.

Today when I begin to feel the same quickening of my self-actualizing energy, I allow the tingling sensation or inner move-ment to spread through my body. I no longer interpret these feelings as anxiety as I once did; I now realize that I will move naturally into an inner level of profound silence and peace, thus allowing a needed level of information to emerge from my inner guidance. This inner silence may emerge through my dreams, during meditation, or while I am fully awake. Once I learned to surrender into my inner feelings, they became a very significant feedback for me. On the other hand, when I find myself in a state of worry, doubt, or anxiety, or when I am trying to intellectually convince myself to do something, the inner levels of profound silence and peace are not present, and my body experiences a very perceivable level of anxiety or tension.

Throughout this book I will be interweaving my own personal journey of transformation, sharing how the last seventeen years have paved the way for my present level of exploration, in spite of the fact that my outer mind initially had no understanding of what was happening. As a result of my own personal experiences within the process of transformational psychology, I now realize that through the unfoldment of an inner awakening energy, I began the exploration into my inner post-biological development by merely following an inner self-actualizing guiding structure. Although all individuals will experience their own unique inner journey, they will follow an outer mechanism of change that will be similar.

Much of my personal anxiety, my feelings of incompleteness, and my relentless search for information and understanding were finally being fulfilled when in 1978 this awakening began to move me into directly experiencing my post-biological development. Once I could begin to understand a certain aspect of my development, it would then begin to change automatically. Sometimes I would feel that my inner guidance had left me, or that I was doing something wrong, because I was not able to feel or understand things in the same way that I had earlier experienced them. Later I realized that my inner sensations and guidance indeed were and always had been there; I was merely changing the way in which I received my inner communication. I realize now that it was vital that I spend a great deal of time learning how to read the "map" for each of the subsequent phases of my life.

The first phase of my odyssey had actually begun prior to the experience in late 1981 with a series of subtle inner-awarenesses about the need for me to change both my understanding of my purpose for life and the direction my life was needing to take. A series of significant dreams and other unique experiences which began in 1970 were, as I can now clearly see, the subtle awakening of the inner guidance that was available to me. As early as 1973 I had begun to directly experience this form of inner-directed guidance, as a result of which I was inwardly led through a series of life changes that ultimately altered my career, my personal relationships, and my geographical location.

My second phase of awakening began in 1978, when I was brought into a direct awareness of my own inner guidance (or what I call my soul energy), and terminated with the meditative experience in December of 1981, which led to my resignation from the Mental Health Center in Fort Wayne. During this second phase, I began directly experiencing a series of transformative changes which ultimately altered my physical body in a very profound way and brought a major "jolt" to my outer mind's intellectual understanding of my definition of spirit. These levels of change continued over the next three years.

I began experiencing another heightening of the self-actualizing energies in the fall of 1982 (nine months after opening my center), which then awakened me into another totally new structure of inner human development and creative potential. Within this newly awakened state, I was capable of accessing and experiencing new levels of transpersonal awareness while simultaneously maintaining my focus and movements in an outer awareness. At this point in time, my meditative states merged with and became my outer reality.

I later understood that all of the feelings and perceptions which I had experienced, had been emerging from an inner state of energy or vibration which can be called "unconditional love." Whenever I experienced this state of energy, my outer awareness would shift naturally into a state of unified consciousness. And in experiencing these levels of unconditional love, all of my personality traits, my problems, and my primitive feelings would shift into a newly emerging perception of unity. Thus, I could directly merge with my self-actualizing energy or unconditional love, and this would allow me to maintain the new perceptions as my patterns of living and thinking. These experiences moved me beyond the beliefs that I had so firmly held concerning the structures of consensus reality. They also changed my beliefs about the need for the existence of duality in my life; I no longer saw people or situations as being either right or wrong, good or evil, or one way as compared to another. Through this energetic awakening, I no longer needed to try to be different. I now very naturally saw and interacted with life from a totally different perspective.

As I awakened into my post-biological development, my focus effortlessly shifted from a dependency upon the logical, linear structures of reality. I no longer saw life as a series of problems and diseases. For the first time I was able to clearly and objectively view myself and others from an observer state. I was able to perceive the limits that we have constructed through our cognitive processes, and to simultaneously see the various ways we waste and misuse personal energy both in our need to collect vast amounts of information and in our need to control one another. I could clearly perceive the limits I had established by maintaining my outer perceptions of fears, doubts, and misgivings concerning what I could do or create. The self-actualizing energy shifted my personal focus into an observer state, whereby I was shown how to allow the new inner perceptions to begin their emergence as the new reality for daily living, thus greatly altering the way I interacted and created with others. Through this level of my inner development, I began to sense what others have referred to as the "divine aspect of living as a human being."

This particular phase continued until the late fall of 1985, when yet a deeper understanding of my inner world began to emerge. Within this fourth phase, I became aware that I had the full conscious choice of being able to live and create each day while living from the inner awareness state. I call this experience coexistence, and I believe that this level of awareness is the inherent potential from which man shall live in the twenty-first century. Writing this book, then, constitutes the completion of the four phases of my personal odyssey. And even now, a new level of the same self-actualizing energy is once again beginning to quicken within me as I feel myself being drawn into a fifth phase. My first glimpses of this phase seem to be guiding me into a yet more profound inner realm, one that extends even beyond my wildest dreams and expectations. The inner self-actualizing force or guidance is again asking me to make a deeper commitment to a level of continual change, exploring aspects of my Being as a physical, living, transformative self. It is with this excitement that I bring forward this book.

Although the concept of post-biological development is relatively new (Joseph Chilton Pearce, Brugh Joy, John Lilly, Gopi Krishna, and Sri Aurobindo are but a few who have explored it), the process has existed for thousands of years. It is looked upon as a time in one's life when an individual reaches a certain level of maturity and achieves a certain hypothetical level of competency within the outer world. Generally such an individual demonstrates certain leadership abilities and thus is given the opportunity to explore the deeper inner realms. Such individuals have often been the elders in a community, the chief or ruler, a witch doctor or a medicine woman or man. Most of these individuals reached a chronological age that allowed them to become the community leader, although most had been identified at a very young age as having such potential. By today's standards, our leaders must demonstrate a totally different form of leadership— a leadership that evolves through a mastery of verbal and intellectual skills.

With the changing patterns of today's culture and the directions in which we are moving, we now know that this process into post-biological development should be a natural part of young adulthood, constituting our natural transition into maturity. Yet very few individuals ever truly awaken into this level. Why? Do you remember feeling that something very "special" or "wonderful" was about to happen when you were in your adolescence? You might have felt that a certain missing piece of information was going to be given to you. Did you feel that your understanding of life and spirituality was about to change and move into a very special space? Did you sense that with this missing piece of information your life would finally feel and be complete? But what actually happened? As I explore these specific feelings with individuals, I find that many of them have experienced very similar feelings and thoughts around this same age, but rarely did anything change for them.

Upon reaching the period of adolescence, we as human beings have completed a phase of the exploration of our biological and our outer physical world, but we have acquired little or no understanding of the exploration needed within the inner realms of ourselves. Adolescence is the time for questioning concepts of authority and exploring ideas about religious, moral and ethical issues, both on an individual and on a collective level. Few adolescents, though, ever experience any real inner peace with or comprehension of these areas; rather, they learn, just as others have learned before them, to put these issues aside, buckle down, grow up and explore life as everyone else does. Most individuals enter adulthood without an inner sense of accomplishment, security, inner peace, or any real knowledge of what life is all about. I feel that much of this is due to a total lack of awareness of the transpersonal and inner structures that exist within each of us. For it is within these inner energetic realms that our next level of development begins to unfold, our post-biological phase. The first eighteen years of life actually constitute the preparation for the subsequent level of inner evolution that awaits us as human beings.

Pearce in his book entitled **Magical Child Matures**, calls this process "reversibility." During the first 15 to 18 years of life we follow an inner-biologically controlled process of development through our physical, emotional, mental, sexual, creative, and spiritual self. From the time of birth these levels of biological energies are released in each human being by means of an inner timetable. As the individual interacts with the outer environment, inner-biological energies are restructured to allow a learning and maturation process to take place. Both are necessary, as the inner-biological energies must interact with the outer energies in one's life in order for the process to awaken. But as we enter our post-biological development, we are no longer dependent upon our innate biological energies. Rather, we need to begin the "inner journey," allowing the awakening of the inner self-actualizing energy to begin guiding us through the remainder of our life.

For this process to occur, individuals often need, at various conjunctures within the journey, an outer teacher— one who has already awakened to and has stabilized the inner energy. Only an individual who has already stabilized this energy can safely and effectively guide another through the inner creative processes. It is not so much a matter of the outer information (such as books or words) that an outer teacher brings forward during this stage; rather, it is the levels of self-actualizing energy that have been inwardly mastered that become the important tool in awakening the creative potential in others. Throughout the biological phase an individual requires specific and structured levels of linear information in order to build a solid foundation for understanding and mastering outer reality. During the post-biological phase, however, the individual no longer needs the linear information; instead, it is the heightened energies of the outer teacher that carry the potential for naturally awakening the energies within another person. As the self-actualizing energy is awakened, it flows naturally as an inner vibration, awakening one into new levels of non-linear understanding and into the inner perceptions of what life has to offer. This opens us into a totally new process of learning and living. Very few teachers, however, presently exist who can truly energetically awaken the post-biological phase in others. Many possess sufficient levels of outer information and understanding for this process, but few have mastered the necessary levels of energy required to energetically stimulate other individuals and bring forward the outer nonlinear structures capable of naturally directing them into their own inner self-actualizing guidance. No amount of talking can bring forth this next level of development. Only a heightened focused energy from one's heart chakra can accomplish the transition into this next phase!

The odyssey into post-biological development is not merely a passive state of meditation, nor is it an intellectual exploration into ourselves or into the reality that we create; rather, this odyssey is an active exploration into our next levels of human development. Current theories of Developmental Psychology regarding outer biological development do a wonderful job of exploring the physical, emotional, biological, intellectual and moral development of human beings up through the age of young adulthood. But when we reach adulthood, it seems that our development comes to a virtual halt. We are taught that it now takes longer periods of time between each successive stage of growth in order to master our outer world. There exists a massive amount of information and data demonstrating the process of development during our first eighteen years of existence, but very little information concerning the next eighty years. Yet, how many adults ever truly feel that they are masters of their lives? If our current crises in the areas of drugs, alcohol, sexuality, physical and emotional abuse, and literacy are any indication, then our level of mastery or comfort is neither very steady nor very complete.

With the level of maturity that is achieved at about the age of eighteen, we are able to interact with other human beings on an intellectual, emotional, physical, sexual, financial, and creative level. We also function within some context of a religious understanding, even though this may take the form of denial or questioning of the use of religious structures within one's life. At this stage of development, we are told that we have reached the beginning stages of adulthood, and we are led to believe that we have now fulfilled the physical, biological, and educational requirements necessary for life. At this point we can choose whether we will move onward and create in the outer world through our job, personal relationships, and family or whether we will move into other institutions for higher learning. We generally are of the opinion that our basic level of learning has been completed. Most people will then live their entire lives focused on the development of physical and material power and the potential it can create for them in their outer world. This can be seen on both an individual and on a national level, and it is also evident that we have applied a similar form of logic in exploring our environment, our national and planetary problems, and our uses of outer space. Unfortunately, in our society, thinking in terms other than of personal power is viewed as being weak or underdeveloped.

Words cannot adequately describe the process of inner post-biological development. What can be described, though, is a process whereby individuals can be guided into their own existing levels of self-actualizing energy and inner silence. It is these realms of inner silence, or unconditional love, that allow us to merge our outer selves with our inner soul-directed selves. At this point, each person begins to experience their own individual blueprint for the inner journey and develops the process of channeling these inner energies into the outer levels of creation. Just as during the first eighteen years of life we experience the natural unfoldment of our physical selves (as physical beings interacting within a physical world), during the remaining years of our lives we are meant to explore living through our inner-directed self in the outer world, learning new levels of inner and outer coexistence. In this context we can all find ourselves in a "win-win" situation in life.

Whenever I travel, wherever I am, I find individuals desiring and awaiting deeper levels of exploration. The process that I describe in this book awakens and develops a level of creativity that is neither based upon one's physical understanding of the world nor upon a process of restructuring reality to fit the current perceptions of what we think our world is. It is, instead, a process of awakening oneself into the heightened order of creativity that emerges naturally from the Divine aspect within each of us. It is a process of awakening into an inner self-actualizing energy, allowing an inner perception of reality to move us beyond the obvious linear, logical, organized world that we have always been taught exists. It is an opening for us as individuals to explore the safety, joy, and excitement of a true inner creative process, allowing us to awaken to "who we are" and "what we are meant to be" as human beings.

The first step I explore in my conference work is that of allowing individuals to experience the differences between their inner and outer awareness, and the ease with which they can access the inner spaces. They become aware of how the mind or intellect directs their perceptions, both as to what reality is and as to the potential of what their physical body is normally capable of performing. As they open into higher self-actualizing energies, or soul directed inner guidance, they can experience for themselves how easy it is to maintain and expand the inner control they have over the brain, nervous system, and other physiological and perceptual processes. Individuals are continually amazed at how easily they can shift into a level of expanded awareness and how they can maintain these levels for long periods of time while performing other outer tasks. They are able to observe themselves as well as others around them. And they soon realize that they have the choice of living within the soul-directed inner guidance (a self-actualizing energy) or of allowing the mind or intellect to take over and to once again feel confined within limited parameters of perceiving, feeling, and living.

As I first began to awaken into the natural expanded inner states, it took a number of months for me to find a level of mastery and comfort with the process. But once I allowed the awakening to occur, I was able to monitor and observe my own thoughts, feelings, perceptions, and physical body from a perspective of unity. It was only through the inner spaces that I understood the concept of "inner power" versus "outer power" in my interactions with other people and with my environment. While being guided by the self-actualizing force, I was able to observe and comprehend the importance of individuals working together. I was able to observe and understand how my current perceptions actually were hindering many of the projects with which I was involved. From this inner depth I was also shown a new set of perceptions and beliefs that would allow me to function and create from a totally new perspective. Through my inner-awareness I came to understand how I could effectively assist others with the awakening process. I realized that what I thought in my outer awareness was being productive was, in fact, counterproductive in accomplishing my goals in working with others. From my outer perspective I was absolutely sure that certain individuals would never really be able to change, and although I wouldn't tell them so directly, I held very little belief for their transformation. Through my inner guidance I was able to move into an observing state from which I could see why a given individual was doing what they were doing, and why I was perceiving them in such a limited way. From this perception evolved new ways of perceiving and interacting with them. When I allowed the new inner awareness to emerge into my daily life, I was surprised at how quickly my life, as well as the individuals with whom I had contact, changed. Suddenly things functioned very smoothly at a totally new level of efficiency and cooperation. In most instances, it wasn't necessary to directly share these new awarenesses with others. It seemed that if I changed and understood something differently, others around me also changed. This is what I am referring to when I say that an "inner sense of power" emerges when an individual learns to really feel and believe differently. What I am talking about is neither "positive thinking" nor "hoping for something to change"; rather, it is a belief that exists naturally within individuals once they begin to truly awaken into their own inner self-actualizing potential.

Through the explorations in this book you will experience for yourself that you are truly a human energy system and that you indeed do exist beyond the boundaries of your own skin. Ultimately you will learn how to direct this energy into the discovery of your own inner self-actualizing pulse. As this awakening occurs, you will begin to experience your own energies emerging directly from your heart chakra, allowing you to experience fully what it means to awaken into your Divine aspect, your soul-directed inner guidance. Only through experiencing this inner shift of heightened energy can new perceptions and an inner understanding emerge, thereby automatically shifting current structures of reality and awakening a higher order of creativity.

We can easily enter into our inner transpersonal realms once the "whole triune brain" is awakened and expanded. As the self-actualizing energy emerges, you will understand how all perceptions are dependent upon the specific areas within the brain that are activated, and how a limited inner awareness is due to certain areas of the brain still being dormant. You will be amazed at being able to experience the process of your brain's awakening and of feeling yourself move into new levels of inner synchronization. There are many levels at which the brain can synchronize, each one of which allows us to perceive life and the varied levels of reality differently. Once the triune brain is vertically unified into a single operating system, awakening into the inner transpersonal realms becomes safe and easy.

Throughout the biological phase, our outer awareness is influenced by the thoughts, feelings, and images that have emerged from the information to which we have been exposed. In many cases, we may have very little direct recall of the presentation of this information. We are bombarded with so much stimulation and awareness that the conscious mind cannot be aware of all that is being processed. Researchers describe man's brain as being able to actually process millions of images within mere milliseconds. Our bodies contain a base of organic substances similar to those that are found throughout the entire universe. Our outer awareness is not what we think it is, since objects as well as people seem to be very different and disconnected from each other. But from our inner awareness, we can begin to understand and directly experience a similarity and a connective relationship between physical objects, people, and the environment as a whole.

As the heart chakra begins to emerge as the new foundation and the primary level of inner focus, functioning in conjunction with the whole triune brain, it will automatically allow us to perceive and directly experience new levels of awareness. Initially we will perceive and feel this as a series of inner sensations. Just as we have learned in the past to translate our outer sensations and awarenesses into words and objects, we will similarly be able to translate our new inner experiences and sensations. The new sensations will eventually be translated into words, images, feelings, and behaviors, as well as into new body structures and movements. What was previously perceived as being impossible or difficult to achieve, will be altered very easily when operating from one's self-actualizing inner force. This process will begin the awakening into a heightened order of creativity that will be reflected not only through outer artistic creations, but will also change the way we learn and how we perform various sports and other activities. The process allows new forms of physical behavior to be accomplished, in addition to altering the learning and processing of all new and previous information. Thus we open into living at new levels of human development.

Each one of the respective "triune brain structures" allows us to perceive and interact with life differently. Each area allows us to perceive images and experience various sensations within both our outer life and our dream cycles. Each area of the triune brain is activated at differing times during the sleep cycle, allowing us to experience different forms of dreaming. The areas vary so greatly in what they perceive and create, that this will be explored in detail in the chapter entitled "Our Brain As A Transducer Of Reality." Man's triune brain structures can be viewed as paralleling the stages of evolution, moving from the ancient reptilian (or old brain) to the mammalian (or mid-brain), and then to the neocortex (or new brain). When these three areas are unified with the rhythm of one's own inner heart energies, we tap into the emergence of the expanded inner realms and awaken to the states of unconditional love. Through the unification of the "triune brain" and heart energies, we can begin to experience ourselves and all outer events as an interacting energy system whereby individual consciousness is integrated with all of nature. Thus we can perceive how naturally every aspect of life flows within a series of synchronized events.

Each one of us can experience how the brain functions as a transducer for the energy that awakens within the heart and extends beyond the boundaries of the skin. We can experience for ourselves that this becomes the key to understanding how the events and perceptions that occur outside of us are translated into what we feel, sense, think, and become. The production of all images, whether outer or inner, is identical. It is the brain that takes the images from the physical world, labels them "outer," distinctly separates them from those images that are created through our dreams or imagination (not to mention those abstract images that emerge through our inner creative energy), and then labels the latter "inner." But the brain reacts and organizes both kinds of information in precisely the same way; from its perspective, any given image or input is just as real as any other. The brain responds first to an inner light, which then connects to either the outer or inner stimulus of light. When it connects to the outer stimulus, we call the image "outside of self," when it connects to an inner image, we call it "inside of self." Regardless of where the stimulus is focused, the images create the same level and intensity of electrical impulses, and of biochemical and hormonal changes. All forms of images and all perceptions of reality are our personal interpretation and reaction to our world, and each area of the triune brain reacts and creates a different form of imagery. As I will discuss later, this is one of the major points in understanding Transformational Psychology.

I have also personally experienced how the brain changes roles throughout the course of living our lives. When we reach that stage of development which we call adulthood (around eighteen years of age), the brain no longer is meant to continue in its role as the primary focus of one's awareness. It is ready to begin a shift into a secondary role as a receiver or messenger of information, becoming the communication link between the physical body and its activities as they relate to our outer awareness. Its primary focus is to communicate one's inner self-actualizing energy, or that aspect of the Divine. Through my own personal exploration I have established a direct opening into my self-actualizing energy through the utilization of my "heart chakra" and the unifying of my triune brain. When I allow my focus of awareness to shift into an inner perspective, the self-actualizing energy awakens and allows me to shift into whatever perception I am needing at that particular moment. I now know that this deeper energy has always lain dormant within me, slowly awakening when the time was right, regardless of what I did or said. Many individuals spend an enormous amount of time rigorously trying to awaken this aspect of themselves. Others may go through life without any conscious outer awareness that such an inner aspect even exists, and then suddenly they will begin to awaken to this inner creative force. Whenever I shift into the perspective of stress or worry, my triune brain has already shifted into its old ways of perceiving and thinking. Until I allow my brain to move back into the state of being a messenger, my current perceptions and feelings will not change.

There are many books containing specific practices and activities outlined to facilitate the awakening of the inner self-actualizing energy. In my own consultations with numerous individuals, I have not found these practices for awakening one's inner energies to be helpful. What individuals today are truly needing are ways to live and create from an inner focus of awareness. They must learn to shift out of the erroneous perception that outer reality is all that there is. By learning to live from an inner quiet and focused state, when the deeper inner energies do awaken (and awaken they will), individuals will then be prepared to explore various new perspectives of life. Meditation alone does not fully prepare us to live at a heightened awakened energy, nor does it prepare us to follow our own inner-directed soul guidance while maintaining contact with the outer world. Therefore, we initially need to explore the awakening of both the brain and the heart chakra in order that the brain may assume its role as a transducer of reality. This allows us to maintain our outer awareness while a natural shift simultaneously occurs in our inner-awareness through our self-actualizing pulse.

The second phase of my personal journey began in 1978, with a series of synchronized events that are continuing yet today. This phase evolved as a result of awakening into my self-actualizing energy and then allowing this inner guidance both to change my physical body and to begin the awakening of new structures within my brain. The first time I began to directly and consciously experience this shift within my brain, the role of being a messenger or transducer of reality, was in late 1977 and early 1978. At the time, I was reading a number of books dealing with the reeducation of one's body and the interplay that exists between the mind, brain, and nervous system. I found this information to be exciting and stimulating, but at the same time, frightening. Through reading and attending several seminars dealing with body reeducation, I had begun to directly experience the ease with which my body could move into, and allow itself to be restructured into, a new level of physical integration. (I discovered, however, that the focus of my consciousness could just as easily restructure my body into levels of tension, pain, and immobility.) I found the discovery of the power that existed within the focus of my thoughts, feelings, and images to be exciting. I was also amazed at how easily various events in my life could change my physiological functioning.

As I continued my exploration, incorporating a variety of different approaches and methods, I was amazed at the changes that were taking place in my body. I remember reading one book in particular by Ken Dychtwald entitled **Bodymind**. In it he revealed how he had been able to develop arches in his feet after having been flat-footed his entire life, thinking that this was an hereditary trait since his father had also been flat-footed. Ken had begun to explore the concept that the condition of being flat-footed was the result of the psychological orientation of how he grounded himself in life. By drastically altering his psychological structures of being grounded, both with himself and with others, the conditions of his feet began to change over the course of the next three years. Ken had realized that he had the choice of either taking direct physical measures to correct his feet or of realizing that his feet were the outer representation of a deeper inner structure that was needing to be changed. He had chosen to explore the latter and had allowed his feet to reflect the changes that were occurring in his life. Ken now has arches in both feet! This was a stretch in credibility for me. I knew that human beings indeed possessed the capability to change things, but to the extent that Ken was relating? And if what he had done was possible, what else could we change in our lives? I later understood that when a change is being desired from within our inner-directed soul guidance, a heightened self-actualizing energy begins to emerge that will allow change to be transmuted in very short periods of time. And through the heightened energy, we can perceive how the new psychological structures are opening in our life. This constitutes the direct awakening of our inner creative force.

There actually are three options available for bringing about change. The first is to work directly on the problem, regardless of whether it is physical or mental, and to intellectually try to determine what to do. The second is to develop the understanding that all outer problems have an inner dynamic that represents and holds together what we perceive the problem to be, and the journey then is to allow ourselves the exploration at the inner level. (This is what I believe Ken was exploring.) The third possibility, which is the focus of this book, is to allow an inner heightened energy to emerge, and to then allow it to indicate what the issues and structures are that need to be experienced in order that the next level of transformation may occur. It necessitates focusing only on that which emerges from within the heightened energy state. And that which emerges may not be what you are expecting nor what you would like to be exploring in your life. But when you allow the inner direction to be your guide, you will alter and change things you would not have dreamed possible. Any one of the three choices is possible; and, of course, choosing to do nothing actually comprises a fourth choice. By which means do you most easily create—problem, underlying dynamics, or inner-directed soul guidance and a heightened energy?

It was at this particular point in my life that I began to experience the first direct awakening into my own level of inner-directed guidance and the inner force of my self-actualizing pulse. I found that whenever I was reading a book, an inner voice inside of me would begin to dialogue about the physical changes that could take place in my own body. This was both frightening and exciting. It was one thing to finally accept the fact that Ken and others could move into this type of change; but it was another thing to feel that these changes were possible within my own body and life. Through the direct experience of this heightened inner self-actualizing energy, my physical body began to change, which altered many of my current perceptions of life.

During the next nine months I experienced an inner battle and dialogue that created a great deal of mental confusion and emotional stress. The crux of the dialogue revolved around determining "who was in charge of whom." Whenever I was exploring some quiet inner space or was reading a thought provoking book, I felt an inner battle waging between two aspects of my brain. One aspect expounded about how the new ideas I was considering and exploring could not possibly exist. It was very logical and rational, reviewing for me all of the training and education I had experienced in understanding what constitutes the Mind and the Body. In actuality, this inner voice helped me to rationally understand how the new ideas contradicted everything that I had been taught to believe. The second aspect of my brain conveyed that indeed all of this did go against virtually everything that I had been taught, but it also made clear that what I had been exposed to all of my life had been extremely limited! It referred me once again to Jerome Frank's book, **Persuasion And Healing** (which I had read in graduate school), in which he relates that throughout the world there are many means of healing for which we have little or no explanation. Even the teachings of the Eastern perspectives are quite limited in their understanding of the inner processes that were beginning to emerge from within me. My rational aspect then proceeded to describe how my life would be one of chaos if I allowed such perceptions to become my reality, and it made very clear that if I dared to open into this new realm of thought "nothing that I currently knew could remain the same."

This, as I said, continued for nearly nine months. Near the end of this period of turmoil and confusion, I was in the process of reading a book by Don Johnson entitled **The Protean Body**. However, each time I picked up the book I found that I could read no more than one chapter. Something within me kept pushing me to complete each chapter, but once I had finished the final word of the chapter, I would find myself pulled into a deep inner meditative space, where I would remain for an hour or more. During this period of time, I would be taken on an inner journey through the same areas of my body about which I had been reading. I would be shown how that particular area of my body could be restructured in its movement and also be restructured into the rest of my physical form, all without having to suffer through any in-depth form of physical therapy or Rolfing. Upon emerging from the meditative inner space, my whole body would be tingling. Even more exciting, those parts of the body about which I had been reading, and that had subsequently been taken through the inner process of restructuring, were actually physically changed. It was not merely a matter of the physical structures seeming different to me, but other people also noticed the physical changes in me. Let me cite an example of such change that initially created strong feelings of confusion and stress.

I had moved into an inner space through which I was exploring the restructuring of my hips and legs. During this inner restructuring, I was shown an image of myself sitting in what I later recalled having read about as being a full lotus position. Although I had never taken a class in yoga, I had once tried to move into this position, causing myself great physical pain. In the past, I had experienced very little success in finding my body to be even flexible enough to move one leg up over the other. I remember thinking that something like this would be impossible. I knew individuals who had attempted for years to master the lotus position and could yet barely achieve it. So how was I going to be able to move into such a posture? As I moved out of the inner space, I immediately felt compelled to actually try to physically move into the lotus position. I sat down on the floor, positioned one leg and then the other, and there I was, sitting in a full lotus position on my very first attempt! As usual, immediately following this new feat came the emergence of that old rational voice from within my

brain shouting "Enough is enough— now look what you've done."
And the other familiar voice was proclaiming even more loudly,
"But see what possibilities are open to you. How can you deny
this?"

The internal debate raged over the next few days, but I was
afraid to share any of this with anyone. On the third day I
remember sitting alone outdoors and shouting at the top of my
lungs, "O.K. I believe. I'll explore and see what my potential is, no
matter where it may take me!" At this point a profound level of
inner silence and peace moved through me and I then effortlessly
moved back into my full lotus position and stayed there for several
hours. When I got up, I felt that I had moved through something
major, but I was not at all sure what it was. However, the one thing
I did know was that my body felt great, and I continue even today
to possess this same level of flexibility. And that other rational
voice has never returned! Sure, I do question things at times, and
I occasionally move through periods of doubting about our full
potential as human beings. But when this occurs, it is easy to
recall this particular experience, as well as many others that I
have since explored, and thereby render the doubts back into my
inner silence.

By the end of 1978, virtually the entire left side of my body had
moved into a full level of restructuring, especially noticeable being
the changed bone structures in my left foot. For the first time in
twenty years the toes on this foot were physically straight. And at
this writing, the right side of my body has achieved similar degrees
of restructuring. Without relating a long and detailed story, let me
explain that by the time I entered high school, doctors had made
it clear that I needed major surgery on both of my feet in order to
realign defective bone structures that caused me a great deal of
pain and discomfort when standing and walking. However, I never
truly felt comfortable in making the decision to have the surgery,
and consequently just resigned myself to the fact that the suffering
would be a simpler and easier route. And suffer I did! My middle
left toe had curved under my second toe to the extent that only a
third of the toe was exposed below the middle joint, and major
callouses had formed around and under my feet. But all of this
changed as a result of my inner exploration. I found once again that
the change was exciting, but also frightening. My outer mind told
me that this whole process was impossible and, with the exception
of those individuals who had seen me before and after the change,
anyone with whom I discussed it had a hard time believing me. To
them it made absolutely no sense and defied any sort of logical
explanation. All of the changes took place through an inner
awakening of energy and an inner-directed soul guidance that

actually directed my physical process of change. This heightened energy also shifted a number of my beliefs and attitudes about many structures of reality. It was at this point in my exploration that I truly began to comprehend what <u>awakening</u> <u>one's</u> <u>creative potential</u> was all about!

After a period of time, however, my outer mind once again began to create doubts, and I proceeded to question everything that had happened. My overall feeling at the time could be aptly described by the comment, "Ah, come on now." I admitted at this time to being sufficiently naive to allow myself to contemplate and ponder what potentials might exist within me, but changing something like my feet extended beyond the point of being naive. Yet, another inner aspect continued to guide me through a series of changes that even today are still taking place.

Back then I had never placed much emphasis on changing the physical body. However, as I continued with my own odyssey, I realized that my physical body was reflecting my inner changes. Sometimes the feelings came forward very loudly and clearly, directing me in what to do. At other times I merely had an inner sense that something was needing to be changed. For example, if I had been searching for some specific information on a topic, I might feel myself drawn into a certain book store; and as I browsed, a book would literally fall off the shelf, wherein I would find the information I had been seeking. I have on occasion even been shown an inner image or vision depicting a page from a book with which I was not even familiar. Later I would be drawn to searching for the book and would find the exact information on the page that I had earlier envisioned.

I will share at this time just one other change regarding the transformations in my physical body. At the end of 1978 I began to receive inner guidance and information directing me to remove my glasses and explore a similar process of change with my vision. On January 1, 1979, I took my glasses off. During the following six months I experienced more outer and inner changes than I had ever thought could be possible. One day I put the glasses back on and wore them for several hours. It felt as though there was a burning weight on my eyes, and I took the glasses off and have never again worn them. Without them I now read, write, drive, and see life like I have never seen it before.

Many people confuse their inner guidance or soul-direction with their own ego identity and their hopes, wishes, and fears. In the explorations of this book we will investigate ways to distinguish between one's soul's inner direction (or self-actualizing energy) and the ego's desires. This will evolve through that level of inner silence that is ever present. If you receive inner information about changing something, or about moving in a certain direction, and you find that the changes you are exploring are creating additional stress for you, then I feel you need to question whether this really is the right focus for you. I have come to realize that when we choose to allow valid changes to move via the process of transmutation, where a heightened focused inner-directed energy emerges, there is very little stress present in one's life. When it is the proper time for something to change, nothing will prevent it from moving you, and you will experience a quietness inside whenever that direction is emerging through your inner guidance. On the other hand, stress is created when you allow yourself to live through your old habits, deep levels of past experiences, and your intellect or outer mind. You cannot fight true transformative change, and when it is ready to move, it moves!

So let's once again consider the question about "Who is in charge of whom?" When I am focused within my inner states of heightened self-actualizing energies, it seems possible to create absolutely anything at all. At some later time, though, when that level of energy is no longer present, the doubts and fears do return. Thus we will explore how to shift back into the inner spaces and allow the inner perceptions to emerge as our directions for exploration, avoiding being caught in the lesser energies and perceptions of other choices of reality. I am now able to determine which state I am in, and I find that it is important to allow myself the time and energy to shift back into the inner-directed focus for my daily living. One of the basic requirements of Transformational Psychology is to be able to distinguish at what level of focus one is living at any particular moment in time. The process we are herein exploring allows us to easily shift our focus from the lesser energies of an outer focus into an inner-directed focus, where there will be no dilemma about who is in charge, for inner and outer become one and the same.

Through my own odyssey, and through the explorations of Brugh Joy, John Lilly, Wilder Penfield, Joseph Chilton Pearce, Carolyn Conger, Richard Moss, and others, I have come to realize that the awakening of our creative potential resides within the heart chakra of each human being; and, as this force is awakened, it will move us beyond all levels of intellectual understanding into our true potential and possibilities. The brain is the transducer for this information. We have direct control available to us to reorganize and attune our brain to the inner rhythms of the heart chakra and to thereby allow our consciousness to emerge into the next phase of our inner development as human beings.

We sometimes forget (or may not even be aware) that our concepts of time and space are actually determined by our culture and are, in truth, really subjective states. If a culture predominantly focuses upon outer reality, then time is something that is measured in a linear process based upon what we call outer "clock time." Those in the culture all "know" that it takes a given amount of time to accomplish something and that the physical body can change and do only so much. We are truly only limited to the concept of time to the extent that it is based upon our inner beliefs, attitudes and perceptions.

A good example of this was the breaking of the four-minute mile in 1954. Just a few months prior to the accomplishment of this feat, there was a large amount of research being published from numerous research centers throughout the world affirming the impossibility of running a mile in less than four minutes. Most of the studies focused on the physical and biological limitations of the human body as rendering impossible the accomplishment of such a feat. Within months of all of this publicity, Roger Bannister of England, broke the record of the four-minute mile. In the ensuing years, runners throughout the world, including even high school seniors, were able to duplicate this feat. What happened? Roger Bannister defied being caught in the mental limitations of what others were saying. Rather, he decided to see for himself what potentials truly did exist in the expansion of the human body and mind. He believed that it was possible to run a four-minute mile, and he set out to prove his beliefs. And with that, others were able to do the same in their realization that the barriers were actually mental, not physical or biological.

Jean Houston, in her book entitled **The Possible Human,** has a series of exercises that allows an individual to explore the subjective nature of both time and space. Within the human mind-body process, an inner focused workout of half an hour is as effective as a physical workout of half a day or more. Many people actually progress faster by first utilizing an inner workout for learning to fine tune aspects of their sports activities, and then these ideas can be applied to the outer workout. This concept is one that I will be developing throughout our journey, allowing us to become aware of the limitations that we ourselves have established. We will explore how subjective our concepts are of both time and space and will explore ways to alter these ideas. We will directly experience the inner dimensions of these two concepts and how they can directly change our beliefs, attitudes, and perceptions as they relate to our outer world.

As I've said, we have a natural capacity to move into a level of inner-awareness that allows a heightened energy to emerge. When we are focused in the space outside of self, we see and experience ourselves as "stopping" at the boundaries of our skin. But as we awaken into the self-actualizing force, we automatically open into a new level of energy and understanding. This inner energy force can be directly felt through one's voice, eyes, and hands, as well as by the mere presence of an individual. As we learn to shift and live from the inner self-actualizing force, one's entire physical body begins to naturally vibrate this inner force of energy. It can be both felt and experienced by individuals, as well as measured by special equipment that has been developed over the last few years specifically for this purpose. This level of energy is also referred to as an electromagnetic field, and over the years, NASA and other public and private research groups have been able to measure shifts in electromagnetic energy. Individuals who have been trained to both feel and visually perceive electromagnetic fields also validate the accuracy of the machines. Or should I say that the machines validate the accuracy of these individuals?

Other research has shown that two individuals who are "open" to one another can influence each other's brain waves over a distance of several thousand miles. Additionally, other studies involving the process of remote viewing have also shown that individuals are not separated by the dimensions of space and time in being able to locate objects and sense another individual's perceptions from across the United States and even into Europe. Many of these studies have been sponsored through the joint cooperation of our government and Stanford Research Institute. Space is limited only by what we perceive it to be. From an outer perspective we know the boundaries, but through an inner shift, it becomes boundless. Later, I will explore this from the perspective of physics, the wave and particle theory, and quantum mechanics. For now, let's work with the idea that regardless of what you believe time and space may encompass, there exists much more for us to explore. Whether you are a skeptic or a firm believer, simply open and explore your possibilities.

Our consciousness is always in the state of directing one's own electromagnetic field through its thoughts, feelings, and images, as well as interacting with other individuals' energies in a similar process. As one is awakened into the self-actualizing pulse, the inner perceptions will become much more refined. We have a natural capacity for allowing these inner energies to restructure both their own perceptual sensory process as well as the perceptual sensory process of others, so long as the other individual is open to the inner shifts. Through the awakening of the inner creative energies, one's mental, emotional, physical, and spiritual understanding of self and others begins to change. Shifts in inner-awareness can alter the way we think, feel, and move physically, thus allowing the total human system to be brought under the volition of an inner guiding force. I believe that humanity has experienced similar processes of restructuring during other time periods in our history, most notably during the Renaissance, as we previously discussed.

Many individuals expound about the physical, emotional, mental, and spiritual aspects of self, and yet few individuals ever fully experience this. Each one of these aspects of self actually exists as an energy system that can be both inwardly and outwardly seen and felt. As you experience these differences in your journey, it will greatly alter your understanding of yourself, and will automatically open you into a new synthesis of the inner creative force. Each one of the subtle energy bodies will become as real to you as what you currently perceive and experience your physical body as being. Through the exploration of the subtle energy bodies, you will master even greater levels of personal transformation and inner guidance in your life.

There are five major layers of subtle energies: the physical or kinesthetic level, which represents your own physical body; the subtle energy body that is identical to your feeling or emotional state; the mental energy body that represents your intellectual abilities (some call this your causal body); the spiritual or potential energy body, which represents the direction of your self-actualizing energy; and the living unified self energy body, composed of the unified energies of the spiritual, mental, emotional, and physical, which is focused in the everyday living world. Bringing our new living unified self energy body forward into the outer world allows us to experience life from a new inner focus of awareness. Each of the subtle energy bodies can be brought under the volition of one's inner-directed soul guidance. As this begins to develop, you will awaken to an understanding of how easily your perceptions of any outer situation can change based upon your level of inner-awareness and the awakening of the inner self-actualizing force. As your perceptions and physical capabilities become easily altered, you will realize that your existence as an energy system is not an isolated event, but that you coexist as a collective energy system. In this system each individual's perception is in a constant state of synchronization with other individuals and with all of nature. The synchronization of the triune brain and its focus in the heart chakra allows mankind to perceive and understand this deeper aspect and purpose of being human.

Most individuals process information through an intellectual and/or verbal mode. In our culture we only acknowledge brilliance, power, and leadership in those individuals who have mastered the intellectual and verbal framework. Individuals who are highly creative, or who are considered to be geniuses, do not perceive and experience life in the same way as others. They think and sense life through a series of images, feelings, and kinesthetic movements that are different.

Many creative individuals, however, have only developed one sensory mode of expression. Many find it difficult to verbally communicate their inner senses and understanding of information into an outer structure of reality that can be understood by others. As we move into the deeper levels of the inner self-actualizing energy, it becomes important to allow a total system of communication to develop.

As we focus on the whole triune brain and the awakening of the heart chakra, we will automatically begin to communicate through a variety of modes, many of which either did not previously exist for us, or were only slightly developed. Individuals, as they awaken, will learn to shift easily between all levels of sensing, allowing themselves the full range of communication abilities. To change from one mode of sensory dominance and communication to another requires the activation of latent electrical, biochemical and hormonal changes within the brain's circuitry. But through the processes that we will be exploring, these changes will evolve very naturally.

It is important that you do not become frightened and that you do not try to stop the development of new modes of sensory communication within you. As the inner self-actualizing energy begins to awaken and emerge, allow yourself to follow the natural course of events that are opening to you. In my own life and in the lives of others who have awakened to and can sense these inner levels of energies, there is a consistent acknowledgement that any shift or change in outer awareness is always preceded by a shift in inner awareness. A new level of energy will always precede a shift in our outer visual, auditory, verbal, or kinesthetic awareness. As you learn to voluntarily shift your awareness into the heart chakra and the triune brain, an automatic restructuring of your inner-awareness will occur, opening you into a new level of inner focus. This new awareness will always begin with a new level of both inner and outer sensations that initially are felt and experienced within the brain, nervous system and physical body. As the sensations develop, they will awaken new psychological and emotional feelings that will allow you to experience a new part of yourself. Through this inner reeducation, you will be able to both understand and share the new aspects of yourself with others, and you will welcome the ensuing changes in your life.

CHAPTER TWO

EXPANDED INNER SCREEN
AND QUADRANTS

I would like to begin this chapter with EXPLORATION #2: THE EXPANDED INNER SCREEN AND THE HEART CHAKRA. This process allows you to directly experience the shift from the outer focus of one's mind into the focus of one's inner-directed soul energies. I customarily present this exploration within the first hour of my seminars so that individuals then have a basis for anchoring the dialogue that is to follow. Although initially this exploration will last about twenty minutes, by the time we progress through the next several explorations you will be able to move through the same process in less than two minutes. View each one of these initial explorations as being part of a training session which is vital to your awakening into the self-actualizing energy and to the exploration of the inner spaces I have been describing. Once these energies begin to awaken, you will soon be able to move into the spaces easily and quickly just by setting the intent. So before you read further, allow yourself to create a tape for this exploration, or have someone read this exploration to you as you follow the instructions.

"With your eyes closed *** become aware of that space inside of you *** for some people, this space is dark *** for others, it contains various patterns or shapes *** some see geometrical patterns *** some see light *** some see only a grayness *** others see very vivid colors *** it makes no difference what you visually see; the important element is what you feel, sense, and experience *** visually draw a circle around the space that you are aware of right at this moment *** draw a circle several times going in one direction, encompassing that inner space *** *** now draw a circle in the opposite direction encompassing the same space *** *** how does this space feel *** how does your body feel while you are focused within this space *** ask the space to expand *** ask the circle to become larger and to expand into a larger inner space *** *** ask that inner space to expand once again *** *** *** how does the inner space feel *** how does your body feel within this expanded inner space *** ask the circle to shrink back to its original size *** become aware of how limited this space now feels *** what happens within your body when you are in this normal limited space of yourself *** ask the circle to expand again *** and again *** ask it to expand several more times until you feel that you are the center of that circle *** *** ask to expand until the circle is all around you *** become aware of how your body begins to change *** notice how your breathing naturally slows as you move into the expanded space *** sense and feel a circle being drawn within this space *** even though that space is much larger than you can actually encompass in a circle *** sense into the dimensions of this inner space *** draw a circle in the opposite direction enclosing the same expanded space *** *** draw a horizontal line and a vertical line, dividing the space into four equal quadrants *** *** become aware of the center point where the two lines intersect *** *** this is the point where we will merge and unify our energy *** *** become aware of that center point being focused between your eyes *** *** become aware of how your body feels as the center point focuses between your eyes, at the third eye chakra *** now feel that the center point is dropping down, and is focused at the center of your chest *** this focal point is from the heart chakra *** become aware of how you are beginning to feel and what you sense when the focus is at your heart center, right in the middle of your chest *** ask the space to expand once again as you maintain the heart-centered focus *** *** feel that point deepening even further into your heart center *** *** sense and feel a revolving crystalline structure of emerald green light slowly turning within the center of your chest *** *** feel and sense that the point at the center of your chest is creating a series of waves *** a series of emerald green light waves *** expanding from the center of your chest, going out in all directions through your body *** *** become aware of how easily and quickly your body changes *** *** your self-actualizing pulse is now being awakened *** *** ask it to open you into your inner-directed soul guidance *** *** ask again, if you wish, for your inner screen to expand *** just through the process of asking, while you are within this space, it will automatically happen *** *** become aware of the inner quiet that naturally emerges *** whenever you are within your expanded inner space, let the feeling of the emerald green crystalline structure expand from the center of your chest and allow the waves of light to move throughout your body and beyond it *** *** now we will explore the four quadrants of your expanded inner screen *** draw a vertical line dividing your screen into two equal halves *** draw a horizontal line dividing your screen into four equal quarters *** begin with the upper left quadrant *** focus on the center point of your screen and follow the line up to the top, follow the curvature of the circle to the left until you reach the middle line, and then move back to the center point *** allow yourself to become aware of and to explore the space within your upper left quadrant *** *** now let's explore the lower left quadrant *** from the center point follow the vertical line down and the curvature of the line up on the left to the horizontal line and back across to the center point *** *** explore the space within your lower left quadrant *** *** now explore the lower right quadrant *** from the center point follow the line down, follow the curvature up on the right to the middle line and back over to the center point *** explore the space within your lower right quadrant *** *** become aware of how this space feels, not just in front of you, but on the side, below, and behind you *** you are the center of this space *** *** now the upper right quadrant *** from the center point move all the way up and along the curvature to the right, down to the middle line and back into the center point *** *** explore the space within the quadrant *** *** bring your awareness to the center point once again, letting yourself be the center of that space *** ask that to deepen at the center of your chest at the heart chakra *** become aware of what you are feeling ** *** let the center point become smaller and smaller *** follow the focus of the center point *** some people begin to feel a movement or tunnel *** or a space that is created within, in which they are traveling *** this is the beginning of the feeling of merging your outer and inner awareness into one inner focus, being at one with your inner-directed guidance *** *** bring your awareness back to the upper left quadrant *** think about yourself getting dressed this morning *** think about the step-by-step process you went through after you got out of bed this morning *** *** going to the bathroom, dressing, eating, communicating *** keep your focus in your upper left quadrant as you become aware of all the things you did this morning *** *** let that image go and bring your awareness into your lower right quadrant *** go through the same process of morning activities that you just thought about *** become aware of the movement inside your body now as you review those same images *** review once again the same step-by-step process of what you did this morning *** keep your focus within the lower right quadrant *** are you aware of feeling these things within your body right now *** *** as if you were physically enacting the different movements at this very moment *** *** let that go and bring your awareness back into the upper left quadrant once again, and think about the same process *** when people are thinking and reviewing things while focusing within this quadrant, it appears only as a mental process *** now shift your focus again into the lower right quadrant **** as you create this same image, sense, feel, and experience the movement inside of you *** feel the changes occurring in your own body that accompany those thoughts *** feel and experience the physical sensations that are being created right now *** *** now bring your awareness into the lower left quadrant *** review the same situation again *** notice as you focus within this quadrant that you begin to once again feel the emotions and feeling tones from this morning *** notice how this feeling tone was not present, or at least was not as strong, in the other two quadrants *** *** allow yourself to deepen into the feelings and emotions within this quadrant *** now move back into the lower right *** review the same things*** are you aware how the body awareness is heightened *** move again into the lower left *** again notice the heightened emotional awareness *** move to the upper left *** notice the presence of more thinking or mental awareness than what existed within the other two quadrants *** *** now move into the upper right *** try to repeat the same process *** *** most people lose their images, feelings, or sensations within this quadrant *** most cannot sense or feel or experience anything from their past when they are within the upper right *** or what they do sense is not very clear, or may be different than the image or focus that was created from the other quadrants *** let the image go now *** maintain your focus within the upper right quadrant *** ask to experience an energy, a feeling, or a sense of unconditional love *** a profound space of inner quiet and peace *** ask it to become deeper than any outer space you have ever experienced *** allow the energies of that profound space of unconditional love to emerge within your upper right quadrant and experience the movement within that space *** *** let that inner feeling shift into the upper left quadrant *** become aware of how quiet your mental inner dialogue can be within this profound space of unconditional love *** *** know that you can experience this peace, as well as an even deeper, more profound inner peace *** *** allow this profound inner quiet to emerge, and experience the movement within this space *** let that shift down into the lower left quadrant *** ask that to deepen into a profound inner feeling of quiet *** allow the feelings of that inner quiet to emerge from your heart, and sense how you feel within this quiet space *** *** shift the focus into the lower right quadrant *** allow yourself to feel that profound inner quiet and unconditional love within your body *** allow the inner quiet to deepen into your body right now *** *** bring your awareness to the center point, ask that feeling to merge and unify *** feel the center point deepening into the center of your chest *** and ask that feeling to emerge inside of you *** allow a profound quiet and inner peace to be fully present *** unifying your spirit *** your mind

*** your emotion *** your body *** ask to feel that inner peace rippling and expanding from the center of your chest through your body to the tips of your fingers and toes *** *** and ask that feeling to expand and to go deeper within you *** ask it to move through your nervous system, muscles, and related organs *** ask it to move into your cellular level and to spread through each cell of your physical body *** ask it to move into the atomic and subatomic levels within your physical form *** ask to deepen and merge with the inner self-actualizing pulse or energy of your soul *** *** ask this energy to begin to expand and move at this deep level throughout your physical form *** ask it to move beyond the physical boundaries of your skin *** radiating from the point deep within the heart chakra at the center of your chest *** ask that feeling to expand and connect you with all of time and all of space *** *** become aware of how your body is feeling and sensing within this space *** ask to go deeper and just allow it to happen *** *** ask your body to feel very heavy and warm *** *** ask that your body feel warm and light and energized *** just let it happen *** *** become aware of how your focus automatically changes your physical body and your awareness *** ask for this space to remain open within you *** *** ask it to remain light, energized *** ask that this level of inner-awareness remain open and merge with and become your outer awareness *** always remaining focused from within *** then when you are ready *** allow this emergence to move you into your outer awareness and open your eyes *** *** allowing the inner-directed soul guidance to be with you in your physical form *** allowing your perceptions and awarenesses to continue to move from this space within."

When individuals complete this exploration, they never fail to be amazed at how easily they can shift into the inner-directed focus. Even individuals who have previously explored other forms of relaxation and meditation find that they begin to touch a deeper, more grounded space within themselves. Many individuals report a feeling of losing touch with the boundaries of the physical body as it seems to become much larger or expansive. Some report experiencing changes in specific areas of the body, while other areas remain the same. There really is only one "correct" result to be achieved from this exploration, and that is for you to open to the experience of something different each time you explore the inner spaces. This will open you to feeling or sensing whatever inner exploration is ready to emerge from within you. You will rarely find any of your experiences to be repetitive. So, if you are "doing it correctly," each exploration will be different. Many times you may have similar experiences, yet each will have a unique quality for that moment. This exploration will require less time after you explore the next chapter, and by the time we move into the exploration of "Awakening Your Triune Brain," it will take less than one minute to set this inner stage. One of the most important things to be learned from this exploration is to allow your self-actualizing energy to become awakened and to allow it to begin to be constantly present within you. As this is achieved, you will automatically have moved into the observer state, and you will begin to perceive and sense things in life differently. Take the time to explore this aspect so that it may become a part of your daily life.

Let's discuss some of the specific points that we have just explored in order that your outer mind can begin to attain some level of understanding. Once you begin to explore the expanded inner space and the heart chakra, you will begin the shift from your outer into your inner self-actualizing focus of awareness. For this to occur, it is necessary to shift the brain into the energy of the expanded inner space. Maintaining your former level of inner space (that of your screen being in front of you) will not allow you to fully experience, or even create, many of the explorations we will be exploring. The expanded inner screen opens you into a deeper and more expansive brain-body connection. While within the outer awareness state, the brain is the receptor for the stimulus of one's outer awareness and feeds this information into the body. We will later explore what it means for the brain to move into the role of being an intermediary messenger or transducer of energy. This occurs naturally as we shift into our inner self-actualizing energy and as we allow the inner-awareness and experiences to become our dominant focus. We will also explore how an inner-directed soul focus can actually change the physical body. By shifting the brain, you will be able to easily experience the sensations and awarenesses I have mentioned.

When I first began to explore the process of imagery in the late 1970s, I was instructed to visually see the images as being created on a large screen in front of me. This space was described to me as being similar to a large television or movie screen. By late 1981, however, something had begun to change within me, and I was no longer experiencing the large screen as being in front of me; rather, it now seemed to surround me in all directions. It was above, below, to the right and left side of me; I felt as though I were in the center of a large sphere. I discovered that when I shifted into the center point of my screen, I experienced direct and profound physiological changes. The inner changes occurred faster and were deeper than I had ever previously experienced, and my body changed accordingly, becoming a direct manifestation of the inner images and feelings. I initially had been taught to direct my images and feelings toward whatever it was that I wanted to create. Sometimes this was effective, but most often it was not. As the self-actualizing pulse was awakening within me, I began to realize that the feelings and directions I was receiving from within my inner guidance were in direct conflict with the images and feelings I was consciously determined to create. Whenever these differences arose, stress and tension resulted. As I learned to let go of my outer thinking and its well-planned direction, and learned to surrender into the spontaneous inner images and feelings that were emerging, I always experienced immediate changes in my body, my perceptions, and in the direction I would take in my outer world. And whenever I noticed that my inner screen appeared out in front of me, rather than surrounding me, I perceived little or no change taking place in my life, and there was a corresponding increase in my levels of stress, irritability, and physical tension.

As I deepened with the concept of the expanded inner screen, I was amazed at how quickly things changed, and I began to experience a heightened awareness of all my outer senses as a new world of inner sensations was emerging. As you begin to experience the heightening of your own outer senses, it is important that you allow yourself to experience and feel the sensations all around you, both outside and within. You will notice that each of the respective quadrant areas is not simply in front of you, with you in the center; rather, it can be felt and experienced above, to the side, beneath, and behind you. These quadrants and the resulting inner images and sensations are not isolated events. They consist of the layers of energies that you are constantly emitting, which allow you to be you! Many individuals find it difficult to allow these awarenesses to be brought into the physical body, and this can cause difficulties at a later point in one's journey. The sensations and feelings that you experience are you, so allow them to move freely both within the deepest parts of yourself and within what you sense as being your outer awareness.

During the exploration, as we brought our awareness into the center point (the fifth part of your expanded inner screen), did you notice the different feelings and sensations that automatically emerged from your third eye or forehead, and then how different it felt when you moved your central point of focus to the heart center? In order to fully actualize the potentials we will be exploring, it is very important that your focus be at the center of your chest. It is from this perspective that you will experience the deeper feeling of unity that allows you to merge with the different aspects of yourself. This will allow you to bring the elements of spirit, mind, emotion, and body from your meditative states into your daily living. Whenever you become aware that you are not experiencing the deeper feeling of unity, ask that the point of focus lower itself into the center of your chest (or heart chakra), and when it has shifted, you will be able to sense a distinct difference. As the heart-centered focus point becomes more finely attuned, you will begin to feel a quickening of an inner motion inside of you. It will feel as though you are being drawn inside of yourself. I describe this feeling as being similar to the hyperspace I first perceived in the movie **Star Wars**. In fact, the first time I saw this on the movie screen, I shouted, "That's my inner space!" However, instead of having to move outside of me, it moves deeper and deeper into my inner-directed space through the heart chakra. If this feeling of being drawn inside of yourself should frighten you, once again adjust the center point of your inner screen directly into the heart chakra at the center of your chest, and you will automatically feel the warmth and nurturing energies begin to emerge.

Throughout your journey, you will become increasingly more aware of the importance of your focus being maintained at the heart chakra and of what the expanded screen can mean for you. Utilization of these processes can facilitate the alteration of physiological processes, the shifting of one's perceptions, and the understanding and experiencing of one's self in a totally different way as a human being. And as you learn to live from this inner perspective, you will then experience for yourself what it means to move into the next level of inner human development. At this point of exploration you, as is the case with most of those who explore this process, are probably beginning to feel something different within you, although you may not be able to verbalize just what it is.

The inner quadrants provide an opening whereby you can directly experience and change various aspects of yourself. They also provide you a direct access to various other layers of consciousness that simultaneously exist as a part of every human being. Each of the four quadrants is connected to a different area of the triune brain, and each quadrant will, therefore, allow you to directly experience a different set of feelings, sensations, and awarenesses. I will continue to deepen and modify this concept as we move through our journey, but for now just allow the following generalizations to guide you through each quadrant.

The upper left quadrant represents our mental or intellectual thinking. The energies from this area help us to interpret our current attitudes, beliefs, and the way we perceive ourselves and life in general. We can recall past linear events in a very precise fashion when we are focused within this quadrant. We rarely will experience events either physically or emotionally while maintaining our focus in the upper left quadrant. The focus of this quadrant allows the intellect to be reeducated once we have moved into our inner-directed soul energies.

As we shift into the lower left quadrant, we automatically open into our personal feeling tones and emotional sensations. This quadrant is the most difficult for us to initially become aware of due to the high emotional personal energy that is present for most individuals. Most of us have traditionally experienced only our "primitive emotional responses." But once we develop an inner-awareness that emerges from our self-actualizing energy, we will then understand the power that exists within this new level of heightened human emotions — a level which is capable of bringing us into a state of unity and inner direction. Being focused in the lower left quadrant will allow us to develop a "feeling" sense of unconditional love and what it means to be heart focused and awakened to one's "inner sense of power."

The lower right quadrant allows us to experience the inner sensations and movements of the physical body. It assimilates the physical movement at that very moment. This allows us to develop a kinesthetic sense of ourselves. The stronger our heart-focused kinesthetic awareness, the easier it will be to live from the heightened state of inner-awareness.

In the upper right quadrant most images and sensations of past events either disappear or become unfocused. This quadrant opens us into the first level of contact with our inner self-actualizing potential or inner-directed guidance. It brings forward the energies or sensations of what an inner-directed focus is, while initially, the other quadrants tap into what has previously been created. Once an inner shift occurs, the energies of this quadrant begin to alter the other quadrants into a new perception of who we are and what we can begin to create for ourselves. As individuals focus within this spiritual quadrant, profound feelings of inner quiet emerge naturally. Many individuals achieve a new depth in both relaxation and inner silence.

The forms of relaxation that I will be exploring with you are, for the most part, very different than those generally practiced. The goal in our explorations is not to move the body into a profound state of immobility; rather, the purpose is to energize the body into a state of unity and inner movement that holds no tension or pain. The upper right quadrant plays a vital role in this process because an inner bodily sense of fluidity is initially awakened from the spiritual quadrant. We then can take this energy and, by bringing our awareness into the center point of the expanded inner screen and allowing it to move into the heart chakra, can thereby allow the energies from each one of the quadrants (spiritual, mental, emotional and physical) to unify as a synchronized living energy within our physical form. At this point an even deeper sense moves through us, allowing the physical form to change and match the inner-directed sense. The expanded screen and the maintaining of the heart focus allow this to develop. At this juncture we have then brought our outer focus into an inner-awareness, which allows us to live at a level of heightened perception. By exploring the triune brain and the nervous system, we can deepen this into yet another level of synthesis. It is therefore important that you build an inner history and become familiar with the concept of the inner screen and its quadrants. Thus you need to repeat the exploration with the inner screen and quadrants several times before you begin the process of allowing the inner self-actualizing energy to "awaken" you through a shortened or abbreviated form.

Current research on body language shows us that individuals have a tendency to look up at the ceiling when they are trying to recall something from their past, as if they were going to find the answer written on the ceiling. When individuals attempt to verbalize about uncomfortable feelings, they have a tendency to glance down or to look at their toes for their response. Recall for yourself how natural it is to move your focus downward or upward in trying to get in touch with different feelings, past memories, or various sensations. Through my inner guidance I have come to realize that this has nothing to do with head or eye movements; in actuality, we feel a natural inner pull to move our awareness in a particular direction in order to gain the easiest access into that particular inner part of ourselves and awaken specific areas within the brain. (Recall where those four respective quadrants are located!) Individuals report that they automatically begin to experience the inner sensations and changes that occur with a particular image when they focus within a certain quadrant. They begin to feel, sense, and experience an inner movement of the heightened energies that are attached to each one of these inner spaces. This process will readily allow the transformative energies to emerge that are necessary for man's post-biological development.

As you allow the shift into your inner-directed guidance to evolve, it will no longer be necessary to try to guess at or arbitrarily create what you think needs to happen. Instead, you will begin to explore the process of "asking." In the exercise when you asked for feelings to go deeper, did you notice that indeed they did deepen? When you asked that your body feel very heavy and warm, did you feel it become heavy and warm? When you asked for it to feel light and energized, did you sense that it indeed did become light and energized? This constitutes one of the major differences between exploring the triad of the Soul/Mind/Body within Transformational Psychology and the practicing of traditional forms of relaxation. In most relaxation techniques the outer mind or intellect is the director and creator of what one desires to achieve. And when this is the case, the body moves into a space that becomes very difficult for most people to live with. But when one shifts into an inner-directed guidance, a lightness of feelings and a different form of unity begin to emerge— a unity that allows you to move into and maintain the focus of the inner space in your everyday world.

I have explored these processes with numerous athletes, artists, and musicians. They have all been amazed at how easily they can overcome their inner blocks by opening into the inner spaces and surrendering control to their own inner creative potential. They are especially pleased once they can allow themselves to maintain their focus within the inner space even while they are performing. Some individuals actually become upset because they can so easily move into the space— merely asking is all that is necessary. Traditionally most people have learned to be creative through a dedicated "push" energy in life, and they subsequently find it difficult to release into a process that just "pulls" one along in a loving and nurturing way— that is, when one allows it! Asking will become the key in your exploration.

One of the greatest differences between inner-directed soul guidance and outer mental control can be seen by looking at what happens in the breathing process. I spent a number of years teaching different forms of breathing techniques. But once I had been guided into the expanded inner screen and heart chakra exploration, my breathing patterns automatically began to change. Previously it had always taken me a number of weeks, through diaphragmatic breathing and progressive relaxation methods, to teach an individual how to begin experiencing levels of profound change in relaxation, concentration, and focus. This was especially true in order for them to become proficient enough to utilize the process in everyday life. These former methods, which are still practiced by many, all focus on the body and nervous system first becoming relaxed and then sending messages to the brain that the body is in fine condition. Meanwhile, the brain is usually interpreting events through one's inner thoughts, feelings, and perceptions, which generally are in total conflict with the messages of the physical body. Consequently, for relaxation to be effective, the brain must shift its focus to believing in the information that is physically being experienced through the body and its breathing, rather than believing the other perceptions that are present. But I have found that by working with the expanded inner screen and heart chakra, individuals are able to shift their focus through a very direct process, one that will automatically alter every physiological system in a matter of minutes, without any focus on the physical body—not even on breath control. In fact, some individuals actually become startled because their breathing moves so quickly into a deep and quiet state that they sometimes feel it necessary to take a deep breath to be sure they are still alive. When individuals attempt to use outer breathing techniques in conjunction with these new methods, they actually slow their progression into the awakening inner spaces. So allow yourself to put aside your old beliefs and ideas, and just see for yourself what transpires. Physiological changes, as well as other changes, will occur within the first several sessions of exploring this process. And as you allow yourself to deepen in this first level, you will begin to experience the potentials that exist in allowing yourself to shift your awareness from the outer control of the mind into the inner-directed guidance of your soul's energies.

Recall that we earlier looked at the three choices we have in order to bring about change. The first two choices explore looking for change to occur either through directly solving the existing problem, or through identifying the underlying causes that exist and allowing the change to occur at a deeper level. Both of these methods imply that one's outer mind or focus is capable of bringing about a solution to the problem. The third approach to change, which I call transformative change, necessitates our understanding that all problems are an energy, an energy that holds a lower vibrational quality that becomes a highly diffused energy created out of the confusion of the outer mind. By exploring the process of "transmutation" and initiating "The Expanded Inner Screen and The Heart Chakra Exploration," we are able to bring forward a heightened and focused energy that will allow us to shift our awareness from the outer focus of the mind into an inner focus directed by the energies of our soul. Whenever we find ourselves caught at the level of a problem, we can be sure that our focus is outwardly directed and that we are searching for solutions through the outer mind. This clearly signals that our focus of energy is not at the level of the heart chakra.

Once we have established an inner connection, we can then begin the process of bringing forward the heightened energies through the quadrants. The process of exploring the quadrants will change and deepen with each new exploration, but for now, it will suffice that you explore this at your current level of awareness. By focusing upon the potential or spiritual quadrant (upper right), you are asking for the emergence of the heightened energy that is needed for the new direction we are exploring. Do not be concerned if you have no idea what that direction will be. The sole purpose of focusing within this quadrant is to bring forth the heightened energy and to allow yourself to remain focused at this level until you experience a stable quality of the energy. Some individuals may begin to see images or receive an inner-direction at this time. That's great! Others will not see or understand anything at this point. They sense only the feeling of a heightened energy. That's great, too! The mere emergence of the heightened energy is the vital key! Once you feel a completeness in the spiritual quadrant, allow your focus to shift into the mental quadrant (upper left) and ask that this heightened energy merge into a new set of attitudes, beliefs, and perceptions that will allow you to live out your new direction. (Again, do not focus a great deal on the specifics of the process; the focus should be on the new energies of this direction.) When this feels complete in the mental quadrant, ask to move into the emotional quadrant (lower left), and allow the heightened energies to shift your focus from your outer emotions into your inner feeling state of unconditional love. Through this awareness allow yourself to feel and to know that you can live out your new direction. Once this feels complete, shift into the body quadrant (lower right), and allow the heightened energies to merge into your physical body, bringing about the inner sensations and move- ments that will be needed for your body to carry out the new directions. Remember that our physical bodies are always living out our current perceptions, and in order to create something new, a new body energy, inner image, and a physical change is needed. When this feels complete, move into the center point, expand your screen and feel that deepen within your heart chakra. At the same time, ask all four elements to unify into a living state—spirit or potential, mental and new beliefs, feelings of unconditional love, and your new physical body energy. At this level of your explora- tions, ask to feel, sense, or see the new direction that is emerging for you, and ask to experience yourself living from this inner direction in all aspects of your everyday world. Do not attempt to control or direct the feeling or image; allow it to emerge and pull you into the inner-directed guidance that dwells deep within you. As the energy is heightened it will set your new focus for you, and this is when you will begin to experience a clarity in the image or feel a specific sense of new direction beginning to emerge. If the energy is not fully set at its appropriate level, more inner exploration is required before any new action will begin. It will, however, always emerge, and you will sense and know when it is set for action.

Take the time to go through this exploration on several different occasions so that you become familiar with the expanded screen, quadrants, and their respective energies. Allow this exploration to become your new form of basic centering. Explore this process throughout your day and prior to reading this book.

CHAPTER THREE

EXPLORING PERSONAL TRANSFORMATION

My first direct awareness of transformation began in 1973 when, within a few short weeks, I gave up a secure and successful career in business to enroll in a Master of Science program in Pre-Clinical Psychology. When I finally came to the realization that it was time to quit my job in the business world, my outer mind went into a frenzy. Yet, another part of me knew that this was the right decision, one for which I had long been inwardly preparing. Since 1970 I had been experiencing a reoccurring dream in which I was being asked to switch careers and move into the area of psychology. These dreams were so strong that the feelings accompanying them would often stay with me for weeks at a time. However, my outer mind felt that such a drastic change would be an impossibility. I had recently married, and I had a number of financial responsibilities, not to mention a commitment to complete a four year scholarship. My employer was eagerly awaiting my return. My parents and close friends felt that I was being irresponsible in even thinking about a change and insisted that it was time to get on with my life. From nowhere within my outer support system was I encouraged to enter into a new life direction.

As I settled down and lived with these strong feelings for several years, the recurring dreams continued, but the theme had changed. I no longer was being asked or given a choice. Instead, in the dreams I saw myself suffering a series of heart attacks and, through this illness, I was being forced to change careers. I was frightened at first by these new dreams, but as my outer mind took charge I was able to rationalize them away, or so I thought. Then, due to a series of unexpected events I learned that I was being reassigned from my current job and was being moved into a new phase of management training. That evening, my dream emerged again, but much more directly than ever before. The series of dreams had always been vivid, but this one was something else. Even now, as I relate this experience to you, it feels every bit as real as it did that evening in December of 1973.

The first part of my dream was brought forward as a series of statements: "Change careers now or else! There is no longer time to turn back. If you continue with this career, expect to be DEAD within ten to twelve years!!" This was followed by a series of images showing me the direction that my life would be taking if I failed to take heed. What should I do? The outer part of my consciousness discounted the whole experience as being due to stress, fear of change, and a host of other logical causes. But during the next several days, the feelings became so strong and vivid that I knew I must follow them. I resigned from my business position and began to search for a program in psychology, in spite of the fact that I had no idea what being a psychologist actually meant! Once having made my decision to enter graduate school in the field of psychology, I immediately moved into a level of profound calm. If, however, I began to ruminate and question my decision, the anxiety would instantly return. Thanks to this feedback, I began to learn to follow the guidance from the inner part of me. During this time in my life I had no conscious understanding of what these various inner feelings were all about, but I did know how different it felt at last to experience the levels of inner silence and peace in contrast to the levels of stress and tension that I had known for so long.

Over the course of the next several weeks I was inwardly led through a step-by-step process, contacting a number of individuals which allowed me, in a matter of weeks, to be enrolled in both an undergraduate and a graduate degree program at two different schools. Whenever I tried to think about all that I needed to accomplish, I would panic; and yet, when I shifted my focus and followed each piece of the inner information, taking direct steps of action, a series of synchronized events would always open to me, moving my life in totally new directions. Prior to this point in my life, change had always been a difficult and painful task for me. However, this monumental change turned out to be the easiest and most profound transition I had ever made, despite the fact that my intellect was continually asking, "How did all of this happen?" Even today, as I continue to trust in surrendering to this inner part of myself, the events of my life progress just as smoothly, and I am always able to deepen into the next phase of my awakening odyssey.

After completing my degree in 1976 in Pre-Clinical Psychology, with a primary concentration in human learning and development, I continued with specialized training in psychoneurological testing geared towards learning disabilities and brain damage, along with specialized intellectual testing to round out my diagnostic and therapeutic skills.

My outer job as a clinician focused on misdirected behavioral patterns and aiding individuals to adjust back to their "normal" ways of living. My inner focus, however, was a burning desire to understand how the brain interacted in the learning process. I wanted to explore the process of self-actualization. I couldn't stop wondering how the human brain functions in what Maslow describes as a "peak experience," and I wanted to know what happens within the brain that allows us to function at the levels of self-actualization. I spent endless hours thinking, reading, and talking about these processes. Little did I know that by the spring of 1978 this phase of my learning would abruptly end. No longer would I be experiencing my quest as merely an intellectual and hypothetical process. I was about to find myself actually involved in the direct exploration of the deeper inner realms of Soul/Mind/Body transformation. Through the awakening of my inner self-actualizing energies, I was to begin my own personal transformation. This, in turn, would drastically alter all of my firmly held concepts concerning outer reality, traditional psychology, and brain functioning. Life as I knew it would never be the same!

As I began to experience levels of inner change, I realized that each of us inherently holds the means to naturally incorporate a variety of experiences and awarenesses in our process of structuring outer reality. I learned to incorporate these new awarenesses into my relationships, my career, and the everyday events of my life. My greatest challenge was to allow my physical body to move into a process of continual change and restructuring that was led by an inner mechanism— a mechanism which I later came to call my "inner-directed guidance." All of these changes initially both frightened and excited me.

Since that time I have come to realize that the means for personal transformation can only occur as I move into and explore the post-biological phase of development, opening into the levels of heightened energy. I discovered that the pathway for my own personal transformation had always existed within me (as it does within you) and that it could be safely awakened through the exploration of the heart chakra and the triune brain. This awakening gave me the opportunity to merge with and become one with my own inner self-actualizing pulse, or that aspect that is often called the Divine or inner-directed soul guidance. As I consciously chose to cooperate and move through this spiritual emergence, I found that I could no longer hold onto the old belief structures that defined who I thought I was. Through these explorations, I saw, felt, and experienced what I now understand to be our purpose of being human— a living and expanding human energy system guided by the energies of our inner soul force. I then stood, as others before me have stood, on the edge of yet another inner evolutionary breakthrough—that of "living as an expanded human energy system and being awakened into living at a heightened level of creative human potential." Having experienced these new levels of inner-awareness since 1978, I have never been able to "stuff" my life back into its former comfortable, predictable, secure, but boring box.

Within each human being there are two primary forces of energy. The first, and most obvious of these, is the actual physical energy, which guides the biological and physical growth and maintains the structure of outer reality and creativity. The second force is the potential, or self-actualizing energy, which lies dormant within the heart chakra, waiting to be awakened in order to guide each of us into our post-biological development and into a heightened order of creativity. The utilization of the heart chakra energy shifts one's focus from the outer reality, wherein the basic function is the maintenance of biological and physical necessities, into the awakening of one's inner self-actualizing pulse. This allows the focus to shift into an inner reality, allowing an inner-directed guidance to emerge which can subsequently restructure one's outer awareness into a new level of unity and livingness.

Individuals are able to enter into this process of personal transformation regardless of their previous occupations and varied levels of intellectual understanding. Each individual enters the process of awakening while being focused at their own unique level of awareness. But once the self-actualizing energy begins to fully emerge, both stabilization and excitement emerge naturally as one shifts into and utilizes the heart chakra as the primary focal point for consciousness. Each specific energy center is directly linked to a specific focus of consciousness as well as to a specific psychological focus or orientation toward reality. The process of directly shifting one's awareness into the heart chakra actually begins the movement of being within the observer state of exploring the new, heightened perceptions of unity. When we are dealing with our primitive emotional feelings, the focal point of energy is within either the solar plexus or the splenic chakra. As we move into the process of becoming very intellectual and perceive life through intellectual perceptions, we are focused through the third eye center, while sexual thoughts and feelings are focused through the lower abdominal and root chakras. Thus, exploring the ability to shift the focal point of one's energy directly into the heart center (located at the center of the chest cavity), allows us to automatically alter our perception from that of an outer focus into the observer state of focus, thereby experiencing a level of human emotion and feeling that emerges from unconditional love.

As you have already begun to experience through Exploration #2, the combined effect of shifting the focus into the heart center and of opening into the expanded inner screen will allow you to perceive reality from a different and more unified perspective. This shifting into and utilizing the heart chakra as one's primary focal point of reference toward reality constitutes the primary emphasis of Transformational Psychology. At a later point I will discuss the process of shifting one's focus through the various energy centers in order to experience how easily our five senses and outer perceptions can be altered.

All persons who awaken share a similar process as they allow their inner focus to shift into the heart center. Through an awakening brought forth from the heightened self-actualizing energies, individuals will learn to experience, move, and create from their own "inner uniqueness" as the process emerges through the heart. Through such an awakening, I have encountered a totally different perception of what it means for me to be human. And all who travel this journey similarly find that their current perceptions of life, along with their habitual structures of living, no longer seem valid nor fit within their new awarenesses and experiences. As individuals learn to explore new perceptions, behaviors, and physical body changes, they automatically begin to experience the new levels of post-biological development. This, in turn, allows them to construct a new foundation upon which to base life as it evolves from the inner-awareness states.

As an inner self-actualizing energy begins to awaken, individuals experience an automatic alteration in their perceptual framework of both themselves and of the situations in which they are involved in life. One moment they may be stuck within their old habits of thinking or perceiving through their outer focused intellectual mind, and just moments later can begin experiencing the inner movement of the awakening energy and can immediately gain new insights and perceptions. For example, one of the first realizations that I experienced in 1978 was that my own perceptions of reality had become very fluid. Traditionally, when I had been focused upon a problem, the only thing that existed for me was that problem. But I now discovered that if I shifted and allowed the inner-awareness to emerge, the problem no longer held any substance. I came to understand that my perceptions were "state-bound," based upon whatever I chose for my focus. But when I was able to release that particular focus by allowing an inner heightened energy to emerge, another perception or level of consciousness would always emerge to take its place.

Eventually I realized that many levels of reality exist, and that each one of us is always perceiving life from our own particular focus, which is paralleled by an inner alignment of specific energy centers. This interaction can easily be seen in groups where participants explore highly charged emotional issues. A number of varied perceptions or points of view exist for any one particular situation, and it is interesting to observe how determined people are to hold onto their own perceptions as being the "right ones." And yet, each perception is always correct, since it emerges through the filters of a given individual's history. For example, a similar process occurs when you misplace your keys or a report. The more panicked you become, the more futile the search. However, another person can enter the room (one who is not "hooked" into your panic energy) and quickly find the "lost" item, sometimes right next to your hand. Or it can be even more frustrating when you later go back into the room, find the missing item where you had previously looked, and then wonder "who put it there," since you know it had not been there several minutes before.

We all have a choice as to what reality we will focus upon, though few individuals at any given moment believe that any other perception can possibly exist. Our emotionally charged perceptions are created through a narrowing of our focus, which is the result of old perceptions, habits, memories, and an inner righteousness that dictates that "this is the way it should be!" As we choose to allow the energies of this self-actualizing force to guide us, there emerges a heightened perception of cognitive functioning that eliminates the old habits and preconceived patterns of thinking and brings forward the choice to experience something new. Instead of allowing the outer mind to be in charge of rationalizing and analyzing every piece of information and then trying to make a decision based upon these outer facts, this awakening energy allows an inner synthesis to emerge which guides the intellect and emotions into new levels of understanding. This process changes the way one gathers and integrates information, and it opens the outer mind to a level of inner synthesis. This, in turn, awakens us into functioning at a heightened level of creativity. The outer intellectual and emotional mind is never eliminated, but rather, moves into a heightened state of cognitive functioning which is now in a continual state of being educated through the levels of energy that are emerging from the inner-awareness.

This process parallels man's first phase of biological development, during which time the outer mind was in a constant state of learning through the assimilation of information obtained through one's outer awareness and perception of outer events. As we now move through the phase of post-biological development, our process of education is changing. We will no longer base our learning on the recall of past information nor on perceptions based on old habits or outdated information. Rather, each action or thought will emerge from within, allowing the outer mind to continue functioning, but from a totally different source. The intellectual and emotional processes are part of our individual identity. However, we have the choice of operating from an outdated, habitual, limited, and primitive set of feelings and thoughts, or of awakening into an inner self-actualizing, creative, intuitive spark. The choice is always ours!

At the present stage of man's development, human beings are usually guided and motivated by their emotions, feelings, and personal needs, which may not always be in the best interest of their deeper, inner personal growth. In most instances, we are unaware of how easily we are manipulated by our more primitive human emotions, and thus we rarely perceive reality for what it is. At times we experience life through a filter or a cloud that distorts what our perceptions are trying to convey. At other times we use the process of denial or the repression of our feelings to such an extent that the outer mind or intellect takes over and once again distorts our outer reality. Regardless of the ways we experience this distortion, there exists within us, on a deep and personal level, a desire to change and move into a level of personal transformation. Most individuals will eventually tolerate the emergence of change if they experience a very severe personal crisis, but few openly welcome personal transformation or search it out. Most, instead, sit back and explore change through the process which I call the three "C's" of conflict, crisis, and chaos. Through this process, change always comes through a reaction to some actual or perceived event in life. By reaction, I mean that we neither change nor do anything different until great pressure or pain motivates us to do so. Even once we have acknowledged that our lives are "falling apart around us" and do finally surrender to the idea of change, we still have a tendency to move slowly and cautiously. Notice that the word <u>reaction</u> contains the exact same letters as does the word <u>creation</u>. The only difference is the positioning of the letter "C." By learning to shift the letter "C" out of <u>reaction</u> and allowing it to come first, we open into an inner "seeing" that will automatically move us into a process of <u>creation</u>.

In all living systems, change is always continually present. Without it, we would not survive. Yet, most individuals fight change and instead wait for the energies of reaction to emerge. Few individuals realize that a choice always exists as to how one chooses to change. It can be through the process of reaction, where crisis, conflict or chaos motivates us, or through the process of creation where we inwardly desire and search it out! When we are doing things out of our old habitual patterns and are holding onto our current perceptions as being the "only right ones" (even though it may not always feel good), we are waiting for our reaction to move us. When we choose to shift into a new inner C-ing and allow a new perception to emerge, we are moving into an inner-awareness based upon creation. Initially the same amount of energy is required to actualize the change. Waiting around for the reaction to occur, however, usually feels more traumatic since there is a buildup of the tensions or heightened energy necessary to change something. In creation we opt to awaken first into an inner C-ing, and then follow our inner creative energy; in reaction we utilize the three "C's" as our motivators and consequently must reevaluate life and its direction, hoping to move or change it into a creative direction. How do you initiate change in your life?

When I made my decision to change careers in 1973 I chose the inner creative path for change, rather than waiting for outer life events or an illness to take charge. If I had been sick, my family and friends would have supported me in my decision to change. However, my outer appearance was healthy, emotionally I was stable, and mentally I was alert. Who supports a drastic change when things are going well? At the end of the first year, during which time I had finished my undergraduate work in psychology in addition to completing twelve graduate hours, a similar feeling began to emerge, asking me to change schools and geographic location. Admittedly my first reaction was "Why now?" Then through a series of unexpected events I found myself being drawn to a small midwestern college in Fort Wayne, Indiana, and through another series of dreams I knew that it was now time to leave behind my personal relationships with family and friends, my possessions, and "whoever I thought I was." With very little financial security or outer resources, I physically, emotionally, mentally, and spiritually moved! This move initiated a domino effect of change that clearly showed me the importance of following one's inner direction and timing. Although I was quite frightened at the whole prospect, everything once again fell into place, and by January of 1975 I was living in Fort Wayne, Indiana.

During the ten weeks prior to my move, I had begun to have a series of dreams about writing a book concerning a different form of psychology that I would be exploring and developing while in Fort Wayne. My outer mind and my friends had a wonderful time laughing and teasing me about these dreams, and after I graduated in 1976, with no book written, I thought I had failed. Little did I realize what was yet in store for me over the next eleven years. I have since faced several other decisions requiring major change in my life. I eventually chose the inner creative pathway, although once I procrastinated so long that a near-death experience was necessary to motivate me back into a creative process for change.

Hopefully you can begin to sense and understand that these changes which I have been sharing were not conceived or mapped out by my outer mind. Nor did any outer part of me try to create or direct them. Some inner guiding force was at play in opening me into new levels of my inner self-actualizing development. There is but one simple criteria which I have found that works in distinguishing between the feelings of the energies of my inner guiding force and those of my personality directing and wanting the change—the former works! Under the direction of my inner guidance I find that all of the necessary pieces fall into place for me in such a way that I myself obviously could not be directing the entire process. The only thing required on my part is to create a level of inner silence, remain inwardly focused while I allow my self-actualizing energy to emerge, and then take direct action upon what is needed at that particular time. I always know when I am moving in the right direction because of the feedback I experience. When I follow and act upon the inner guidance, I continually feel a level of inner calmness and an expansion of my energies. On the other hand, anxiety and worry enter whenever I follow my intellectual or more primitive human emotions, or whenever I try to retreat to the habitual patterns held by my outer mind. It was important for me to learn to distinguish between the two processes, and I soon became aware of how easily the inner feelings of quiet and calmness emerged if I followed my inner guided path. Sometimes I would try to intellectually convince myself that I felt calm and inwardly quiet, but I always knew and felt the difference between the two.

As I now look back over the years of my personal transformation from my present vantage point, I can see that the changes in my life have always been preceded by an option to choose the creative path. And in some cases I did choose this pathway. However, in many instances I ignored the signs and chose to wait for the reactive path to emerge. Nevertheless, I can see now that I always had available to me the necessary levels of inner information and the opportunity for allowing the synchronized events to guide me easily through any approaching change. Having once opened to the creative pathway, I could more easily distinguish it and thus choose to follow it more often; but whenever the reactive path emerged, it became more difficult to trust what was currently emerging as being all right! In either case, a heightened level of energy from my inner-directed soul guidance was always available to shift me out of the confusion of my outer mind and into an inner self-actualizing direction, if I would just allow it.

I finally began to understand that whenever a so-called problem emerged, it was not because I was doing something wrong, but because I was doing something right! With this attitude, I could maintain my creative focus and at the same time perceive what was currently blocking me from moving on with life. Actually, any block that I "suddenly" encountered had always existed within me, but I was often unaware of it until it began to emerge. When something is ready to change, it will always emerge into the outer awareness because the time is right for the change to occur. At that moment, we have the full capabilities for implementing the change easily and swiftly. But if we view the situation as being due to something we have done wrong or if we are upset that change is again being required of us, we will miss taking advantage of our inner timing and will only make change more difficult at a later point. Each piece of information always emerges at its own level of inner timing, in conjunction with a heightened focused energy to move us into a new level of awareness. This constitutes the process that is called transmutation, whereby all of our perceptions and information will automatically begin to change either by choosing to move from within the inner creative flow or by choosing not to move at this time, which will automatically initiate the traditional reactive cycle for experiencing change. Regardless of our choice, change will occur.

Most individuals try to maintain their old levels of behaviors, and then wonder why nothing seems to work or why, when at a later time they choose to act upon the prior information, it no longer seems to fit with their new levels of perception. Nothing in life stands still. We are continually being asked to update our levels of inner information and to explore new resolutions to our perceptions. This allows our reactive energies the opportunity to easily transmute to a new and exciting creative pulse. The observer state opens the doorway for the heightened energies of transmutation to enter, which form the pathway into our ever present creative self-actualizing pulse. If we had not been ready to change, no awareness or alternative course of direction would have emerged in the first place.

I perceive that all of our so-called "problems" in life are not really problems at all; rather, we have made a choice to perceive the situation from a particular perspective. A heightened creative energy is naturally present at the moment of change, but if this needed change is not acknowledged, the creative energy is perceived as an energy of disorganization or confusion. For most of us it is usually a major crisis or problem that attracts and holds our full attention. And even then, we may decide not to take any immediate action. If we can begin to perceive that all reactive energies are merely a creative energy being manifested as a lower vibration, then we can understand the importance of letting ourselves move into the observer state and of allowing the process of transmutation and heightened energies to shift us into our new creative potential. Through the observer state it is first possible to find a level of inner peace and to feel the energies of unconditional love. From the perspective of this inner-awareness, we can observe what is currently happening in our lives. We can find an inner balance and subsequently open into perceiving new levels of unity. Once we are able to perceive a situation differently, we can feel secure in allowing the heightened energy to emerge. In this way, one can become a new and different person and can comfortably live at the new levels of inner awareness. If we should choose to focus back into the level of the problem, the process will reverse itself and we will find ourselves experiencing the same old feelings and thoughts.

We truly have the power to create our own reality, but we must choose between a reality that is based upon perceiving life from either the level of unity and the energies of unconditional love or from the levels of duality, whereby we get lost in situations we think will never change. Transmutation allows us to truly change the way we live if we will but allow a part of ourselves to transform into a new identity and thereby create a new set of perceptions regarding who we are. As this new awareness is allowed to emerge, we will move into a peaceful synchronization with the people and events in our lives. If we do not allow the heightened energy to emerge, a different pattern of synchronization and events will evolve. Nothing in life is ever an isolated event, and we are continually in the process of change. How will you choose to change and interact in your life?

For me, the self-actualizing pulse results in a feeling that some inner part of me is pulling me along a certain creative path. Throughout my life, I have understood very well how to "push" myself along a path in order to accomplish a given goal. As long as I was doing the pushing, I had some sense of where I was going. This constituted what I used to call creativity. However, whenever I achieved a so-called creative goal through this form of push, my initial feelings were always focused upon whether it was really worth all the stress, tension, and pain that was created in order to achieve the end result. Through the process of awakening into my self-actualizing energy or inner creative pulse, I may not always know the end result, but I know that it feels right. Whenever I am being guided along my inner path, the inner silence, calmness, joy and excitement make up for any lack of outer knowledge.

Today I can accomplish many things with a level of ease and excitement that years before would have been very difficult. I used to find myself moving in a certain direction or creating things in a certain way, and my intellect would be in a constant state of turmoil. My outer mind just knew that I would never be able to accomplish those things. And as long as I was caught into those old feelings, my inner perspective would remain lost. But once having experienced the emergence of my inner awakening energy, I have never again felt alone in what I am creating or doing, and as I allow the "inner pull" to move me, I naturally move into the directions that I am needing to explore. Other individuals tell me that this process of living from one's inner guidance requires a great deal of trust. I usually smile at this, because at least now I know that the direction toward which I am moving will always work out for me and will inwardly be very successful. The process by which I previously created actually required greater trust just to be able to keep pushing and straining along each step of the way. My relationships with others, especially with my family and close friends, are very different when the inner self-actualizing energy is guiding me than when I am moving out of the push energy.

I have learned through my own struggles that the process of transformative change can be simple, easy, and fun. And I have learned that transformative change is available to every human being. I know, however, that it is much easier to accept this at a time when one is not faced with a series of reactive situations in life. In my own personal work with individuals afflicted with a life threatening illness, I have found that the majority of them will not allow their lives or their communication patterns to change, even under the emotional reality of death. In fact, most individuals react so negatively to ideas of change that they admit that they would rather die than change what they feel and think. They fail to understand that the illness is asking them to do exactly that— change or die! And through the process of dying, one changes!

It is difficult at first for most individuals to realize that physical or psychological illness is actually a gift that is helping them to focus on new levels of transformative change in their lives. The changes that are being required through the mental or physical illness are announcing that one still has time to do something different; if not, you would already have died. The major problem that both psychology and medicine face is that of a system that will always fail. From a medical perspective, each one of us is going to physically die, and from a psychological perspective we will continue to develop stress while other aspects of our psychological patterns continue to emerge. This is a given of life, at least at the present stage of our human development.

What would happen if psychology were to cease focusing upon the criteria of achieving a stress free state and cease looking for a system that is free from psychological crisis? What would happen if being able to move through points of personal transformation were of key importance, regardless of how long it might take an individual? What would happen if we were to view these aspects of reactive energy as being something wonderful and important that was happening to change the way we organized our world? What would happen if professionals focused on teaching individuals how to change their inner psychological makeup and perceptions about living, rather than hastily medicating them so they could cope? In my opinion, a focus on personal transformation should be the primary emphasis in the field of psychology. This would not be a process which focused on doing something "right;" rather, it would be a process whereby when some difficulty did emerge in one's life (for whatever reason), the deeper inner dynamics would always revolve around the focus of a major transformative change in the individual's life. The period of difficulty would be viewed as a signal that individuals need to awaken and explore a deeper inner focus for their individual existence, and that they need to allow the heightened energies of their inner guidance to emerge and direct them into a new life path. It would not be seen as a time just to give up and live out the pain; nor would it indicate that one should just resign themselves to coping with their current levels of feelings, communications, or relationships.

This same process would also evolve in the area of medicine. The physical illness would be viewed as a part of the personal transformation, with time being devoted to the physical, mental, emotional, and spiritual dimensions of the individual's life. Many doctors today believe that illness and other physical problems will begin to change as the personality of the individual is changed. And when it is time for an individual to die, they will die quickly and with a sense of inner purpose and peace. Individuals need to learn to participate fully in their journey in order to feel that they have some level of control over and within their lives.

The prospect of personal transformation is frightening to most individuals because of the "unknown feelings" that emerge. Yet this sensing into the unknown has a great deal to do with experiencing the heightened energies that encompass this level of change. Even something as simple as a bud of a flower opening into full bloom requires an enormous amount of energy. Just because the outer mind is not aware of the heightened energies does not mean these levels of transformative energy do not exist. Being unaware of the inner sensations often causes us to automatically react to change with a negative or adverse reaction, without really

:rstanding why. By not allowing change to emerge as a natu-
ow of life we create a false sense of security. As a result, we then
o....1 allow our intellect or emotions to run wild, creating a wide
array of responses to life but never creating anything that is
actually new. In most cases, we just continue creating or structuring our same traditional perceptions of reality.

Regardless of whether it is through a reactive or a creative
choice, individuals need to fully participate in their personal
transformation. The process of awakening one's creative potential
allows individuals the choice to fully participate in the journey that
is evolving within their lives. I have seen many individuals with
similar patterns of illness (either physical, mental, or emotional),
whom the helping professions then attempted to "treat" in similar
ways, totally ignoring the deeper underlying dynamics that are
at play in each unique human being. The process of Transformational Psychology, on the other hand, is not to "normalize"
individuals. Rather, it is to allow them to awaken into their own
inner self-actualizing energy and, within this process, to allow an
inner guiding force to direct them into their next level of personal
transformation. Reactive energies are merely the feedback announcing that change is needed— NOW!

It has taken many centuries for us to begin to understand and
prove ideas that we have inwardly "known" were valid. Very little
of what we have observed in the last several hundred years is
actually new or resembles a true inner creative spark. Sure, our
technological advances have made great strides, but we are still
debating and struggling with many of the same issues as before—
war, religious rights, sexuality, our purpose in life, the vastness of
the universe, and so forth.

Much of what we call technological advancement has little or
nothing to do with humanity learning to live together on the same
planet in a creative and inwardly harmonious way. Remember that
during the last Renaissance change continued as the major focus
for several centuries, thus allowing every aspect of life to evolve into
new structures. Since that time, these ideas have steadfastly
remained the basis upon which all civilization must exist. In reality
though, many of those ideas were merely the next phase of a very
broad evolutionary process for understanding ourselves, as well as
our relationship to others and to our world. We are once again in
an evolutionary process of understanding ourselves, others, and
our world from a new and broader base. This time the level of
change will materialize through a new evolutionary structure that
will alter the very fabric from which life as we know it has evolved.
Our exploration in this new Renaissance involves opening to a

totally new inner self-actualizing heart-centered force within us. We must then allow a new inner perception of self to emerge into the everyday existence of our lives. When we reach this level of transformative change, we will have evolved to a point where our inner-awareness can emerge as our outer reality, allowing us to live and create from totally new levels of creation. Individuals initially respond to this concept with either panic, chaos, or great excitement. How do you respond to the concept of this new evolutionary level of transformative change?

We can open naturally into the heightened energy of our inner guiding force. When I first opened into this deeper dimension, I was awed by the depth of understanding that naturally emerged. The energies of my inner guiding force moved me beyond all levels of intellectual comprehension and opened me into experiencing a vastness of feelings and emotions that few individuals ever experience. These new "feeling states" are what I earlier described as being the energies of unconditional love. Within the new levels of awareness, I was able to feel, experience, and live within an expanded awareness of unity. I did not have to try to create this state. Rather it was, and always is, present and available to me as long as I allow my focus to shift and move into the inner self-actualizing pulse. Both mystics and physicists discuss this unseen "force" of energy and view it as the essence out of which all reality, as we know it, manifests. This force of energy exists at various levels, and it cradles the seeds of our creative, self-actualizing process and holds inherent within itself the ability to "awaken" us.

In exploring the inner spaces with terminally ill individuals who have been living primarily through a reaction process, I have encountered many who are suddenly able to sense and experience the inner feelings and heightened energies even more easily than can many "healthy" individuals. This I believe is due to the fact that during a serious illness or crisis, a part of one's consciousness moves into a reaction state and simultaneously opens one to the gift of an inner awareness capable of guiding them through the awakening phase of their own odyssey. This only happens, however, if we choose not to get caught into what we think is developing out of the physical crisis, and learn instead to explore the inner realms that can move us beyond the perceptions of illness.

When the outer focus of one's personality is present, we can feel our fears, doubts, worries, apprehension, and confusion. These feelings exist as a result of choosing not to change and of being determined to hold onto our old habits in thinking, feeling, and doing. As individuals open to the energies of their inner self-actualizing force, they experience a series of transpersonal feelings opening them into an awareness of knowing. This is the point at which the personality and the energies of one's soul, or Divine Essence merge. Although our vocabulary cannot adequately describe these aspects of awareness, once they have been experienced, words are no longer necessary. When you are in the presence of an individual who is within the expanded energetic states of unconditional love, you are aware that something feels different. The presence of unconditional love can also be felt in objects and in services because a heightened order of creative energy has emerged and manifests itself to all that is present. From the inner self-actualizing states of unconditional love emerges the source of all inner knowing.

The process of Transformational Psychology also explores deep levels of transformative change in the physical body by allowing the self-actualizing force or the energies of the inner-directed guidance to emerge into all physical activities. This allows the body to evolve and change in its physical appearance, size, and ability. I relate these changes to sports activities and other instances when individuals experience a sudden and dramatic shift in awareness that automatically changes their physical form and allows them to manifest additional physical power, strength, and endurance. Such changes occur without any outer conscious thought; they just naturally emerge at critical times. Michael Murphy describes such events in his well-documented book **The Psychic Side Of Sports**. I believe that these and similar changes are a part of man's inner evolutionary process of awakening into the beginning levels of post-biological development. This allows the energies of our inner consciousness, or soul force, to become more involved in guiding both our physiological and our outer physical changes. Large numbers of individuals are already awakening into this internal shift and are allowing themselves to transcend to abilities beyond even their wildest imaginations. Through such levels of physical restructuring we can learn to expand our current physical movement and capabilities, as well as increase our endurance in sports, exercise, and creative living. We will be in a constant state of defining new potentials or vistas for ourselves in our mental, emotional, physical, and spiritual understanding of "who we are" and "what we are to become!"

Before we continue, I would like to guide you through two separate explorations so that you can experience for yourself the power of change that is available through this process. The primary focus of these two explorations is to feel and experience the ease with which the physical body can change to reflect the focus of one's inner self-actualizing force. If possible, use the pre-recorded tape or make your own tape of EXPLORATION #3:

PHYSIOLOGICAL SELF-REGULATION. If not, first read through the exploration and then experience step-by-step what it has to offer you. And don't forget to have fun with it!

Sit back in a comfortable, quiet position *** close your eyes *** allow your awareness to move into the center of your inner screen *** ask that your inner screen expand *** ask it to expand several times until you feel the screen around you, with your focus at the center of this inner space *** *** ask the boundaries and the quadrants to emerge *** ask the center point of your screen to move into the center of your chest, your heart chakra *** ask the crystalline structure of emerald green light to emerge and begin to pulsate at your heart chakra *** ask to feel the waves of the pulsation move from this center point throughout and beyond your physical body *** ask it to go deeper and just allow it to happen *** bring your awareness into your intellectual quadrant, the upper left *** ask that an image of an outdoor scene emerge, one that is very quiet and relaxing for you *** one where you are alone and feel comfortable being alone *** it may be the mountains, the desert, the ocean, a farm, a lake, or any place that brings forward an inner sense of relaxation *** move your awareness into your emotional quadrant, the lower left *** ask to feel, sense and experience the warmth of the sun and feelings of relaxation within you *** *** shift your awareness into the body quadrant, your lower right *** ask to experience within your body these feelings of relaxation *** *** shift your awareness into your potential or spiritual quadrant, the upper right *** ask to fully experience these deeper feelings of relaxation *** bring your awareness into the center point and ask to unify these profound feelings and experiences of relaxation within yourself, within the potential, mental, emotional and physical aspects of your being *** *** ask it to move deeper within you, and just let it happen *** *** ask that feeling to move through your nervous system to the tip of your spine *** ask it to spread to the tips of your fingers and toes *** *** bring your focus into your lower right quadrant, your body quadrant, and feel that your lower right quadrant and your left shoulder, arm, and hand are one and the same *** and ask in a very gentle way that your left arm and hand feel warm and relaxed *** maintain your focus within your body quadrant, your lower right, and ask that feeling to go deeper *** ask it to deepen more, moving all through your left shoulder, arm, and hand *** sense and feel the warmth and relaxation *** allow your body quadrant to be connected into your left ankle and left foot *** sense that your left ankle and foot are warm and relaxed *** ask it to go deeper *** allow the body quadrant to be focused on your lower back, on the left side only *** sense that your lower back is relaxed *** and feel the whole left side of your body as being connected to your lower right quadrant *** ask it to relax *** *** ask it to go deeper on your whole left side *** *** allow the focus in your lower right quadrant to include both shoulders and shoulder blades *** ask them to relax *** feel that your shoulders are heavy and warm *** connect your right foot and ankle into your lower right quadrant, asking them to relax *** now feel your entire body as being within your lower right quadrant *** and ask the entire body to go deeper into the profound states of relaxation and deep warmth *** *** bring your focus into your lower left quadrant, and ask to get in touch with the deep feelings of profound relaxation *** and feel this within you *** bring your awareness into the upper right quadrant, and ask to experience a deeper, more profound level of relaxation than you have ever experienced before *** allow that energy to deepen within the inner space of this quadrant *** bring your focus into the center of your expanded inner screen *** and ask it to unify you into a deep and profoundly relaxed state *** spirit, mind, emotion, body *** bring your awareness into the potential quadrant, the upper right *** become aware of how you're feeling right now, mentally, emotionally, physically *** ask to be able to move yourself into this same space within a matter of two minutes or less *** *** see yourself tomorrow sitting down and in a matter of two minutes or less, recalling the step-by-step process of bringing back this feeling and moving back into this level of profound relaxation in the quiet of your mind, your emotions, and your body *** *** bring your focus to your lower right quadrant, and become aware of how the body feels when you are deeply and profoundly relaxed *** shift to the lower left, your emotional quadrant, and ask to experience emotionally these profoundly relaxing feelings *** move to your upper left quadrant, the intellectual quadrant, and experience the knowingness that you can create these total feelings and even more in less than two minutes *** bring your awareness to the center point *** and ask that you can unify these deep inner profound states within less than two minutes, spiritually, mentally, emotionally, physically *** ask that your body go deeper, and let it happen *** ask your body to become very heavy and warm *** ask your body to feel light and energized *** ask that you remain inwardly focused, light, energized and inwardly alert *** ask this feeling to remain and to become your outer awareness *** *** and when you are ready, allow the inner awareness to become your outer reality and open your eyes.

Most individuals are surprised at how easily their inner focus can alter the physiological processes of the body. As individuals experience the outdoor scene, they report tension and aches leaving areas of their back, neck, shoulders, head, hands and feet (often replaced by feelings of warmth), along with a slower, more rhythmic heartbeat and breathing pattern. Many are surprised at the various levels of relaxation that they sense within themselves. As we begin to explore different areas of the body through the expanded inner screen and physical quadrant, layer upon layer of relaxation begins to emerge, bringing individuals into deeper levels of inner unity. They are amazed at how easily the body can shift from being very cold, stressed, and tense into feeling light, energized, and relaxed. When you are focused within the inner spaces, and the self-actualizing pulse is guiding you into the deeper levels of inner-awareness, the physical body changes very quickly and easily to whatever the focus is. Just by asking to move deeper, you move deeper. Even with a great deal of work and concentration, it would be difficult to create these same levels of physiological change; but through the process of moving into the inner self-actualizing pulse, just "asking" allows it to occur. As we begin to open and live at the levels of inner-awareness, our physical bodies will reflect the inner changes through a fluidity in movement and relaxation. For this to occur, the physical body will become very different from what it traditionally has been and currently is. Even those individuals who have practiced other methods of relaxation are surprised at how quickly and deeply the body can be altered through this process.

In EXPLORATION #4: MIND-BODY EDUCATION, we will explore how to allow the emergence of an inner feeling or image that will let the physical body first experience a series of inner movements and then will allow the body to be physically altered, gaining a level of flexibility and physical change in the muscles throughout the body. The most important directive for this exploration is simply to not try too hard. Be open to the concept that just relaxing and allowing an ease in movement will greatly reeducate your muscles into the movements for which we are striving. If you can, listen to this exploration on a tape. If not, read through the exercise and take the time to explore each step. Remember, each one of these explorations is structured to allow you to slowly shift into a deeper awareness of your potential.

"Choose a location about three feet in front of a wall where you can stand with your hands stretched out in front of you and can freely move your outstretched hands around your body without touching a wall, object, or another person *** *** allow your hands to rest at your sides *** place your feet comfortably apart *** you will keep them in this position for the entire exploration *** move your right arm and hand out in front of you at shoulder height *** hold your head and eyes so that you are looking down your hand to the tips of your fingers *** keeping your eyes focused on your fingers, slowly move your head, arm, fingers to the right as far as you can comfortably go *** be sure you do not move your feet from the ground and do not force the stretch *** be sure your head and eyes are still in line with your arm, not ahead of your arm *** visually mark this spot on the wall *** bring your body, head, and arm back to the starting position *** lower your hand to your side *** *** this time you are going to keep your eyes, head, and focus straight ahead *** again raise your right hand and arm to shoulder height *** slowly move just the right hand and arm to the right, straight out from your body *** now bring it back in front of you *** allow your hand and arm to move slowly but freely back and forth, to and from this position, six or seven times *** remember to keep your head and eyes focused straight ahead *** *** *** good, now lower your arm and let it rest for a moment *** we are going to repeat the same hand and arm movement again, but this time your head and eye focus is going to move to the left as your hand and arm move to the right, and when you bring your hand and arm back in front of you, your head and eye focus will also be in front of you *** do this movement six or seven times, slowly but freely *** *** most people are not familiar with this feeling, so allow yourself to experience the sensation of it *** *** now lower your arm and let it rest for a moment *** again put your right arm and hand up at shoulder's height in front of you *** your eyes are looking down the arm and focusing on the tips of your fingers *** slowly move your head, eyes, arm, and hand as far as you can to the right *** did you easily go past your first visual mark on the wall? *** now visually mark the new point to which you moved your arm *** bring your head, eyes, arm, and hand back in front of you, lower your arm and let it rest *** *** *** now we are going to explore the left side of your body *** put your left hand and arm straight out in front of you *** with your eyes, follow down the arm to the tip of your fingers, allow your head, eyes, arm, and hand to turn easily and slowly to the left as far as you can *** do not move your feet or strain *** mark this point visually on the wall *** bring your arm back in front of you, lower it, and rest a moment *** now close your eyes *** everything you are now going to do will be experienced through your expanded inner screen and the physical body quadrant, the lower right *** do not physically perform any outer movements unless I ask you to open your eyes *** ask your inner screen to expand several times *** focus your inner awareness at your heart chakra *** now ask it to deepen and feel the pulsation of the emerald crystalline structure moving throughout and beyond your physical form *** bring your awareness into the lower right physical quadrant *** explore the remainder of this exploration from this inner space *** ask to Feel, Sense, and Imagine (FSI) that your left arm and hand is being raised in front of you *** (FSI) that your head and eye focus is straight ahead *** (FSI) your inner left arm and hand moving to the left, until it is away from your body *** (FSI) it moving back in front of you *** now (FSI) that same movement slowly and freely, six or seven times, with your head and eye focus remaining directly in front of you at all times *** *** **** allow your inner sensory hand and arm to rest *** again raise your inner sensory left hand and arm and as you repeat this movement to the left, (FSI) your head and eye focus moving to the right *** and as your left hand and arm return to a position in front of you, (FSI) your head and eye focus also being back in front of you *** slowly and freely repeat this movement six or seven times *** allow yourself to fully experience and sense each one of these inner movements *** *** *** now sense that your inner left arm and hand is in front of you and that you are looking down the inner sensory arm with your inner eyes and focusing at the tips of your left fingers *** now (FSI) that your hand, arm, head and eye focus are moving slowly to the left, at least one foot or more beyond that first point on the wall *** allow yourself to fully feel, sense, and experience this *** hold this for a moment *** bring your inner arm back in front of you *** now open your eyes, physically raise your left arm out in front of you, and direct your head and eye focus down your arm to your finger tips *** now slowly move your left arm and body, in the manner that you just inwardly sensed, to the left until you move past your previous mark on the wall, noticing how easily you can move beyond that point *** hold this for a moment *** bring it back *** rest your hand and arm *** most likely you were able to easily move a foot or more beyond your first mark *** close your eyes again *** raise your inner sensory right hand and arm, and focus your inner sensory head and eyes at the tip of your fingers *** allow the inner sensory right hand, arm, head, and eye focus to move to the right and to go past your last mark on the right by a foot or more *** hold it *** bring it back *** keep your inner sensory head and eye focus straight ahead and move your inner sensory right arm and hand six or seven times back and forth to the right, slowly and freely *** *** *** once again (FSI) your right hand and arm moving to the right while your inner sensory head and eye focus move to the left and back again, six or seven times *** *** *** once again focus your inner head and eyes on the inner right hand, arm, and fingers out in front of you and (FSI) moving them together past the last mark by another six inches or more *** hold it there *** bring it back *** now open your eyes, raise your physical right hand and arm, and focus your eyes and head on the fingers *** slowly move the physical right hand, arm, eyes, and head past the last mark at least six inches or more *** hold it for a moment *** return it to the position in front of you *** lower and rest *** <u>close</u> <u>your</u> <u>eyes</u> and repeat the same process with your inner sensory left hand, arm, eyes, and head, moving to and beyond the mark to your left *** repeat as before, first with the inner head and eyes focused straight ahead, moving the inner sensory left hand back and forth slowly and freely *** *** *** then repeat with the inner head and eyes moving to the right, and the inner sensory left hand and arm moving to the left, back and forth, slowly and freely, six or seven times *** *** *** (FSI) raising your left hand and arm, with eyes and head focused on fingertips and moving beyond the left mark six inches or more *** hold it *** bring it back *** <u>now</u> <u>open</u> <u>your</u> <u>eyes</u> and physically go through the process *** how far did you go? *** return and rest."

I am continually amazed at how easily we can reeducate our bodies into more expansive movements just by breaking down some of the habit structures that we have created in life. During the initial phase of this exploration, utilizing the right side of the body, we isolated a series of movements in order to allow ourselves to gain greater freedom. We very seldom move just our hand and arm without having our eyes and head move in the same direction, much less having them move slowly in opposite directions. But by doing this, we break down a set of habits within our mind-body connection and in so doing gain a foot or more of flexibility in our movement. This concept was first introduced to me by Moshe Feldenkrais in 1978, and since then I have explored numerous possibilities in the reorganization of body structures as a means of handling the levels of change that are needed in order to awaken into a heightened energy state. What I find exciting is the ease with which the left side of the body changes just through the use of the expanded inner screen and body quadrant. Nearly everyone achieves the same or better results through the use of the inner process than what they achieve with the actual physical movement. By continuing to explore each side of the body, utilizing only the inner sensory movements, the body is able to automatically reorganize into new levels of inner awareness and movement. Did you notice that at some point in the exploration you were no longer directing the inner movements, but instead had moved into the observer state and were watching as the movements were inwardly occurring? If you began this process, that is great. Allow yourself to continue to explore the process of this inner part creating the inner images and inner movement for you. If you were not able at this time to sense these inner experiences, don't worry. After several additional explorations you will automatically be sensing and allowing this inner process to evolve.

Become aware of how your shoulders, neck, and eyes now feel. How about your feet, thighs, and pelvic area? The simple process you just experienced restructures the entire body. Some individuals are able to gain two to three feet of flexibility and can allow that to remain for hours and even days before the body once again restructures itself back into old patterns. Physical stretching exercises can never bring the same level of change as quickly nor as easily. Allow yourself to think back to a course on physiology and the body, and recall all that must take place internally in the brain, nervous system, and muscles to release this same amount of tension and restructure the body into a similar level of flexibility. But by utilizing the expanded inner screen, all of this happens with little or no direct physical movement. Such is the inner power that resides in the inner self-actualizing energy within each one of our hearts. It directs the body based upon the inner focus which one is maintaining. An organized focus will direct the body in one direction, while a confused focus will direct the body differently. What we will be exploring later will lead to an understanding of how an inner-directed focus can allow the body to restructure in much deeper and more profound ways.

I sincerely hope you can begin to understand that your body is indeed a reflection of your focus, and that later you can accept it as a reflection of the awakening that is occurring within you. You may be one of numerous individuals whose outer mind or intellect cannot readily accept this understanding of the physical body; if so, you may begin to rationalize these ideas into a structure that feels more comfortable for you. Be open within yourself. Allow yourself to experience what can transform, one way or another. Later I will ask you to try this entire exploration again, but without any outer physical movement at all until the last test, allowing all direction to emerge from your inner guidance. This will allay your skepticism. But first we will need to awaken some other areas within the brain and nervous system to facilitate such an emergence.

Just what is this heightened order of creativity to which I have been referring? Is it something that can be outwardly taught, as in mathematics or science? Or does this level of creativity extend beyond an intellectual understanding of who and what we are as human beings? The way in which most individuals describe creativity has nothing to do with what we are exploring in this odyssey. Within this new framework, we are opening into the next phase of our post-biological development where creativity is not something that the outer mind manufactures, nor is it something we can create by sitting around and talking about it. It is a process of moving into an inner awareness or self-actualizing energy where we move beyond any outer form of what we think, and open instead into the world of possibility and knowing. The outer mind instinctively wants to grab hold of the idea and say "yes," but this automatically begins to limit the degree of "real" potential that can exist. Awakening into the inner creative force is a process of <u>knowing</u>, not thinking.

As the awakening process begins, we automatically extend beyond what we previously have been taught or have experienced as being our concept of self or personality. This form of creativity is not solely dependent upon our physical biological development, nor is it dependent upon what we call spiritual development. It occurs by allowing the energy of the spiritual or soul aspect of ourselves to emerge in our physical form. This emergence will ultimately allow a type of human being to evolve that is not dependent merely upon the biological needs of the species, but is instead one that moves into the collective needs of humanity where each individual is able to develop his/her own special uniqueness as a human being. As this develops, we then naturally evolve into allowing the collective form of humanity to change, creating a new way of living, interacting, and communicating. This development evolves through the heart chakra of each and every one of us, for the heart focus allows the spiritual energy to merge with the physical body, and thus directs the existing perceptions of ourselves in a totally different way.

Our goal at this stage of human development is to become aware of our specific and isolated pieces of information, and to allow ourselves to move into a universal level of understanding. We must move from the concrete, linear way of doing things into the nonlinear and the abstract, from the physical levels of creating or thinking to the subtle levels of knowing and allowing things to emerge on their own accord. We can no longer allow ourselves to push our way through life with our basic focus being on the end result; rather, we need to open into the process of the journey and realize that how we allow something to manifest is ultimately much more important than the resulting manifestation.

CHAPTER FOUR

TRANSFORMATIONAL PSYCHOLOGY

I recall in early 1980 walking through a bookstore and being drawn to a particular book on the shelf entitled **Joy's Way: A Map for the Transformational Journey**, written by W. Brugh Joy, M.D. When I initially touched the book I felt an electric shock move through me, a sensation I had felt many times during the previous three years, but never as a result of just touching an item. Prior to this, such sensations had been experienced only during my personal inner explorations! I was instantly overcome with an expanded, awesome feeling of excitement and fear. I sensed that if I were to read this book, my life would never be the same. My outer mind, of course, reasoned that this was ridiculous, but some inner part responded differently as I spent what seemed an eternity in reading the first fifty pages of the book. I wanted to underline and understand every word, but each time I began to read, I would experience feelings of being drawn into an inner meditation. This was similar to those experiences I had felt in 1978 when my physical body first began moving through the various forms of change. A part of me became frightened, and I subsequently put the book down and soon forgot I had it. Then early during the summer of that same year, I was again drawn to the book. This time I poured through it within a few days. For the first time since 1970, I at last understood why I had been drawn into the area of psychology. In this book Brugh used the term "Transformation" to describe a similar journey that he was exploring, and he saw the total process as being TRANSFORMATIONAL PSYCHOLOGY. Psychology for the first time made sense to me!

Thus it is that I am sharing with you these first awarenesses of mine concerning Transformational Psychology. Few individuals have ever heard of it. There is no recognized division of Transformational Psychology in the American Psychological Association, although there is a division of Transpersonal Psychology. However, being a professional member of the Division of Transpersonal

Psychology, it is evident to me that few individuals in the field are even aware of the Transformational process as Brugh outlines it. Brugh's way of bringing forward Transformational Psychology has been the only model that resonates at a deep level within me and parallels my own inner path of purpose.

Although some forms of psychology do include a discussion of the spiritual or divine realms, few, if any, directly empower the process of opening into the inner-directed energy of one's soul and then allowing this awakening to guide one's own individual purpose. It has only been within the last nine years that I have directly experienced this self-actualizing energy from my own soul and that my outer mind has felt secure in the unfolding of this odyssey as a result of these direct experiences. This model for me is very real; it is not another theoretical construct of what the personality is or could be. Rather, I myself have personally experienced the ideas and inner spaces that Brugh describes as Transformational Psychology. I have seen them work in my own personal exploration, and I have safely guided thousands of other individuals into the various levels of this same journey. I will not go into the details of Transformational Psychology, as Brugh does a more than adequate job of describing this in his book. I will, however, summarize my own perceptions about Transformational Psychology, and also relate the process through which I have evolved while allowing and assisting other individuals to awaken into their own self-actualizing pulse— into the energies of their inner-directed soul guidance .

In order to fully understand Transformational Psychology, we first must begin with a literal understanding of the word psychology, which means the study of the Soul. I always thought it interesting that the founding individuals of current psychology, such as William James (who is viewed as being the "father" of modern psychology), strongly believed in and explored both the "spiritual" and the "psychic" nature of man. Yet, these ideas are touched upon in very few areas of psychology, and they are virtually never directly explored. In Chapter Nine of **Joy's Way**, Brugh discusses the foundation of the Transformational Process:

> "The principles involved in the unblocking of the soul's flow can be applied universally. In this widespread sense they are the basis of a psycho-physical-spiritual therapeutic interaction called Transformational Psychology.... Transformational Psychology is nothing less than the study of the transformation of the soul— the freeing of the soul into natural expression. Its fundamental focus in the treatment of the human being is the mind that has somehow walked into a closet, closed the door, turned out the light and instantly forgotten all these events."

In understanding Transformational Psychology, one must realize that we are no longer exploring just the mind-body interaction that has been the foundation of holistic health over the last fifteen years. We are exploring the triad of Soul/Mind/Body. The "soul" is that part of us that moves out of spirit, that inner essence or Divine Essence, a higher intelligence of ourselves being brought forward into our physical form through an energetic vibration. This is the inner self-actualizing pulse which I have been describing. The "mind" is actually a two part system, one part being the intellect or outer mind, and the other being our emotional or feeling nature. I distinguish these as being two separate parts of mind, since each part is very real and at times has its own direction and ideas as to what it thinks or feels should be happening. The "body," then, is the physical part of us, which we perceive to be composed of solid matter. Our physical body is actually in a state of constant vibration, truly representing our densest form of spirit.

In the triad of Soul/Mind/Body, the soul and body are always in a state of perfect balance and know exactly what is needed for our inner growth as human beings. Even within the most severe forms of illness and pain, the body is still truly in a perfect state of balance, manifesting exactly what is necessary at the moment in order to provide us feedback as to what needs to change. The physical body is actually an energy, a vibration, that is in direct connection with our inner guiding soul force. When an illness or some other disruptive energy merges with the body, it becomes the feedback announcing that the mind (intellectually and/or emotionally) is at some level holding back a deep change, and that a new level of information is trying to emerge from one's inner-directed guidance. The illness or state of "being out of balance" represents one level of energy or vibration in our journey, and indicates that the mind is ignoring the deeper inner messages and directions that exist and need to come forth. Under the mind's direction, our body is then guided through the process of cultural and learned behaviors, which are quite limiting. It is not that the body is "sick" or has "let us down"; rather, we have allowed the mind to be the key director, while our body becomes the direct feedback for a greater interplay of underlying forces. But if we allow an inner-directed energy to emerge, it will gently "pull" us in a different direction and open us into a new set of perceptions, energies, and directions for our life. As we move naturally into a heightened energy, this new force of energy will be experienced both in our consciousness and in our body, and in most cases, illness cannot exist at this new level of heightened energy.

I have explored the process of change through a heightened level of energy with hundreds of individuals inflicted with various forms of life threatening illness, and I have seen many of them move in totally different directions once they allowed the new inner direction and energetic restructuring to emerge. As they opened to new levels of energy, they began to experience a level of inner knowing and guidance that allowed their lives to become different. Richard Moss, M.D. has written a series of books that deal directly with the process of illness and how the heightened energies can be converted into new concepts of health. A good starting point for reading on this topic is his book entitled **How Shall I Live**.

Within the Soul/Mind/Body triad, it is the mind that is always in conflict with the other two elements. The mind is comprised of that aspect of the outer self, the personality or the subconscious, that is made up of one's personal learning experiences and memories, and that is also influenced by the individual and collective process that has evolved over the last fifteen to twenty thousand years. It is the activity of the mind that is always out of synchronization with the inner growth or purpose of the soul. The soul, being the most advanced aspect of our self, understands the true purpose for our creative potential as human beings. The soul knows the inner blueprint for our development and when one's soul energy is allowed to flow freely, life moves unhampered by the mind. This free flowing energy of one's soul directs the physical body and also synchronizes our outer events into one unified system. When the mind, however, decides to take charge and direct this system, either through its intellectual and/or emotional parts, the body and other outer events in life no longer move smoothly. Each human being is meant to explore the process of surrendering into the freeing nature of the soul's energy.

The exploration of awakening your creative potential begins the process of opening into one's purpose in life and initiates the unfolding of the inner-directed energy of one's soul into the physical form. As this occurs, the body is in a constant state of transformation, changing in varied ways to reflect where it needs to be at any given time. We rarely know what our physical body is really all about. It is important not to get caught up by cultural or outer mind definitions concerning what constitutes one's body, not to mention society's criteria for beauty and attractiveness. As we awaken to the soul's direction, we begin to unfold into an inner understanding of what the body represents. And as we open into the energies of our inner guidance, we can allow our physical form to be sculpted through this force. It is important that we not be caught up by the outer illusions of physical appearance, size, function, or attractiveness, but instead, allow a natural inner illumination to ignite and to continually flow throughout our physical form.

In the death/rebirth cycle, transformation is always achieved either through the physical death of the individual, or through the death of old perceptions, habits, and beliefs. From this perspective, illness, crisis, and changes in outer events can never be looked upon as being wrong; rather, such circumstances become the feedback announcing that a part of the mind is being asked to change and that the process of transformation is emerging.

I feel that it is important to give some consideration here to the death/rebirth cycle, for I have so often seen in my own life, and in that of others, that when we become frightened about inner changes, it always centers around the death/rebirth issue. Once I had finally formulated my own conclusions regarding this issue, I immediately experienced new levels of creative freedom and an awakening of unlimited energy. Thus, to deeply appreciate the levels of transformative change, one must always begin by finding an inner peace and resolution concerning their own death/rebirth issues.

By opening into an inner resolution of the death/rebirth issue, individuals are then able to perceive, feel, and know that in every aspect of life, nothing truly dies— only its outer form changes. Even through physics we know that matter cannot be destroyed; it can only be transformed in its size, shape, and density. A similar understanding can occur through the process of transformation when we inwardly know that nothing ever dies. Through a deep inner realization of the process of death and rebirth, we understand this process of change as the foundation for the transformational journey. Through the inner release of what we think the physical form is and what we think our mind's perception of reality is, we become free to explore our true inner potential and awaken into the next level of human development where new possibilities of living allow us to transcend our present boundaries.

We all think we understand reality, but as Buckminster Fuller helped me to understand, we actually know very little about the nature of reality. Despite all of the books, research, and lectures throughout the world that have dealt with this concept, man's intellect has been able to discover only about 2% of the true nature of reality, while the other 98% of reality yet awaits our discovery. A whole new world of discoveries awaits mankind, but this will not evolve through the processes that are currently being explored. If you can begin to grasp the dimensions of this statement, then you can appreciate at some level of your consciousness the importance of change itself, of the resolution of the death/rebirth cycle, and of freeing up and expanding your concepts of what the body, mind, and soul are. You will thereby be able to allow yourself to open into an inner awareness that is infinitely vast and contains far-reaching potentials for all human beings.

In previous chapters I have used such terms as heart chakra, heart-center, in one's heart, and the word energy or energies. What I am referring to here is not your everyday awareness of energy or of the physical organ of the heart. Rather, this concept involves understanding a very complex system of the deeper or "true" nature of man's physical, emotional, mental, and spiritual self. Our information on the system of chakras and energies has its origins in the Eastern philosophies and mystical teachings dating back thousands of years. Although only limited research on this topic has been done in current scientific circles, NASA, The University of California at Los Angeles, and other research laboratories have proven the existence of these interpenetrating energy fields in and around the body. As a result, totally new areas of medicine, which are related to the area of psychology that we are exploring in this book, are being discovered. This current wave of scientific exploration, however, has yet to uncover any information that has not already been known and passed on through ancient mystical teachings.

When I first moved into teaching the process of energy transfer in 1981, I was able to determine the positions of the chakras or energy centers through the senses of sight, sound, smell, and touch. I was able to scan and determine their positions, in addition to becoming aware of the layers of energy that surround the human form. We usually think of the body as being a solid mass. We need, however, to understand that the physical body is actually composed of interwoven patterns of energy bodies that are in a constant state of fluctuation or vibration. Through physics, we know that the body is composed of a vibrating particle field of energy, localized or focused in a way that allows us to perceive and experience the body as a solid object. Around each vibrating particle field of energy exists a wave field of energy that holds the structure in place. Individuals can learn to see, feel, and experience these different vibrating fields of electromagnetic energy. Many individuals think that the wave field, or what is often referred to as the aura, is created by the movement of the particles, or the solid object. However, the wave field around the object is actually vibrating at a higher frequency, thus allowing the creation of the solid, particle field to emerge at a slower vibrating frequency. Our brain, as a transducer of these vibrations, interprets the various energy frequencies through the chakras, nervous system, and sense organs, thereby allowing us to experience the particle-based vibrating field of a body as being a solid mass. Please understand that I am simplifying this concept and am merely offering an overview, eliminating many detailed inner steps.

To further understand the concept of energies and how our focus of awareness or consciousness interacts with them, we can presently find a number of physicists who explore a similar process through their understanding of quantum physics. Fred Wolf, in his book **The Body Quantum**, explores the ideas of quantum physics, the observer effect, the consciousness of an individual, and how one interacts to interpret and create the reality and physical structures that are perceived. In his Introduction, Wolf defines the "body quantum" as follows:

"The word 'quantum' refers to a whole amount of something. Thus, the body quantum refers to a whole amount of something important governing the whole human body. That something is consciousness. It is my contention in this book that consciousness acts in a quantum manner inside our bodies. It acts to produce all the various activities we enjoy that make up our lives, be they extraordinary or dull.

Thus, quantum consciousness is the observer effect in quantum physics. What this means is that the action of simply observing something alters the thing observed in a sudden and disruptive manner. This change is reflected in quantum physics by changing that which is probable into that which is certain.

...Because we humans can think and are able to gain conscious control of our lives, the mind-body interaction is extremely important and necessary for our understanding of the body human. It is my contention that by understanding the physics of the body, specifically, how quantum physics and the observer effect are involved in the body human, we will be able to gain healthier and happier lives."

He further states that:

"Through the eyes of quantum physics, one can see that the mind also begins to emerge as evidence of the ancient 'soul'— that which governs and regulates the invisible atomic and molecular processes of life. These processes govern the living movement of matter in the body, both consciously and unconsciously. Here I put forward that the mechanism for governing the living movement of bodily matter arises through the effect of quantum physics, especially, the effects that observation has on matter."

The structure of quantum physics also focuses on exploring the shift into an unconscious inner-directed force of "soul" as the next level of understanding our development as human beings. According to Wolf:

"Even though modern science has provided a great number of detailed maps of the body, the experience we call life is no clearer now than it was centuries ago. However, I have lately begun to wonder if the age-old dream of uniting the soul of life and the body of inert matter is possible through the new physics."

For our purposes we will accept and utilize this as one of the basic structures of our foundation for exploring the awakening energies of transformative change. Through our odyssey, we will personally experience what this means. For now, it will suffice that you be able to accept the idea that your consciousness, however it is directed, will have a direct impact on the creation and movement of both your physical body and the reality around you. Understand that if your consciousness is directed through your outer mind, one focus will emerge; if your consciousness is inner-directed through a heightened self-actualizing energy, a different reality will emerge. And realize that these processes are continually evolving, regardless of whether or not you are conscious of them. The worries, doubts, fears, and inner chatter of the outer mind process have the power to direct this movement, just as the layers of inner silence and self-actualizing energy have the same directive capability. The choice of which one is allowed to be the director is always ours.

Individuals who perceive and experience subtle forms of energy also confirm many of the ideas that we are exploring here. They confirm the fact that the physical body is in fact created both in the midst of and as a result of these interpenetrating energy fields, and that its existence and density is in a constant state of flux based upon the interplay of the energy fields and one's focus of consciousness. These individuals can also discern the process of illness in the energy field even before any trace of illness exists within the physical form or before laboratory testing can detect any imbalance within the body. This is the sort of information I was given in my earlier meditative states, which I then explored with other individuals. My knowledge of the chakra system initially emerged through my inner-directed soul guidance, and then later, books and individuals moved into my life to help clarify the ideas. Although some individuals can visually perceive the movements of energy within and around others, most individuals with a little training can at least learn to feel and sense the direction of these currents of energy.

Through my own extensive work with the chakras, brain, nervous system, and human energy systems, I have found Brugh Joy's work to be the most complete. He describes energy centers that other authors omit or feel are unimportant, and in **Joy's Way** he describes a process of exploring these centers through what he calls the "spiral meditation," which I will later discuss in more detail. For now, it is sufficient that you understand that these vortexes of energies, or chakras, are associated with both the development of the physical body and with the movement of energies throughout the subtle energy bodies, and that they can thus open us into an understanding of our inner world. The energies are directly connected to the way we have learned to focus our consciousness, and with every shift in our focus there is a parallel shift in our energies. As we explore our post-biological development, we are meant to fully experience these shifts in awareness and thus allow a greater freedom of choice in the directions we take in life. We will later explore how directly focusing upon the different energy centers will greatly alter our perception and sensory abilities in everyday life. Even if you find it difficult to accept the concept of energy centers or chakras, you will still be able to experience all of the different explorations of our journey together. For me, however, an understanding of the system was a necessity, for only through this process was I able to make sense of the experiences into which I had awakened. It provided me with a context for understanding how my brain could produce many of the images, feelings, and experiences I encountered both within myself and in my outer world.

For the purpose of this exploration and your own personal journey, I will always ask you to focus at the center of your chest, at the "heart chakra." This focus allows you to effortlessly shift from your everyday awareness, and from the structures that are created from your outer mind, into the direction of your own inner self-actualizing energy or guidance. This constitutes the first level of shift that you will explore in your journey. If you are already familiar with the chakra system, I ask that you please put aside any judgements and just allow your awareness to shift into the heart center and explore the differences for yourself. If these areas are completely new to you, do not initially allow your outer mind to question or try to understand; simply allow yourself the exploration. You will soon begin to develop an understanding through the ease of your own experience in exploring the profound and beautiful inner realms that exist. Remember, reality, from the perspective of the heart, is very different than when it is perceived from any other center. And the only way that I have found to move easily and safely through one's inner self is by awakening into the heart chakra, which then becomes the focal point of the journey.

In 1983, through a complex series of events, I moved into a near-death experience. My wife, Ilene, was with me at the time, and later related to me what had transpired outwardly with my body, which I learned was similar to the inner changes I was experiencing. I cannot fully explain the cause or details of this experience, but will briefly relate that my physical body began to move through a rapid deterioration of its physical structures. Its robust color of vitality and warmth transformed into a dull, cold, rigid, whitish color in a very short period of time. I inwardly felt myself falling into a spiral that felt endless. Although time seemed to pass slowly, what my outer mind perceived as being but a few minutes was actually more than three hours. As I was moved deeper into the inner space, my physical body progressed through all of the stages that resemble physical death. During this time, Ilene kept her hand on my chest and focused a stream of energy into my heart center, and at some point I at last reached the bottom of my inner spiral. Throughout the course of the experience I felt no pain, fear, or panic. I felt as though I were being cradled by some unseen energy force that was carrying me through the inner dimensions of life.

Once I reached the bottom of my inner spiral, I heard a familiar voice speaking to me about my choices as a teacher and the ways in which I had previously chosen to create during my life. I was shown a series of personal events that had transpired over the past several years, reviewing the choices I had made, and I was now made aware of other alternative choices that had been available to me. I was being given the opportunity to choose the direction my life would take as a teacher. One choice required that I give up my old patterns and perceptions, wherein I taught out of fear and pushed myself through life, and that I move instead into exploring with myself and with others the vast potentials we as human beings have. This would be done by undertaking an exploration of the "heart chakra" as a living process united with the inner guidance that is continually available to us. The other choice involved teaching through the process of healing my own physical body of the damage that I could incur from this near-death experience, thus exploring the transformative aspect of the "heart chakra" and the body changes as they evolve through physical illness. Either way I was going to be exploring the process of heightened energies that evolve through the feelings of unconditional love and the heart chakra, in addition to exploring the ways in which one's perceptions change and transform as a result of these self-actualizing energies. I immediately felt overwhelmed at the thought of either choice, and yet I knew exactly what was being asked of me. A part of my outer mind wanted to say yes, with the hope of having time later for further consideration. But this was not to be the case, for the voice clearly said, "There is no time for procrastination. The decision must be made now!" Having received this ultimatum, I vowed "Yes" with a level of conviction that resonated from the deepest part of my Being, and I felt a new wave of energy cradle me and move me upward through a similar spiral and back once again into the confines of my physical body.

Although words cannot truly and adequately describe this level of interaction, it was the most loving force of energy that I had ever in my life experienced. And I now understand that the choice was not one of either/or; rather, it was really a question of choosing how I would create. I had a choice between succumbing to illness and an infirm physical body or of evolving through the consciousness of the "heart" and creating positive bodily changes and new directions in my life.

After this experience, I no longer had any fear of the death/rebirth cycle, and I truly understood the level of love and safety that exists in life. All previously held perceptions were now seen, felt, and experienced differently. This did not require days, weeks or months to be integrated into my life. That very evening I understood! Kenneth Ring has a wonderful book that describes the process of near-death experiences in the context of personal transformation called **Heading Toward Omega**. If you have ever had a near-death experience, and have not allowed yourself to integrate this into your life, I would recommend your reading Ring's book as an aid to understanding a very important element of personal transformation.

One can learn to move into the levels of unconditional love in ways less dramatic than a near-death experience or physical illness. But regardless of how one moves into the inner realms, the important thing is that one does move, thus allowing the vibration of the awarenesses to automatically educate the mind into new levels of understanding and perception. Until this occurs, one's living process is merely a process of intellectual stimulation, and every time one faces the space of unity or unconditional love, panic will set in. However, once the resolution of the death/rebirth cycle has been accomplished, the individual no longer panics, and can enjoy the process of shifting the mind into the nurturing inner-directed realms of the soul. Through this surrender, one can remain and live within the inner-awareness and allow this same inner force to emerge through them. The mind, though, cannot begin to intellectually comprehend this more expansive energy or heightened order of creative functioning in our journey as human beings, and thus it usually panics at both major and minor directional shifts. Through its panic, it then blocks the very essence of change that is needed in order to fully understand its survival. This is the irony in the journey of the mind. If it releases itself into the inner guidance of the soul, it is reeducated into a new and inner depth of understanding and is allowed to create within this broader overview. On the other hand, if it blocks this flow, it becomes increasingly confused and more limited in its scope of understanding, until at last the confusion becomes so great that illness or crisis begins to manifest. If the mind refuses to let go of its current perceptions, the physical body takes over, and eventually dies. Either way, the mind is in a constant state of personal transformation.

Over the past ten years I have explored transformation with many individuals who are physically dying. Many of them, once they experience this inner understanding, find a level of inner spiritual psychological peace that allows them to live out their remaining time at a level of "psychological and spiritual health" that few individuals ever attain, not even those free of all signs of physical illness. Again, the body, as it is brought under the direction of the soul, with the mind moving simultaneously into the inner guidance, experiences levels of inner peace and instinctively knows that something else does exist. A dear friend who recently died, shared with me, just a week prior to her death, the fact that after all the years of talking about unconditional love and about the transferring of energies, she finally understood what I meant by the energetic state of human feelings called unconditional love. And through this inner understanding she was able to move into a state of inner peace with the death/rebirth issues. When individuals have not personally resolved the death/rebirth issue, any form of change appears to the outer mind to be life threatening and overwhelming, and the mind thus desires to hold tight and block all change, no matter what the cost.

Most individuals try to achieve a level of transformation either through thinking and/or talking about the changes, or by allowing the intellect to be educated (or saturated) with additional outer information. We fail to understand that if all of the information in the world were collected and fed into the intellect, it still would not be sufficient to transform it into the energies of one's inner soul guidance. Throughout the process of the development of our biological and physical capabilities, the use of outer stimulation is beneficial. Others guide us through walking, speaking, toilet training, and many other key levels of development. Throughout the educational process, outer teachers are important in bringing forward the stimulation needed to create new levels of intellectual achievement. Through such stimulation, we always can choose how to use and to what depth to explore these areas of achievement. However, the intellect cannot initiate the awakening of our inner creative potential. We need another form of teaching to be able to awaken into this level of development.

Just as we have begun to explore the interweaving of four basic layers of energies that comprise a physical human being (the spiritual, intellectual, emotional, and physical energies), David Bohm, a theoretical physicist, views all of creation as moving from one pulse of energy which he calls the <u>holomovement</u>. He advocates that the entire creative process emerges out of this holomovement. According to Bohm, the outer manifestation of reality moves first from the unseen energy forces of the <u>implicate order,</u> where the wave field of energy exists, into the particle field of energy. This manifests into the physical form and is called the <u>explicate order</u>. The creative energies move from a process of the <u>generative order</u>, a vast inner space of unseen energies that holds within itself the totality of all possible outcomes of reality. This level of generative order moves through both the implicate and explicate levels of reality as a self-actualizing pulse of energy. This inner awakening pulse directs the wave energies of our blueprint in the implicate order into a direct physical manifestation of particle mass which is interpreted as an object, perception, or event within the explicate order— outer reality.

I believe that each area of the triune brain interacts as a different medium in functioning as the transducer of various layers of energy into what we would call our physical reality. The generative order can be sensed when the whole triune brain is transformed into one inner synchronized pattern through the energies of the heart chakra. As this self-actualizing pulse of energy deepens, it merges with the generative order of energy via the subatomic levels within us, and will eventually emerge as a heightened order of creative functioning. As this self-actualizing pulse is inwardly released, the neocortex portion of the brain begins to interpret the force as a superquantum wave that awakens our inner blueprint. This is stored as a nonlinear process. Within this blueprint our individuality is held at heightened levels of creativity that can only begin to emerge through our post-biological development.

In the course of our normal development, we awaken the first layers of our blueprint through our outer process of education and behavioral learning, which encompasses the 2% of outer reality. However, we still lack the larger inner perspective of who we are and what our inner creative potential is, which allows us to explore the other 98% of unknown awareness. As the first level of inner energy is released, it awakens the implicate wave potential of energy within the mid-brain. This allows the mid-brain to begin to take on the unseen structure of energy and guide the movement of particles into a physical form of reality that is eventually translated through the old brain as outer reality.

To summarize, one's physical interpretation of reality is based upon the inner self-actualizing pulse of energy that stimulates the inner blueprint within the deep levels of our awakening energies. When we are focused only within an outer perspective, the levels of inner-awareness are not available to the outer mind, and the mind directs and orchestrates the energies based upon its habitual patterns of learning. As we open into the levels of inner silence and allow our heart chakra to fully open, we can release and become aware of the deeper structures of energies that are continually present. Through this awareness, we can allow the inner guiding pulse to pull us into the inner directions of our soul-body connection. Without these levels of awareness, we are left solely to the emotional/intellectual process and must keep guessing as to which direction life is pushing us.

As we begin the process of awakening the triune brain and tap the energies of our creative potential, we will move easily into a new level of heightened creativity. If the areas of theoretical physics entice you, you may find David Bohm's book **Science, Order, and Creativity** to be stimulating. The integration of these concepts into the triune brain is a result of my own personal journey and explorations, which also parallels ideas from Joseph Chilton Pearce's book **Magical Child Matures**.

This groundwork is the basis for our explorations of the triune brain, nervous system, heart chakra and other energy centers. The intellect merely reshuffles or creates a very limited degree of creative potential from the space of outer reality, the 2% factor. The process of awakening into the 98%, and into the inner direction from one's guidance, is a process of allowing a heightened, more refined form of wave field energy to emerge in our lives. This higher form of energy begins the process of guiding us into our inner realms, as will be further discussed in later chapters. For now, allow yourself to open into the understanding that this form of education will be drastically different from any other forms of education you can outwardly recall. And yet each one of us, in our earlier developmental years, experienced a similar form of learning. We all know that if a child is born of English-speaking parents, and is raised in France where the only language spoken is French, when the child is ready to begin speaking, French will be his/her natural language. Man does not hold any genetic structure for a particular language. What we do hold is the capability for language, and the environment to which we are exposed then awakens that structure and guides it into one's outer framework. Our early years comprise the period of normal creative development.

This same process is similarly awakened in many areas of our lives. Many of the things we hold as being "sacred" or as "truths" are only so because of the outer structure to which we were exposed. Being exposed to a different outer stimulus can change any part of us into someone else. Regardless of the culture or geographic location, when we as individuals are exposed to the awakening of our "potential energy," we experience similar processes. Our origin and outer training make no difference. Our inner world is not directed by any outer country, culture, language, location or religion. Rather, we all possess what is actually a universal process once we awaken into the inner creative potential. At long last we can become a unified planet, with one focus and one inner consciousness that is guided by the inner feeling states of unconditional love. Mystics and sages throughout time have described the desire for a similar global process, as has every major religion throughout the world. Our universal heritage is awakening from within, and this constitutes the next developmental phase for mankind.

The basic process of awakening begins through an inner timing mechanism that can be stimulated as a result of direct contact with an outer teacher through whom this energy or presence flows, or it can be initiated through books or tapes that carry the same inner energy or presence we have been describing. Once we begin to open into the inner states, each of us then has the potential to bring this forward into all aspects of our lives. However, the levels of inner information and awareness cannot emerge when individuals are experiencing life from a reaction energy. The process of reaction blocks the inner creative flow and keeps one locked into the outer structures. Breaking away from the reaction energy is the basic purpose of the explorations through which I will be guiding you in the process of Soul/Mind/Body Explorations. This process, utilizing a heightened or unified vibration of energy, allows the mind to feel safe in letting go and transforming itself into the next level of awareness.

The key to transformation is allowing the new expanded vibration to precede any and all outer information or images of change, thereby permitting the mind to transform easily and swiftly. Confusion results if information and experience are brought forward first through words, or at a lower vibrational structure that encompasses perceptions of duality. From this level, the mind is focused only upon the problem itself or upon doing whatever it can to move out of the given situation. Either way, the focus is still at the level of the problem and not within the vibration of unity or unconditional love. Whenever we are focused within a lower vibration, we are viewing reality from primitive intellectual or emotional patterns.

As I perceive the energy centers and their interplay, I can see and understand why an individual maintains a particular level of focus. Each energy center creates a particular focus of reality, and the heart center can shift our perceptions into the observer state.

No amount of talking, thinking, or feeling will transform one into a perception of unity. The energies must always precede the perceptual shift. But either way, the mind will never remain in a constant state; it is always experiencing some form of transformative change.

Individuals who have prior experience with consciousness are surprised at how readily the mind desires to shift into the soul-body direction. The transition occurs easily when individuals learn to alter their focus from an outer to an inner-awareness, unifying the triune brain and shifting the focus into the heart chakra. As they begin to explore the inner awareness, they are able to experience the deeper realms of inner silence.

I have found that there are three distinct, consecutive levels of inner silence that we need to clarify. The first level is that of the mental inner chatter of the intellect. At this level of exploration an individual's intellect is deeply focused on rumination and on all that it perceives it is unable to do, based upon its own experiences or the experiences of others. When this occurs, one's level of self-confidence is very low, regardless of what we may be trying to project. This level of inner chatter represents the "critical inner voice" that is laughing or talking about the impossibilities of accomplishing one thing or another. Individuals perceive the inner chatter as a "critical inner voice" because there is never any sign of encouragement, and even when a choice is presented, it is brought forward as the best choice out of the worst possibilities. This level of mental inner chatter keeps the mind in a constant state of confusion and prevents one from ever receiving any clear inner direction.

We are taught that it is difficult to quiet mental inner chatter, and that it is necessary to spend a great deal of time meditating to achieve a quiet state. However, this is not true. The expanded inner screen process which we are exploring, along with focusing at the heart chakra, allows you to quickly and easily quiet the mental inner voice and begin to explore the first levels of inner silence.

I have found in my work that there is a predictable sequence in an individual's journey in this exploration. After a period of time of being able to quiet the mental chatter and of spending time exploring the inner spaces, individuals will experience difficulty in attaining the inner states and quiet. Suddenly they no longer want to go back "inside" and explore. This is due to the fact that they have automatically opened into a new level of inner chatter and emotional fear. This second stage occurs for all individuals as they begin to move into the next level of their inner guidance, although many will not be aware of why it is happening. The mind quickly and automatically blocks out any fear and will instead bring forward a number of legitimate excuses to explain the sudden change. At this point many individuals psychologically "flog" themselves for not understanding, which will automatically prevent them from experiencing a deeper space. Others, especially if they have had previous experiences at workshops or through study, will be shocked at what they feel moving through them. Although they continually verbalize that this transformation is what they want to achieve, the physical experience of actually moving into that new space frightens them as they touch the wall of <u>emotional</u> <u>inner</u> <u>chatter</u>.

Yet, without moving through this second level of emotional inner chatter, individuals will begin to feel increasing amounts of fear and other unpleasant emotions in their daily lives. I feel this is what takes place with individuals who explore various forms of relaxation techniques— they feel the energy move through them, hit a wall of emotional fear, and then call the experience an "increase in anxiety." However, I have seen many individuals, after understanding and experiencing the safety of their inner space, move through these walls. One can usually identify this emotional chatter level by the presence of a dramatic increase in fears, doubts, misgivings, anger, or at times, misdirected levels of sexual energy. These emotions seem to emerge very easily, often without any outer stimulation whatsoever. The emotional level of inner noise is much stronger and more powerful than is the mental chatter, and when the two are combined, an individual becomes virtually nonproductive. But once individuals deepen in working with the expanded inner screen, in utilizing the heart chakra, and in harmonizing and awakening the triune brain, they are naturally able to quiet the emotional noise, and thereby allow new perceptions to effortlessly emerge from their inner-directed guidance.

At the point of emerging from the level of emotional fear and chatter, one moves automatically into the third level of conflict, that which concerns the physical body. Although one's body is always in a state of balance with one's soul, the mind, through its confusion, begins a restructuring of the body to match its focus, and in so doing blocks out the soul's flow. Until the physical state of the body is brought back under a level of inner guidance, it becomes nearly impossible to maintain and integrate one's inner meditative experiences into the flow of daily life. The presence of <u>body</u> <u>chatter</u> then blocks the higher levels of energy from emerging, which in turn prevents the formation of new behaviors, movements, and perceptions. This is what some describe as "body armor." Individuals will have difficulty remaining focused in the inner-awareness state while performing outer activities so long as this "body armor" is present.

In 1983 I began exploring the direct link between the focus of my consciousness, the expanded inner screen, the whole triune brain, and the nervous system. I was inwardly guided through an exploration in understanding that each part of the triune brain was directly linked to a segment of my inner space, which in turn was directly linked to different levels of energy bodies. When I allowed my inner space to be directed by the flow of energy from the heart chakra, my body armor restructured to hold the new levels of higher energy that were presently emerging, and my perceptions could then easily move into the new level of inner-awareness. But whenever I failed to allow this level of physical restructuring to occur, I found it was difficult to let my meditative spaces emerge into my daily life, and the time I spent in meditation seemed very removed from actual living.

One day I was exploring a direct exchange of energy with my inner guidance through each one of my major chakras in order to facilitate the process of moving through my "body armor" and my current levels of physical inner chatter. Through this inner-directed exploration with each one of my energy centers, my body armor and chatter were eliminated, and I was capable of maintaining these states for longer periods of time. As I opened to this level of inner restructuring, it was no longer necessary to consciously direct the flow of energy through the process. Merely by being in an inner focused state and by just "asking," the energy would direct itself as I learned to focus my awareness under the volition of my inner-directed soul guidance.

The ramifications of this whole process were mind boggling, for I then understood to what degree the outer mind's confusion prevents us from experiencing life directly. I feel that these natural levels of inner-awareness and restructuring are, and always have been, available to every human being. But in order to utilize these natural levels, we must begin to live from a different state of inner-awareness. I have since explored this process with individuals involved in training for various sports. I discovered that they can learn to initiate their particular physical activity from a level very close to this inner-awareness state (which is a state similar to that of a runner's high), and can continue to spend greater portions of their training time within or close to these inner levels. Many experience "hitting a wall" while performing, and I explore with them how to continue what they are physically doing, ask for the natural spaces of their expanded inner screen, focus at the heart center, thus allowing the brain to shift into the inner-awareness needs, and then move directly into the next level of their performance. All individuals who have explored this process have encountered dramatic changes in their physical ability to perform.

With the removal of the body armor, we are again able to move in a fluid manner and can maintain our inner-directed guidance. At this level of inner development, one can allow the body to move into restructuring at whatever level it needs. When this occurs, the individual is living through the Soul/Mind/Body. Individuals cannot merely talk themselves into these levels of transformation; but by opening into one's inner-directed guidance and by allowing the self-actualizing pulse to emerge, life can truly take on new meaning and become exciting. Whenever we are ready to give up the old habits and the old perceptions of who we think we are and what we think we can or cannot do, we can explore the dimensions of our new inner creative potential.

As I moved into the last few months of 1981, I finally felt that I could effectively integrate my personal experiences of the previous four years into my then current job at the local Mental Health Center. I was respected in the community for my diagnostic and therapeutic skills, and during the past several years my work had primarily been focused in the Department of Consultation and Education. I thought I was beginning to understand Transformational Psychology and felt that I was ready to begin integrating the ideas into my life.

Ten months earlier, a group of individuals had approached me about facilitating a class on the theoretical foundations of energy transfer. Although no one in the group had any direct experience or training in energy transfer, myself included, I had at least acquired a very broad base of understanding through my extensive reading. My outer mind frantically rejected the possibility of directing such a class, and yet, a deeper inner feeling kept saying, "Yes, do it!" Once again surrendering to my inner guidance, I agreed to take on the role of facilitator in covering the areas of Polarity Therapy, Therapeutic Touch, and Energy Balancing by Brugh Joy. Prior to the first meeting, I began to read over the information for that night's lecture and I once again was pulled into a deep meditative state, similar to what I had experienced in 1978. This time I was shown the procedure for awakening myself and others into the process of energy transfer and was shown the step-by-step exploration which would allow other individuals to begin awakening into their own levels of sensitivity of the energies. When I moved out of the meditation, I realized that over 90 minutes had passed and that it was time to go to class. I still had not reviewed the written information.

As we met that evening, I began with the theoretical work, but soon something shifted within my consciousness and I began to share the structures I had been shown earlier in the day. Each person in the group began to awaken into a totally new experience for themselves. By the end of the evening I was amazed! A similar process of afternoon meditative instructions for myself, and a subsequent sharing of the information in the evening classes, continued over the next several months as we completed the first two books. The time we had initially set aside for this group exploration had now ended, and we still had not covered **Joy's Way**.

Four of us decided to persevere, and so throughout the remainder of that spring and into early summer I continued to awaken into the exercises and processes of energy balancing. On one particular evening during that summer, Ilene and I made personal commitments to explore all of life through the perceptions of the heart chakra. Later that same evening I felt a profound inner feeling, a feeling that I now can describe as the energies of unconditional love, beginning to quicken deep within me. But I later thought skeptically to myself, "What can all of this really change anyway?"

I was to find out later that fall. In September, I offered a class on exploring The Human Energy System. This brought me a great deal of joy, but I nevertheless felt a discernible sense of incompleteness beginning to move within me. Ignoring the feeling, I shifted my focus into my outer mind and went about the task of trying to make some sort of sense out of the previous nine months. I was about to begin a vacation over the Thanksgiving holiday, when I suddenly experienced an overwhelming desire to organize all of my files and class information from the previous four years. It took a full week of concentrated effort to accomplish the task, and I felt no relief until it was completed. However, as I left for vacation I did feel relieved to know that I would be entering a neat and organized office when I returned. Little did my outer mind know what was in store for me following my vacation. But you are already aware of the subsequent events, as I shared this with you in Chapter One.

At first, learning to move at levels of constant change was not an easy task for me. It was not until the summer of 1985 that I was able to really appreciate with an inner sense of joy the ideas of transformative change. I had done a lot of changing over the previous years, but not without a great deal of screaming and kicking along the way. I can now honestly say that all of the difficulties that I encountered in my own awakening journey were of my own making. If I had been able to trust and listen to the levels of inner guidance that were emerging from within me, the earlier years of my own journey would have been drastically different. But since they were difficult, I can now understand when others discuss their fears, doubts, worries, crises, and traditional perceptions; but I also know that they themselves are the ones creating their problems.

Since 1985 I have learned that as I continue reaching into the inner depths of my self-actualizing energy, I eventually sense that I have reached a plateau. When this happens in my own personal transformation, I know that a new level of inner self-actualizing energy is beginning to emerge. I have learned to recognize that the first signs of inner change occur when I begin to feel an inner sense of being at a plateau. As I allow myself to open into that plateau, I personally feel a profound quiet and a love that both nurtures and motivates me to move to the next level of inner development. But if I shift my awareness into my outer mind, the chatter takes over and everything stops; or, even worse, I move to a point where I am completely out of synchronization and automatically begin living out of crisis once again.

Each time during the past nine years that I have moved into the Soul/Mind/Body Connection my outer mind at some point breaks in and I am faced with the next situation to be explored. At times I may spend days or even weeks living through the energies of my inner guidance, only to once again be suddenly moved back into my outer focus. When this occurs, a new perception emerges that no longer fits into my current perceptions of life. Initially when this happened, I would spend days or even weeks searching, thinking that I had done something wrong and wondering what it was that I needed to do to correct things and bring my life back into unity. After several years with this struggle, I one day heard an inner laugh bellow out with the words, "Maybe you are doing nothing wrong; rather you are doing something right! That's precisely why the new piece of information has emerged. Now you can bring it into the heightened levels of energies and thus learn to perceive it differently." At no time in all of my searching had my outer mind "thought" it was doing something right, and that's exactly why this confusion was occurring. Once I allowed myself to accept a new perspective and followed my inner guidance, change moved quickly and easily. I now know that I am moving and exploring in that 98% of reality which Fuller describes. The next levels of change will always emerge when the timing is right and when I am ready to explore the subsequent levels of my transformation. There is no opportunity within this continuing process of transformation to ever become bored!

Many individuals (Carl Jung and others) talk about the existence of synchronicity, but few ever explore how to open oneself to and remain within an inner synchronized flow. I feel that a similarity exists between the idea of synchronicity and what mystics and philosophers refer to as the process of "living in the now moment." I recall in 1980 teaching a seminar through my outer mind about what it means to live in the now moment. By the time the day was finished, I and the participants were completely exhausted and totally confused about exactly what it meant. What we did know, after completing that seminar, was that what we had experienced certainly had not been living in the now moment.

After having reached such a new high in frustration, I surrendered that evening into my meditative state and was taken through an exploration of feeling and experiencing what the now moment truly meant. Within that state, I experienced having no past history, no memory or habits out of which to live, and no direction as to where I thought my future was going. My outer mind of course panicked, but once again I experienced the force of my inner self-actualizing energy and moved into a wonderful nurturing, calming state of unconditional love. I experienced a knowing that whatever I did and said from that level of inner-awareness would be what I needed at the moment. Oh, the now moment! While in that space, all of life made sense. But when I shifted back to my outer awareness and tried to talk about my experiences, I once again reached new heights of confusion.

It took another five years of exploring that particular inner space before I was able to induct others into the now moment. I first needed to deepen my own experiences before I was able to bring individuals and groups into the heightened level of energy of the now moment. Once they had experienced it for themselves, they were able to understand what I was verbally expressing. This again was a wonderful example in understanding that words are not what is important. Rather, it is the direct experience of the heightened levels of energy that constitutes the only easy means of understanding Transformational Psychology. The words may be helpful to some part of you, but once you experience the heightened energetic levels, the words will always be there. I do, nevertheless, enjoy sitting back and listening to other individuals trying to describe the process with their outer mind.

I have allowed these levels of energies to be present in many areas of my life and have learned to trust that whatever evolves is always right for that particular moment. In so doing, I have experienced deep, profound feelings, and long periods of synchronization in my life. But it is only when we open into the energies and inner direction of our soul guidance that we move beyond the current history that consists of our habits, memories, and body patterns. At that moment, we have available to us a new series of perceptions and directions concerning who we are and what we are doing.

Once within this space, we are living in the observer state, where we can see things for what they are and allow ourselves to act, create, and do whatever is needed. As the mind shifts into the observer state, we perceive, feel, and sense the inner direction that is available to us. From the observer state there are no limits, worries, or doubts about what one can do, say, or become. When the mind shifts from being the observer back into being the one in charge, confusion returns and our meditations or perceptions from within the observer state seem frightening or impossible to achieve.

Individuals explore or cope with this resulting fear in one of two ways. The first way is to react directly through the feelings of fear, which prevents most people from doing anything. The other approach is to simply deny one's fears and emotions. People talk about what they are going to do, but find no energy to take any direct outer action; or if action is taken, it is outer-directed and so nothing other than the energies of the reaction phase seems to work. But we can learn to allow the inner-awarenesses to stay with us and channel this into a new outer expression. Through this awareness, we can allow ourselves to do and say things, and to make decisions in ways that previously would have been confusing. This is why a certain part of us knows that surrendering into the energies of our inner-directed guidance feels right, while another part of us has a field day with images and feelings of fear (that second level of emotional inner chatter).

When we are in the now moment we move into events and situations with other people that create exactly what is needed. However, the timing of these events is important, and we must learn when to take direct action and when we have waited too long, thus necessitating a different direction. So often individuals will receive very accurate inner direction and information, indicating the need for a specific action or creative effort. But as they shift back into the confusion of the outer mind, they begin to experience doubts and delay taking the action that is needed. Then, at some later point, they reconsider and take action upon the old information, which by that time is usually outdated. Few individuals go back into the energies of their inner guidance and update their current understanding. Remember that if we allow ourselves to be always creating from the inner space, we will also be automatically updating the information on an ongoing basis. Initially few individuals achieve this. They go within, bring forth information from which to create, think and talk about it, and possibly at a later point in time, act upon it. Then they wonder why things didn't work out the way they thought they would.

Learning to create from the energies of inner guidance means that our lives will naturally and continually move from the levels of inner synchronization. Whenever I am doing something and begin to push it through, or when an overwhelming emotion or feeling emerges, I know that something within me needs to change to a different focus or perspective. I can do one of two things. I can keep pushing and allow my perceptions of the feelings to become my reality and thus move further out of balance; or, I can stop what I am doing, allow myself to shift back into an inner focus of being the observer, and thus allow the perceptions of the now to move within me. Through this perspective, I can then see clearly what is needed and can change whatever I am currently doing, which may sometimes even dictate doing nothing.

As the various levels of energetic structures began to move through me in 1978, I was also asked to do public speaking for the job I had at the time. At that point in my life, any time I was required to talk about something for several hours, I had to have the material fully written out before the presentation, and I would then read word for word during the several hours of the presentation. By 1979 I was working full-time for the Department of Consultation and Education, so my full-time job was that of speaking publicly and presenting seminars. Now as I would begin to plan out a seminar, I would move naturally into a deep inner meditative state and would feel an outline begin to emerge from within me. I also began to learn how to write from the inner levels, which allowed me to put my inner feelings and thoughts on paper. Many times I would be given a definite structure to follow, as well as an outer timetable indicating when I would be covering the various topics during a given evening. I might also perceive a specific time that I would take a break or stop for lunch during a particular seminar. As I shared this information with others, we always had a good laugh. But over the next eighteen months, the timetables proved to be accurate nearly every time, even to the very minute! Needless to say, I thought this very strange.

At the time, I also had serious difficulties in spelling, and I would panic at the mere thought of having to write on the board during a presentation. But as I began to move into the transformational process, I suddenly found that if I remained in the inner focused and relaxed state, I could spell everything correctly. Never in my entire life had this happened. By late 1981, I was no longer using any notes, outlines, or structures for my seminars; instead, · would begin to create them at the moment I met with each group. All of these changes had transpired as I moved into the deeper inner realms of my self-actualizing energy. I had spent no outer time trying to change any of the structures related to my abilities to speak in public, spell, remember information, or plan seminars.

By late 1982, I had begun a whole different process of verbal communication that allowed me to explore a totally new learning process with individuals and groups. I was consciously aware of speaking to a group, and at the same time I was listening to myself talking to them and understanding everything that was synthesizing within me as I spoke. Today, this process has evolved into an art form for me. Sometimes I begin by exploring no more than one word with a group, and I will then spend the next several days in a seminar exploring and experiencing with them the various levels of both the outer and inner related information.

Over the years I have come to realize that this form of communication and understanding is available to each one of us as we awaken into our own self-actualizing energy. This is the outer expression of the inner heightened levels of creative functioning that I have been describing. Yet, few individuals allow themselves to move into a level of trust at which they can truly be present with a group and share what is needed at that given moment in time, rather than exploring what they might think is necessary for them to be sharing. For myself, this level of trust naturally emerges from the levels of inner silence within me; and when I am not within the inner focused space, it becomes difficult for me to say or do anything. Awakening into such a level of self-actualizing energy is an amazing and wonderful process, so long as we allow ourselves to learn how to live and create from these levels in our everyday world .

Have you noticed that at certain points what I am describing makes sense to you, and that a moment later, as you try to remember, think about, or verbalize to someone else what you are feeling, you become confused? If this is happening, great! Then you are experiencing and understanding the concept of the mind versus the inner-directed guidance of the soul. Your mind will be unable to communicate this information in the ways that you have traditionally been accustomed to relating information. This information can only be understood in what we call a nonlinear process, which means it needs to be experienced within one's self. Very little of our former learning has ever really been experienced within us. Most of it centers around the memorization of what others have written or stated as being correct. Without allowing yourself to feel and experience information, you remain locked within the customary 2% of experienced reality. But if you allow yourself to relax with it, and allow yourself to speak whenever you have an inner feeling or insight based upon those feelings, it will all begin to make sense.

Try for a moment to talk out loud about some of the ideas we have just discussed concerning the now moment. What happens?

Do you become confused? Do you notice the subtle levels of the inner chatter coming back, possibly on both the mental and emotional levels? Whenever the inner chatter is present, there is no inner silence, and very little understanding evolves concerning what we have been discussing. Allow yourself to relax, expand your screen, and your awareness into the heart center, and open yourself to feel and experience something about the now moment. The now moment arrives as we awaken into the heart chakra and the expanded inner screen, with various levels to be explored as we deepen in our inner journey. Allow the silence to emerge and just follow what begins to structure within you. This is the experience of being in the observer state.

You will experience this state by learning to move into your inner focus, utilizing the expanded inner screen and the heart chakra in conjunction with the triune brain. At this level, the inner chatter is automatically quieted and you will shift from a state in which the mind is the primary focus, into one where you are the observer of what the inner guidance or soul is bringing forward in its perceptions and feelings. In order to move into the level of expanded awareness and synchronization, you must begin to learn how to live at the levels of being the observer. At first it may seem that this will be impossible to comprehend, much less to accomplish. And in one sense it is impossible for you to do this. Instead, you need only to allow yourself to be moved into the natural inner states, for without any conscious effort on your part, these inner spaces will automatically open.

Being and living from the inner observer state is the most natural state in which we as human beings can live. I believe that this is, and always has been, man's most natural state for living, but throughout time we have moved away from this natural understanding. In the observer state the mind shifts into the energies being inner soul directed, which allows the next levels of restructuring to begin. This state or focus eliminates the mental chatter, the emotional chatter, and the physical chatter or body armor, and through the deeper levels of the observer state you will then feel and experience a much different inner vibration or energy moving through you. When the mind is operating at the level of confusion, this inner vibration may not be apparent to you, or you may experience it as stress or as an anxiety attack. But within the observer state, it opens into the energetic feeling state of unconditional love. The observer allows the unity of perceptions to enter, while the mind allows the perceptions of reaction to be the focus. Once again, I want to emphasize that as humans we have the choice to observe and be creative, or to react and move into the depths of emotion and confusion. Either way, change will occur.

Throughout this book I will present various processes showing you how the mind moves into the levels of confusion we've discussed, followed by similar processes of opening you into unity through the heightened energies of transmutation. In this way you can fully experience the choices that do indeed abound for us as human beings.

In this and previous chapters I have attempted to lay out a broad overview of topics, not intending to delve into any one area in great depth. Hopefully you now have an awareness of the many changes that will occur in your perceptions and feelings as you begin to explore the new levels of inner development, the post-biological phase. Your intellect may not fully comprehend many of these areas, but as you open and experience the heightened levels of energy, the awakening of your inner creative potential will allow the changes to occur naturally. Some of you may experience fear, that second level of inner chatter, as you awaken into your creative development. I feel this happens because you are ready to emerge into new perceptions and ideas about change, and yet you are not ready to completely let go of your current levels of experiences. Thus, fear sets in. We never experience any perception or feeling unless we are ready to allow it to transform or change within our lives. If we can fully trust this, then the process of transformation moves very smoothly. But if we feel we are doing something wrong, or if we are continually compelled to analyze it, transformation becomes painful and slowly moves into an outer thinking process.

Joy's Way covers in much greater depth many of the concepts upon which we are touching here, and if you desire further information, I highly recommend that you continue by reading that book. The primary purpose of my book is not to focus on the explanation of the inner spaces and the changes that will occur, but rather to focus on the actual process of awakening into the inner spaces through understanding the Soul/Mind/Body Exploration. I refer you to **Joy's Way** and other books as a means of deepening and expanding your outer awareness of the changes in concepts and ideas that you will be exploring in your odyssey.

The exploration into the other 98% of unknown awareness holds the key for developing our true levels of inner creative human potential and to shifting into our next level of human development. And yet, many will choose to cling to the traditional 2% and will barely touch this other inner world. To fully awaken, one must step beyond the 2% and allow the 98% to become home. Christopher Fry wrote a play, **A Sleep of Prisoners,** that describes this process well. "The enterprise is the exploration into God; but what are you waiting for; it takes so many thousand years to wake, but will you wake for pity's sake?" I firmly believe that this current awakening constitutes the next level of our inner creative human development, and that we are presently in the midst of the process of learning how to awaken. The time is now to "wake for pity's sake" into who we are!

CHAPTER FIVE

CHOOSING TRANSFORMATION AS A CREATIVE WAY OF LIVING

The process of awakening one's creative potential is an exploration into the inner alignment of the Soul/Mind/Body energies in a way that allows individuals to perceptually shift their outer awareness into the observer state of inner-awareness. This begins the next level of human development, the post-biological phase, and allows man to attain a heightened order of creative functioning. Today many expound about man's potential as a human being and about how every individual is capable of accomplishing great things and should be able to perceive life as a wonderful experience. I remember in 1977 becoming familiar with the concept of tapping one's potential, and I also became aware of holistic health, biofeedback, transpersonal realms, and other techniques or practices that brought forward the idea of "becoming much more than you already are." I would convincingly think to myself, "Yes, I'm going to be a new person right now, and nothing is going to stop me." I sincerely believed that the person I knew, the person that was right there, and whom I knew as Conrad, was most certainly going to become this unbounded potential. But after many disappointing experiences directed toward creating a new me, I finally realized that the person who was there, right then, was already living out his potential. And this potential had nothing to do with future potential, except as a base camp from which to further evolve. I realized that in order to achieve any one of my inner potentials, I would need to change the ways through which I perceived who I was, my concepts and structures regarding what reality was, the relationships that I had, and how I interacted with life in general. The beliefs, attitudes, and perceptions that I held so dearly as to what constituted reality would no longer be valid!

Hopefully, you can begin to feel into the word potential for yourself, understanding that the person you know as you will be different when you are living from your new potential. The differences will be reflected in your physical body and how it moves and feels; in your emotional self and how you feel and interact emotionally with life; in your mental attitudes, beliefs, and perceptions; and in your seeing vast possibilities for yourself that were previously unavailable. And as your potential changes with the passage of time, you once again will be asked to be different from the you that has evolved. Don't get caught in the trap of thinking that you can stay the same and still be able to create within the 98% of awareness. Much of the stress and anxiety we experience in our daily lives is due to our lack of flexibility and our inability to change quickly and easily. Even living within the traditional 2% of reality requires change. We experience the realities that we experience because we are who we are, and in order to experience something new, we will need to be someone different.

Just reading and exploring this book from the observer state can bring about great changes in all aspects of your life. Change can begin to take place very quickly and easily if you allow it. If you approach reading and exploring this book in the same way that you have read and explored in the past, intellectually you may change and you may even alter some of your perceptions. But, will you really awaken and emerge into the unexplored 98% of awareness? The choice for this type of transformation always rests within you.

What separates us from other existing levels of awareness or reality is the automatic way we live and move within our habits. Our habits transcend all aspects of ourselves, encompassing everything from our mental thoughts, the way we react with our feelings, and the way our body moves, to the level of new inner awareness or guidance that we allow to emerge. Habits cannot change merely by thinking or talking about them or by simply undertaking some new pattern of behavior. Thinking allows new information to be brought forward for the mind to ponder and debate, but rarely will the new information be integrated into one's life. Thinking is merely the result of a rote process of learning. I often ask my university students on the first class day of a new semester if they would like to gamble and retake their final from the previous semester, allowing whatever grade they receive on the new attempt to become their final grade. The test would be the exact same test as was previously taken, but there would be no additional time to review the information. Very seldom is a student willing to take this gamble. Most individuals recall very little of the information they have studied, even when it is as recent as the previous semester's studies.

Most of our educational experiences come directly from other people's information about reality, much of which has never directly been felt or experienced by either the individual trying to comprehend it or the individual relating it. Individuals can rarely integrate such information into something useful within their lives. Until one can directly experience what is being brought forward, deeper integrative levels of learning are not possible.

With each new group of students at the university I find that the initial reaction towards me, as I begin the first several lectures dealing with the theoretical foundation and structures that we will be experiencing throughout the term, is one of viewing me as some "far-out" or "off-beat" individual. I just let it pass and patiently wait until we are ready to begin the direct exploration into the inner spaces. As their self-actualizing energy begins to emerge during the initial explorations, they begin to directly experience what I had been teaching. The looks on their faces after the first few explorations is worth the wait. And by the end of the semester, they are asking, "Why haven't we known this before?" They are surprised at the ease with which they can alter their perceptions and open themselves into new levels of heightened creative functioning. And what I explore with them barely touches the surface of what I am sharing with you in this book.

The only way to understand fully the nature of reality beyond the customary 2% is by directly experiencing it within yourself. You can intellectually think you understand another person's experiences, but it only becomes real through your direct involvement. Over the years I have encountered many individuals who have read various books and have attended a number of seminars on consciousness, but who have never fully awakened into their own inner depths. They have all the right verbal answers and words, but they lack the in-depth exploration. When they begin to experience the various inner spaces, many of them have more difficulty than the beginner who lacks the previous exploration through the outer mind. This is because many people allow the mind to hold them back, thinking they should encounter some certain type of experience. Allow your experiences to be uniquely yours; don't compare them to my own, or to the experiences of others, or even to your own previous explorations. Each exploration is meant to be a totally unique and enjoyable experience for you as you explore your 98% of unknown awareness.

We acquire our current perceptions of outer reality through our physical and biological development. From this perspective we feel that we know and have experienced a great deal about life. However, in this book you will explore how we actually create limits for ourselves and for the people around us. We will also explore the type of paradigm shift that is required in order to live from the next perspective of inner human development. Traditionally the primary understanding of our world is and has been created through an interpretation of our human emotions and feelings. These feelings become the filters through which we interpret and maintain our reality by means of our ideas, beliefs, attitudes and experiences. Only as we learn to shift these structures will we be able to perceive things differently.

I once considered myself to be very liberal in my thinking and my actions, but as I opened into the inner realms of transformation, I became aware of how little I truly wanted to change. So long as I compared myself to the average person and to the structures I imposed on myself within the 2 or 3% of reality that I was exploring, I indeed felt very trusting in my desire to change most anything. But once I emerged into the inner realms of myself and began to experience the actual depth of change that was available, I quickly became aware of my own self-imposed limits, and how conservative I really was. My first reaction was to hold onto many of my old beliefs, especially in the areas of sexuality, my physical body structure, and my emotional relationships with others. These were those "sacred" areas that identified me as me! And yet, these were the very things that imprisoned me within my limited ways of creating. I was willing to give up most anything to attain the changes I desired, but why should it mean these particular beliefs?

The first shift which must occur in most individuals' transformation involves the process of projection. We are not exploring this in terms of the limited sense from which Freud viewed projection, but rather, from a perspective of understanding that all of reality is a projection of our inner consciousness. When our consciousness is focused within the mind, we understand, see, feel, think, and experience life from one form of reality. When we shift from our previous learning and habits into a deeper internal mechanism, our perceptions of reality expand. In understanding this first stage, it is important to realize that reality is a fluid process, and whenever we become aware of something that feels out of balance, our awareness is the feedback that is telling us that something within our realm of current perceptions is ready to move into a new level of integration. Whenever you block the emergence of a new perception or when you focus on an outer perception as being reality, you ultimately must bring forward more and more energy in order to hold to those same perceptions, and through time they will become even more restrictive and more limiting.

The levels of change to which I am referring have nothing in common with the concept of doing something either right or wrong, or with something being seen as another lesson to be learned, or even with certain given circumstances as being some sort of cosmic test to be passed. There exists a natural human desire within each of us that keeps calling us into a deeper meaning of life and greater understanding of who we are. This inner movement, if we allow it, will evolve into a more integrated and synthesized level of inner experience and meaning. The stresses and pains we perceive in life are a result of the part of our consciousness that is choosing to hold onto things and keep them the way they are, in turn blocking the inner self-actualizing forces that are asking us to change.

Pain and stress are caused by a blocking of the self-actualizing energies. Those individuals who can sense, feel, and see energy, report seeing blockages both in the physical body and in the energy levels around a person when the inner creative forces are not allowed to move freely. One aspect of us is saying that we must remain the same, and another more powerful inner-directed force is saying that change is needed now, in order to move us into our next level of inner development. Would you limit a child's body from growing during its primary developmental stages, preventing the emergence of this inherent mechanism? Of course not, and if you did, it would cause a great amount of stress and pain for the child. Yet, each of us limits the mind from growing into its next level of human development and blocks the emergence of the inherent flow of information from the energies of our inner directed guidance. Most individuals confine the mind to a set of perceptions that have emerged from experiences brought forth through their outer development. These perceptions were very productive at one point in time, for they were very deeply anchored in the concept of duality as being the primary focus of reality. These perceptions kept the mind shifting back and forth, from one extreme to the other, repeating the same things over and over until the appropriate behaviors and perceptions were thoroughly learned.

In man's new phase of inner development, the former process of learning can never suffice. We need to let go of our thinking of things in terms of being right or wrong or of being this way versus that. Instead we must begin to experience life as a process whereby each new perception becomes the base for another perception, which in turn becomes the new base for the next perception. Then each perception can extend beyond the concept of duality, and we will begin to encompass an even greater overview in experiencing and understanding life. From this new perspective, our previous perceptions were not wrong; although they were limited, they still played a very useful and vital role in our development. As we move into post-biological development, our initial perceptions of life become limited as we experience the emergence of this inner force of energy that will eventually shift our perceptions into a new focus of unity. The outer mind, at its current level of perceiving, cannot grasp this broader overview because it can only seize upon the duality that it has been taught. As we move into the observer state and go beyond the limits of the outer mind, we open into the new perceptions that will emerge from our own inner-directed soul guidance. As we learn to live from these inner spaces of unity, we will experience the various shifts in perceptions that are available.

The first phase of transformation then requires that individuals refrain from getting caught within the duality of their perceptions, and instead, try to understand that all external perceptions are really based upon a changing internal perspective. This awareness then allows one to move out of the mind's perspective and to allow a heightened energy to emerge. The new energetic vibration will automatically allow one's perception to shift into a new understanding of reality. By completing this first stage of transformation, we will be able to move through, and thus not be controlled by, the more primitive human emotions. Now we will have a choice when we feel ourselves out of balance or out of control. We will be aware that our current perceptions are ready to change. There is no need to blame one's self for doing something wrong or perceiving that you have failed once again in getting it right. One's choice is to be able to experience a knowing that all of this is occurring through a natural inner process of growth aimed toward a new level of synthesis. Through choosing this latter awareness, one naturally moves into the observer state, and very little time is spent feeling stuck within one's feelings and thoughts.

At this present stage in my own odyssey, I am able to function from within the observer state a great deal of the time. This frees up a great amount of time and energy to focus on the awakening of my creative self-actualizing energies from within, in contrast to investing a great amount of energy living in and creating from the reaction phase of life! Whenever I am caught within my mind's perceptions, I always feel that this time it is different, and that there are no other options or perceptions left to explore. I either have to allow sufficient time for my perceptions to shift out of this reactionary phase or I have to ask someone else to point my problem out to me. When the latter occurs, I need to be careful not to shift my focus of anger onto someone else in order to keep distracting myself from the real issues that are involved. Regardless of what I happen to perceive as being the "real issue" when I am in my reaction phase, the issue is always a result of some perception within myself. Once I finally realize that an internal shift must be occurring, I allow myself to move into the observer state in order to clarify my new perceptions of the situation and of reality. Through the observer state, I can then allow the self-actualizing energy to emerge and move me into an inner state of unity. It is from within this state of unity that I can live my life from a new and different perspective— a perspective that is evolving out of that other 98% of my unknown awareness as it is becoming known to me.

The concept of <u>projection</u> opens the door to transformation. The broadest implication for the word projection is the realization that everything outside of ourselves is really a projection of our inner world. With seminar participants I also explore a practical aspect of projection, in which each feeling and thought has a counterpart within oneself. For example, if I become angry at my friend for always being late, I also feel a great deal of anger toward myself when I am late. I will either push myself into being on time and will feel frustrated and angry whenever I perceive that I will be late, or, since I place such an importance on being punctual, I will demand that others hold to the same values, and if they don't comply, beware! This same process also holds true regarding feelings of love or accomplishments that we see in others. We cannot see within another person something that we ourselves cannot also see, feel, and possibly experience for ourselves.

Let's pursue this further with an exploration into projection. Think of an individual towards whom you hold anger, frustration, or other similar feelings. Identify three behaviors that push you into feeling this way. I want you to focus on specific behaviors, not on general statements about the individual. Take a moment to do this before reading on *** *** ***. Now think of three behaviors that you like about this person *** *** ***. Now I would like you to fill in the following blank with one of the three personally annoying behaviors that you identified in the other individual. "I feel anger or frustration towards myself whenever I experience myself (doing or saying) _____." Do this same thing with the other two annoying behaviors. Do you notice any similar patterns of feelings within yourself? Can you begin to feel a similar counter-part within you?

Individuals often refuse to allow themselves to make certain choices because they feel so repulsed by them. This is usually because they are either still maintaining these same behaviors themselves or because they will go to any lengths to avoid exhibiting such behaviors. In either case, projection becomes the means of psychologically dealing with the deeper inner feelings. If this is the case with you, can you see why you become so angry at others for doing what you cannot allow yourself to do? We project our feelings whenever we do not or will not allow ourselves to do something that we see and experience others doing either to us or around us. Thus we ultimately react in exactly the same manner as the individual whose behavior annoys us, thus feeling and doing many of the same things ourselves.

Now let's go back to the three things you liked or admired about that same person whose annoying behaviors you listed. Most people find this task of identifying positive or admiring traits as being more difficult, or even impossible, to do. Whenever a person gets stuck in projecting one certain image or feeling about another individual, it becomes impossible to let an opposite image or feeling emerge. If you experienced this type of difficulty, it usually indicates that your projections are so strong that you have not allowed yourself to see who this other person really is. Whenever we hold an extremely strong belief about another individual, we rarely see any aspect of them other than that one belief. This should provide a valuable feedback for you in understanding yourself and your projections.

When I am counseling with families or couples, I explore the process of projection as a means of again opening the channels of communication. During the 1970s I spent a great deal of time working with adolescents and their families. Each time there was a communication breakdown, I found that it centered around the process of projection. The adult was always projecting on the child to "do what I say, not what I do or am afraid to do." Meanwhile the child was enacting what the adult was actually feeling about themselves or some given situation.

In 1978, as I opened into my inner-awarenesses, the area of projection was the first into which I was guided. I was seeing approximately 125 people in individual or group counseling settings. Through my inner guidance I was asked to place each individual into one of three groups based upon my perceptions of their feelings and their level of motivation for change. One group was comprised of individuals whom I believed sincerely wanted to change. Each session with them was very productive, and between sessions they practiced and explored the things we discussed. Another group of participants was made up of those individuals that I perceived as being semi-motivated, sometimes desiring to change and sometimes not. I perceived the participants in the last group as not being very motivated at all; I felt that they truly did not care and that they were in counseling for a variety of reasons, none of which were for growth and change.

Through my inner guidance I was asked to explore the belief that I too was interacting with each one of these groups and that I somehow also played an important role in either their progress or lack of progress in awakening change. My first reaction was, "How can I possibly force another person to change?" It was explained to me that although one cannot ever force another individual to change, it is possible to hold the inner feeling, energy, and belief that they can and will change in whatever direction is best for their own growth. The role I was to be playing was that of being a catalyst for holding the intent, or inner energy, and the belief within myself that their change was truly possible. It became clear that whenever I was unable to perceive another individual as being able to change, there also existed a deeper inner structure within me that likewise lacked conviction about my own personal abilities. My inner guidance asked me to allow myself (over the next three weeks) to keep focusing my inner feelings and perceptions into the heart as I came in contact with each individual with whom I was interacting. I was inwardly instructed that whenever I found that I was not maintaining this heart focus and whenever my thoughts and feelings wandered back into my previous projections, I was to explore and accept my frustrations as first being within myself, and then explore and accept them within the other person, allowing my perceptions to change until I felt that both of us could be different. All of this was to be done nonverbally and was not to be shared with the other individuals involved. I thought this was ridiculous, but in light of what had already been happening, why not try it.

During the next three weeks something strange occurred. First, I began to feel very different about myself. Although I thought I had a good self-image, I was surprised by all of the new feelings and perceptions that emerged. As I allowed each one of these feelings to change within me, I was shocked at how different I felt. A lightness and love for life emerged that I would not have previously thought possible. With my clients, some automatically stopped coming and did not say why, while the remaining 80% all began to care and to work on themselves with a totally different commitment than before. I didn't have a single client that was not motivated to change. Sure, they still had difficulties in their lives, but they knew they wanted to change them, and they were determined to do so. All of this transpired without directly verbalizing a single word! It was due entirely to the inner shift in my own consciousness.

I later learned that this same process occurs when a teacher is given falsified records concerning the children coming into her/his class. If each child is categorized as being either slow or average, while in reality each child is average to above, within a few weeks the children will be performing at a level consistent with the teacher's previous expectations of the group. The reverse situation is also true, with slower children quickly learning to perform at an average or above average level. Our perceptions, feelings, attitudes, and beliefs about ourselves and others are not idle daydreams or mere inner thoughts; rather, they hold an energy that is so real that we unconsciously create what we feel. Individuals are always capable of choosing to move beyond someone else's expectations for them. However, when an individual assumes the role of authority, or of being the "expert," her/his unconscious feelings hold a very powerful energy or unconscious expectation, and it takes a very strong individual to overcome this powerful unverbalized belief. The responsibility always lies first with those individuals who are in the position of authority; only when they begin to believe in themselves can the situation be easily changed. Many individuals talk a great deal about believing in themselves and in others, but yet very little change occurs in their own lives or in the lives of those with whom they interact.

Throughout the past nine years I have realized that whenever I feel that either I or someone else cannot accomplish something, or that one of us is caught in a state of negativism, I must begin to explore those perceptions or feelings within myself. Sure, not everyone is going to be willing to change or move into their potential, but at least I have the potential of choosing not to hold any unconscious feeling that can further block another's growth. One of the major goals of awakening into an inner creative development is to be able to see clearly from within one's own inner guidance, where only feelings and perceptions of unity exist, and to allow these to be the perceptions and feelings with which one naturally lives. So often people try to talk in a positive manner to one another, when inwardly they hold a very different feeling and perception. Most people feel that the important thing is to talk nicely or say the right things to one another and not to worry about what one truly feels inside, since no one really is aware of that anyway. The other extreme is when individuals share exactly what they are feeling under the banner of being honest, but share in a very cruel way. I explore this dilemma with myself and others by imagining that everyone around me can easily and accurately read my mind, my inner thoughts and my feelings. Therefore, whenever a thought or feeling emerges that moves from my outer mind or from a place of duality within me, I accept the responsibility of first looking at it as being some part of myself and my own feelings about myself, acknowledging that it has nothing to do with the other person or the current situation. I then maintain an inner focus on this until it is balanced and I can once again see clearly what is occurring. Sometimes there are rather painful things I need to share with another person, but when the sharing is truly done out of an inner energy of love, it no longer feels painful, and both of us can feel the difference. Whenever I need to share, but feel afraid or frightened by what I am to do or say, I know that there still is an aspect within me that needs deepening. By utilizing this procedure I do not contribute to another's maintaining a poor self-image or sense of feeling unworthy. As I explore this process with groups and allow them to open into the inner spaces of silence where their own energies of inner guidance emerge, they are surprised at how easily their perceptions shift into a state of unity, and they are even more surprised to discover that their initial feelings had actually evolved from their own projections toward themselves. This becomes the basis for the exploration into deeper levels of understanding one's self.

What would happen if people all around you could read your thoughts and feelings? Is this something you would like? If not, then why hold onto such inner feelings? Let them change, but realize that they cannot change until you acknowledge that what you are experiencing is really feedback about yourself! Once you become responsible for the perceptions in your own life, you will be amazed at how quickly things move.

Can you begin to understand that our only hope for inner peace and calmness resides within our inner-awarenesses, in the exploration of the 98% of our unknown reality? Initially our outer mind perceives only the 2% of external reality, and yet feels overwhelmed with just this amount of information. The inner peace, the calmness, the feelings of love, and the perceptions of unity that mystics describe can only occur through the process of coexistence with the energies of our inner guidance as we are led by means of direct explorations into those aspects of ourselves of which we are unaware. Through the inner-directed energies of our soul we become aware of our internal world, and through this level of coexistence, a certain level of peace, hope and focus is maintained. Through our outer focus, without a direct link to our inner guidance, we experience strong feelings of incompleteness; we begin making comparisons and judgements about ourselves and others, and begin to feel a strong need for our intellect to know and control everything within our grasp. Focusing one's awareness solely through the outer mind rarely satisfies these yearnings for inner completeness.

I believe the brain is the physical counterpart of a deeper and more powerful energetic structure, whose vibrations are within a constant state of organization. The structures of these energetic vibrations will determine the type and level of neurological connections that are created. If the outer mind is allowed to focus without experiencing the energies of one's inner guidance, this directs our perceptions into one type of focus. If we allow our inner guidance to direct and educate us in our outer awareness, it will alter these vibrations into a new set of unified patterns and will allow us to perceive and sense other perceptions of reality. Everything that we need to know is available to us through the energetic restructuring that occurrs from our inner-directed guidance. Through this we move into the heightened vibration of coexistence, wherein we maintain an inner connection while living and moving in our outer world. Life thus becomes a "living meditation." This process of coexistence is made possible through the communication between our inner energetic vibrations and the physical brain and nervous system.

Many individuals perceive that we must move into an altered state of consciousness in order to experience the unexplored 98% of reality. In my own experience, I have found that we are never creating a new or altered state of awareness; rather, we are allowing our awareness to move along a continuum that evolves into various energetic structures that form perceptions and levels of inner knowing that are awaiting discovery. Each one of these levels is maintained by an invisible veil that allows the brain to function at one, and only one, particular level of perception. This veil can be experienced as a vibration, and through this vibration we perceive and experience reality from a certain given perspective.

We cannot open safely into our next levels of awareness until we have first established a new inner vibration. Through the use of drugs, for example, we can force ourselves through some of these veils, but then what should be a naturally safe and exciting journey becomes frightening. Fear comes into play because we have not transmuted most of the projections that exist in our conscious mind at this one particular level, and therefore what we are perceiving through the breaks in our veil cannot yet be compre- hended by our outer mind. Thus we become fearful. The process of transmuting our projections organizes the living vibration within the brain in a very natural way and allows us a smooth journey into the next layers of our inner realms. We never really create another reality; we merely allow the reorganization, synthe- sis, and emergence of something that has always been present within us. This awakens an aspect which has previously been blocked from our current state of awareness by our beliefs, attitudes, feelings, and perceptions.

The concept of reorganization and synthesis is similar to what I encountered when I first learned to feel and experience the transferring of energies. I did not invent the energies. They had always been present because they constitute the reality of what we are physically, psychologically, and spiritually as human beings.

As my mind moved into its observer state, I was able to sense what had always existed. But when my outer mind was in control, or was the primary focus, there existed no awareness of what energy really was. When I first began transferring energy and then allowed my outer mind to move back into control, I would deny many of the experiences I had earlier felt. The mind is so powerful in its construction of reality, that whenever we move out of our observer state it automatically denies or distorts all of our previous experiences. When the energy or vibration first emerges from within, and the outer mind then is allowed to be restructured into new states of awareness, we will perceive feelings of comfort and excitement about our new discoveries of life!

The second shift necessary in transformation involves the owning of each new projection as one's own. In this process we must allow each projection to move into the outer mind, shift our focus into the observer state, and thus own the projection as our own. Next, we allow the emergence of a vaster and more unified energy of unconditional love to emanate from the heart chakra and the synchronization of the triune brain, allowing a new awareness to come forward. The new awareness must then become integrated as a new perception in one's life. When I talk about projection I am referring to each perception of life that holds the forces of duality, wherein something is either right or wrong, good or evil, or should be this way versus that, and that is under the direct influence of one's outer mind and emotions. The best way to understand the outer forces of duality is with an understanding of the inner forces of unity through the energetics of unconditional love. In **Joy's Way**, Brugh describes this radiance of unconditional love as:

"... the energy that uplifts downcast eyes, heals the pain of years of struggle, nourishes the soul in its venture to unite with the spirit, inspirits the mundane and transmutes that which is not to be into that which is to be. It is the essence of the cohesive force that binds all things to God. This love is nonemotional, nonsexual, and nonmental. It has the power to spiritualize instantaneously, imbuing each individual with an expanded experience of universal relationship and universal values. The sensation is one of Divinity, and it does not matter whether rational states comprehend. This Love is the energy that sweeps one towards home, a return to the embrace with God."

This constitutes the essence of one's inner guidance. Within this second stage, every perception of reality is dependent upon an external force. Regardless of whether it is good or bad, it is viewed as a projection and needs to be transmuted into the vaster and more refined vibration of the heart chakra and triune brain. When this is complete, it will be perceived as unity.

The second phase of transformation then is a phase of action, which is very different than meditating and talking about the unity of mind, emotion, body and spirit. This process actually allows one to experience the unity of the inner force of unconditional love as the natural state of living. During meditation we can experience many levels of awareness, and we can see clearly what issues are confronting us and sense the direction that we can take. Leaving the safety of our meditations, however, and moving into the outer world, brings us face to face once again with many of the same issues and events that we earlier were perceiving. If these events are fully transmuted through the heart chakra and the synchronization of the triune brain, we automatically move into the inner perceptions of unity which create a new level of awareness. Many mystics call this state of unity the fourth state of awareness (the energy of unconditional love), through which all interactions with ourselves and others are drastically changed. But if we interact with others and are manifesting and experiencing the same inner feelings of duality as before, then the energy from our meditation has not emerged into our livingness, and thus maintains a different state of awareness. There are always two levels within this process, one being our outer actions and the other our inner focus of thoughts, feelings, and images. If we have shifted our projection into an inner unity, we automatically find an inner calmness, peace, and joy on both of these levels. Many individuals, however, talk about the spaces of unity without ever transmuting their projections, therefore making it difficult to truly interact out of the inner spaces. When a projection is fully transmuted into unity, a radiance of love is present and can be felt by everyone involved. Words can only convey a very small part of this radiance of love.

I believe that the human brain is capable of holding several distinct structures of energetic vibrations. Within a given structure, the outer mind is capable of perceiving and performing various kinds of tasks. Each one of these distinct structures could be perceived as a major form of awareness. Ancient traditions describe six or seven distinct levels of awareness, and within each of these levels of awareness, one would interpret and understand their outer reality and their inner world from a totally new and different perspective. No matter how many perceptions are held at a particular vibrational focus, no form of thinking or feeling will allow an individual to penetrate into a new structure of awareness. And an individual cannot truly open into the levels of unity, the fourth state of awareness, without first experiencing the energies of unconditional love. The brain can only vibrate at the levels of energy that are reflected by the focus of the outer mind and of the personality structures that are currently being explored. The process of the heart chakra and the triune brain allows us to move into the fourth state of awareness that extends beyond the structures of the physical brain, body, intellect and emotion.

At this fourth state of awareness or consciousness, we open into a heightened level of creative energy that encompasses all other possible levels of perceptions. No matter how hard we try to intellectually change our perceptions, attitudes, and beliefs, it cannot hold the energetic vibrations of the heart. To awaken the observer state, the brain begins to move into a new inner alignment that is focused upon the heart chakra, thus allowing the body to move into the inner harmony and rhythm of one's self-actualizing pulse. As this process deepens, we can allow our inner guidance to emerge at another level of energy, which automatically allows the mind to be restructured or educated into perceiving and feeling life from a totally different perspective, one of unity. This allows the brain to organize and function at the new heightened level of energy, and our new outer mind's perceptions of unity can then emerge. We have thus allowed our inner-awareness to become our outer reality.

When we are face to face with life, and our perceptions are firmly focused in the outer mind, the clarity of information which we previously received in meditation is no longer available to us. What we recall from our meditation is usually but a small part of what we actually experienced. However, both levels of perceptions which we have been discussing are always available, and the level upon which we choose to focus is based on the current level of the brain's energetic structure. Will it be focused from the personality of mind or from the energies of the inner focus of one's soul guidance?

I have seen many individuals "think" they are taking direct action based upon their meditative information, when instead they have shifted the information that they have received into a lower vibrational level. At this lower level many of the synchronized events which I earlier mentioned cannot manifest because they require the energy and action that emanate from the fourth level of awareness. Individuals are then surprised to find that what they thought would be working, is not!

Initially there is a fine line in distinguishing between the perceptions of duality and the perceptions of unity. However, the differences in the level of energies which one experiences between the two are really very easy to identify. Through the feedback of the physical body, we can understand which levels we are focused upon and creating from. Unconditional love, the fourth state of awareness, knows "no push" or "should" or "have to." It only knows the nurturing, gentle movements of unity. We have the feeling, when operating from the inner spaces, of gently "being pulled through life" instead of feeling as though we have to create life. By choosing to transmute all of your perceptions (projections), you will continue to explore these differences, and it will soon become very obvious to you how each one of the levels begins to feel inside of you. Your body is truly the ultimate feedback mechanism.

Whenever I am doing individual or group explorations, regardless of the nature of the information I am bringing forward, I am continually in an inner state of unity, observing as I listen to what is being said. Whenever an issue has direct personal meaning for me, I can feel a different energy or an inner shift within my body, and this becomes a feedback signaling that what I am saying also has personal meaning for my own exploration. With this mere acknowledgement, the vibration will evolve into a deeper inner sense of unity, and at that moment I become aware of the new perceptions and understanding within me. If I do not feel the inner shift, I know that the information continues to hold something very personal for me to explore. When I am sharing my insights with another individual, and this inner shift does not occur for me, I usually share with them that this particular information may also have some very personal meaning for me. Whatever the circumstances, I am continually observing my perceptions and am allowing an inner automatic process to operate, thus exploring the new levels of whatever it is that I am bringing forward. Even under the direction of unity, there exist yet deeper levels of perceptions and energy just waiting to emerge.

For more than five years I have actively explored the process of transmutation, and I am continually amazed at the intricate levels of inner working that one's consciousness is capable of handling. My outer mind could never handle the many levels of nonlinear structures and understanding without the aid of the inner vibration of the expanded human feeling state of unconditional love. Based upon my observations and experiences, I am amazed at how capable we are of simultaneously exploring the inner levels of reality and the vast amounts of nonlinear information. During these past five years I have learned to allow the inner state of unity to become present each day in my outer world, thereby allowing the levels of inner synthesis to continue. When this state is present, I no longer hold as sacred the sexual issues, the physical body, or the emotional relationships that I once felt I dared not change. I now can allow them to transform as needed. However, without the heightened energy from my inner guidance, many of the old issues return even as I am learning to live at the levels of coexistence. The fourth state of awareness, and even levels beyond, are always available to us through an energetic restructuring, which we can then learn to maintain. Without maintaining the new levels of energy, though, we automatically reconfigurate any previously attained level of consciousness and move right back into the prior levels of awareness, thus falling back into our old habitual patterns.

One never truly resolves any patterns or issues in life. Transformation does not bring an individual into a state of being "normal" according to outer standards, especially since these standards vary greatly, even within the same culture, religion, or geographic location. Rather, transformation allows one to shift into an observer state and allows the energy to transmute one set of projections into a new set of perceptions; and this new set of perceptions follows the unfoldment and needs of one's inner guidance or soul energy. This allows us to discover who we are and what our inner purpose is. It allows our own uniqueness to emerge as a state of inner unity. Transformation actually brings forth greater individuality, and yet it binds us together with a greater common thread through the energies and feelings of unconditional love. Through these energies and this unconditional love, the deeper part of our soul is satisfied, and we therefore desire to continue awakening, exploring and creating our inner potential. This is the essence of transformation.

As we move through the second phase of transformation, we automatically begin to explore the third phase where there is no separation between inner and outer reality—they become one and the same. What appears to be an external perception actually feels like the energy of the expanded state of unity or love from one's inner guidance. Thus our internal and external perceptions literally feel and are experienced as being the same. The expanded state of unity, or unconditional love, can be present with all perceptions in life, regardless of the outer situation or action that we are experiencing. And when this energetic feeling is not present, the perceptions that we do become aware of at that given point signal the next perception that needs to be explored and allowed to shift into a level or vibration of unity. This becomes the odyssey of Transformational Psychology—the shifting or "transmutation" of all perceptions that exist at the level of awareness of the outer mind into the fourth state of awareness, or energies of our inner-directed soul guidance. This allows the new vibration of human feelings, or that energy of unconditional love, to become the feedback as to what has been transmuted and what is now ready to be changed.

From this perspective, can you begin to understand the concept that the perceptions which emerge do so because you are doing something right, and that they are the next ones you need to explore. The concept that if you do things right and handle situations in life properly you will never become angry or upset is erroneous. The only way to open into the energies of unity and the fourth state of awareness is to allow the process of transmutation to emerge in the everyday events. When you can honor the process of allowing the new information to emerge with excitement and love, you are well on your way in the process of transformation. The process of transmutation is very important in allowing the growth of one's soul to coexist within the physical form. It is no less important than breathing is in allowing the physical form to remain alive. The heightened energy becomes very nurturing to one's outer mind, and the outer mind will rebel with confusion only if the process is attempted without the energy of unconditional love of the fourth state of awareness.

We will be exploring the "how to" process of transmutation throughout this book. I would like to quote a section from **Joy's Way** concerning the Tibetan Buddhist approach to the resolution or transmutation of problems:

"The highest and most difficult [approach] is to transmute the problem—that is, to generate an intensity of energy from a higher, more expanded awareness and to use this energy to force a change in the configuration of the problem's less expanded, less intense energy and thus free the energy that configurates the problem. Transmutation implies a change of the form or nature (of anything) into another form or nature. In this plane, all energy flows from more energetic sources to less energetic manifestations, never in the opposite direction. Therefore, higher aspects of consciousness always transmute lower aspects of consciousness."

The process of awakening to your creative potential is one of direct transmutation of perceptions brought forth by allowing a heightened energy from within your inner soul guidance to emerge and shift perceptions to a new level of inner understanding or consciousness. This becomes a gradual process of allowing your physical vibration to be increased, and at the same time, allowing yourself to be awakened by your own inner self-actualizing pulse. All inner creative energies are a part of the deeper inner awakening of the ancient mystical energies of Kundalini. These deeper energies are inherent in all human beings, and their awakening is based upon an inner timing sequence that is interdependent upon many unconscious forces. It is the deeper energies that allow us to perceive and live within all levels of unity. They allow us a synthesis with our total being. Once an individual's vibration has heightened, many of the perceptions will automatically begin to shift into the inner levels of unity. As the deeper mystical vibration awakens (i.e., the inner self-actualizing pulse), this force is meant to become a very exciting and exhilarating part of one's inner journey. Many researchers in the West believe that every major breakthrough in the sciences, music, art, and other forms of creativity is a direct result of these deeper energies being awakened. The process of awakening is not a one time occurrence; rather, it is a gradual process that will continue to evolve throughout one's life. I believe that as we move into the inner levels of post-biological development, these natural levels of energy will become those that allow humanity to awaken into heightened levels of creative functioning. It is only through this energy that man's total brain and nervous system can be shifted from an orientation that is focused upon physical and biological development into one that is focused upon nonbiological or inner spiritual development. The inner self-actualizing energies are truly as natural to our inner awakening as the energies of breathing are to our outer existence. Carl Jung who spent time exploring the process of Kundalini, also felt that the awakening of this mystical energy would start a world that is totally different from the world we currently knew.

Much of the literature dealing with this topic describes the deeper awakening process as being frightening and powerful. Rarely, however, have those relating the experiences of such an awakening explored the process of learning how to increase their levels of energy and shift their outer perceptions prior to the awakening. Meditation alone does not create a living energy, but the awakening of the self-actualizing pulse prepares one to live in the unity state of consciousness. The purpose of being awakened into the inner force is to allow us to quickly and directly experience the essence of who we are and to directly explore the profound, nurturing, loving process of living at the fourth state of awareness. Thus the awareness becomes the base camp out of which all reality is perceived and allows us to shift again and again into new levels of inner-awareness throughout the journey into the 98% of our unaware reality.

I believe that as individuals choose to explore the process of transmutation and allow the inner creative self-actualizing energies to awaken through their soul, they will discover that the deeper, mystical energies move through them very easily and safely. I have experienced this for myself and have also explored this deeper awakening energy with other individuals over the years. When they allowed the inner force of love to emerge into their lives, the shift in perceptions and experiences evolved very easily and safely. I have known several individuals who chose to experience the deeper forces as being different and frightening and, because they never allowed the heart to guide their journey, they remained "stuck" within the levels of fear. Even individuals who have used great quantities of hallucinogenic drugs have been unable to achieve these deeper levels of awakening. On the other hand, I have known individuals who were doing the most ordinary things, such as walking down the street, when they awakened directly into the deeper mystical states of their self-actualizing pulse. If an individual is ready to awaken, awaken they will.

The process of transmutation is one that is part of our inner heritage and is meant to be explored by every human being. Through the process, new levels of a heightened inner creative energy will emerge which will let us interact with one another out of the inner space of unity. Transmutation is a very gentle step-by-step process which allows the heightened energy to emerge; this then very naturally shifts the energy of a problem, or a lesser configuration of energy, into a new awareness. Individuals can learn to move into the heightened vibrations very quickly and can even allow this to occur during a business meeting, a sporting event, while driving a car, or in any other circumstance of daily life.

We as human beings are not meant to hold onto the limited perceptions that most of us are now perpetuating. We have within us the full potential to shift them at the time of their occurrence, or whenever we become consciously aware of their existence. In order for this to transpire, however, we need a process that will permit us to safely and easily allow the transmutation to emerge. Exploring the Soul/Mind/Body process allows this journey to be a smooth and safe one for you, just as it has been for me and for many others.

Choosing transformation as a creative way of living, however, has not always been an easy task for me. I initially thought that transformation meant exploring the many realms of psychic possibilities, and in the early years I did master and teach others many of the psi phenomena that are popular. I explored the realms of psychokinesis and was able to move and influence objects from a distance. I investigated precognition and past cognition, where I was able to see or perceive events that either had occurred or were going to occur. I practiced telepathy in both the transmission and reception of thought patterns at great distances. I developed clairvoyant perception, seeing the auric fields and chakras of humans and other life forms. I became adept at clarsentience (the feeling of other people's emotions, pains and inner sensations); clairaudience (the hearing of sounds and voices at a distance or from other realms); out-of-body travel; the reorganization of physical illness within my own body and in that of others; being able to sense, describe, and interpret another person's dreams for them; and a host of other experiences. Although these were very exciting to my outer mind and ego, none of them aided me in my inner commitment to transformation! Being able to accomplish such things and teach others about these experiences helped my outer mind to understand that other realms of possibilities did exist, for all of this was contradictory to what my outer mind thought was possible. In 1983, after exploring my own near-death experience, I realized that I had the choice of either fully embracing the principles of living through the processes of transformation and giving up the psychic processes, or of continuing to dabble within the areas of the psychic and never being able to fully embrace the inner world. It was a decision that my outer mind struggled with, and yet my inner feelings automatically said "YES!"

Once I had made my commitment, I no longer had available to me the aforementioned abilities in the area of psi phenomena. One aspect of my ego panicked, but another part of me knew that something even more wonderful was awakening. I found that I could no longer perform any of the "parlor tricks" for myself or other groups. What began to emerge, however, was a deeper awakening and subsequent exploration that made the psi phenomena seem like childish play. I have come to realize over the years that I have not lost anything; instead, I have gained a new world of understanding by choosing transformation as a creative way of living. The outer mind has a very vast realm of psychic possibilities which it can explore all by itself, without ever shifting into the inner-directed soul realms. But none of these psychic processes really helped me to better my own life or the lives of those around me. They were merely places and things to explore. Sure, I had wonderful information for other people, and about my own life as well, but once I had shifted into the energies of my inner-directed guidance, I allowed my own perceptions and capabilities to move beyond the psi process, and the levels of inner information and abilities changed phenomenally.

My daily life is now deeply integrated into the transformational process as a natural way of living. I allow, as much as is possible, my own perceptions, actions, and thoughts to be inwardly guided in order that my entire life, and all the actions which I take, can move within the area of transformation. This I believe constitutes the next stage of our inner development as human beings. Having shifted my focus from my outer mind into my heart center, choosing transformation as a creative way of living has been the easiest and most profound step I have ever taken.

CHAPTER SIX

OUR BRAIN AS A TRANSDUCER OF REALITY

The human brain is the most remarkable organ of the body. Furthermore, we humans possess one of the most evolved brains existing on the earth at this time; only the brain of the dolphin or the whale is more advanced. Yet, we know very little about how the human brain functions, and much less about the purpose of the vast area of neocortex, of which less than 10% is presently being used.

There currently exist two major theories regarding the purpose of the brain and its role in understanding consciousness. The first theory is supported by the Newtonian-Cartesian model and sets forth the idea that the brain is the major structure for the process of perception, with one's consciousness being created as the direct result of brain activity. In this model, everything is contained and maintained within the brain. The other theory is supported by a group of researchers and individuals, including Jean Houston, Wilder Penfield, John Lilly, Barbara Brown, Joseph Pearce, and others who have direct experience exploring consciousness as it relates to the functioning of the human brain. They experience the brain, not as the creator of consciousness, but rather, as being one part of a larger communication system existing between the mind aspect and the physical body.

Wilder Penfield, in his book **The Mystery of the Mind**, describes what he perceives as the potential functioning for the human brain. Penfield perceived the brain's highest mechanism as being one of messenger between the mind and the other mechanisms of the brain. Even Hippocrates expressed the idea that the brain's function is the messenger to consciousness. These individuals denote the term Mind as not being of the intellect, which I call the outer mind; rather, they describe it as a process of higher intelligence, an unconscious process, an aspect of the spirit, the divine, the soul. Their use of the word Mind is equivalent to my use of the phrase "the energies of inner-directed soul guidance." For the sake of consistency, I interpret their use of the word Mind throughout the remainder of this book as being that inner-directed soul guidance or the energy of one's self-actualizing force. Within their theory, the energies of our inner-directed soul guidance are perceived as existing outside of (beyond) the human brain. They also describe the "other mechanism of the brain" as it relates to the basic levels of controlling and monitoring the various functions of the physical body, as the mind contained within the brain. Penfield feels that we will not truly understand what this higher process is until we understand the nature of the energy that is responsible for "mind" or "soul" action. This of course is one of the premises we are exploring in Transformational Psychology.

As we explore the difference between these two theories, we can ultimately see that they are both correct. At certain times we do use our outer mind, which is contained within the brain, for direction and monitoring of the physical body. At other times we use our inner-directed soul guidance, which resides beyond the brain, for information and monitoring of the physical body.

Within the first premise, which utilizes the outer mind, we perceive and interpret all of reality from a singular, linear, sequential pattern, whereby one cannot verbalize, perceive, feel, or think of two or more processes at the same time. Therefore, we accept the hypothesis that we cannot focus our awareness upon two or more ideas and objects simultaneously. Within this premise we believe that we can identify in the brain the existence of a localized biochemical action that is consistent in storing and processing perceptions, thoughts, and memories. Through such an interpretation one could view the brain as being analogous to a "computer," with the brain itself functioning as the hard disk, capable of processing information in a direct and linear way. Thus, we view ourselves as interacting with our world in a mechanistic way, responding in a linear pattern to different stimuli in our environment.

Most individuals spend their entire lives living and thinking within this type of model. This is precisely why many mystics and philosophers portray humans as being "asleep" when we are functioning from the outer mind in walking, talking, acting, and so forth; and being really "awake" when we are "physically asleep." During sleep we have the opportunity to be present with the energies of our own inner-directed soul guidance, and to open to our creative self and to the ability to understand our inner world. Lucid dreaming states play a role in this process.

When we shift to viewing the brain as being the "messenger," the energies we perceive from our inner-directed guidance go beyond the confines of the physical brain, and we automatically open ourselves into a process that no longer defines perceptions through a linear, sequential model. We begin to experience life as a series of simultaneous, or multidimensional experiences. Within this second model we are then able to perceive, feel, think, and experience multiple levels of stimuli at the same time, even though many of the experiences may be nonrelated. When certain areas of the brain are stimulated during specific types of brain surgery, individuals report full recall of a past event and at the same time report exactly what is taking place in front of them in the operating room. Some theories purport that the brain itself holds all information, while other theories contend that it holds very little. Still other theories believe that an outside force of energy, or electrical current, actually organizes a certain set of patterns that encompasses the entire cortex, and that this, in turn, is responsible for all of the information related to perceptions, memory, and potential functioning. If this theory is correct, as I believe it is, then an additional interpretive model of the brain needs to emerge that will take into account these highly developed cerebral functions. One could perceive this model as being the "holographic principle of brain functioning." This concept does not contradict the traditional theories of the brain's functions; rather, it broadens one's understanding and explains many of the phenomena which our current theories cannot yet explain.

Jean Houston, in her book **The Possible Human**, describes a series of exercises for awakening the brain and senses. Over the years, I have explored both her exercises and my own with thousands of individuals in order to awaken them to the possibilities of maintaining simultaneous experiences and thought. As individuals moved through these levels of training, I found that virtually every person with whom I worked was able to clearly hold, experience, feel, and think of many contradictory experiences at the same time. One of Houston's explorations that I regularly use is described in **The Possible Human** as Left Brain/Right Brain:

"Now on the left side of your brain, experience as fully as you can the following scene: you are riding a horse through the snow and sleet carrying three little kittens under your coat, and you are sucking on a peppermint. On the right side of your brain you are standing under a waterfall singing 'You Are My Sunshine' and watching a nearby volcano erupt."

As individuals begin to awaken into such inner simultaneous experiences, they are also able to awaken into a similar process to synthesize information in other areas of life.

These experiences, and many others, especially in the areas of processing and focusing information and in allowing various awarenesses to be simultaneously present without any other visual cues, cannot be adequately described by the theory that consciousness is contained totally within the brain. Through these experiences we can begin to understand our autonomous desire to be free and to interpret reality from our own inner-directed state— a state that holds no boundaries or limits.

Since 1978 I have directly experienced the brain as a transducer of the energy that exists between the inner-directed guidance and the physical body. The brain's function as a transducer of energy allows us to interpret the different levels of reality that we perceive. I believe that the brain takes this inner energy and steps it down to a level at which we can begin to process it. This arbitrary level is based upon the overall vibrational level of the whole brain and nervous system. (Henceforth, when I use the term whole brain, I am always including both the entire triune brain and the complete nervous system as being parts of one operation.) When the brain is within a state of confusion, or even balanced but with an outer focus, the level of vibration we then experience actually limits the experiences that are available to us. As the whole brain moves into different resonating frequencies, it acts as a filter for our perceptions and brings forward a specific focus. Through this filtered awareness, we maintain and structure our world into a series of perceptions that permit us to experience our thoughts, feelings, and interactions only through the filters of right and wrong judgments or other similar duality structures. On the other hand, when the brain functions from the energies of an inner-directed guidance that is moving through the vertical unity of the whole triune system, we process that level of energy differently. Through more highly resonating frequencies, we experience an inner sense of unity that expresses itself through a different series of filters, which subsequently change our thoughts, feelings, and interactions as they relate to that same outer situation. Thus we have choices in the creation of our reality by being able to choose what level of brain functioning we are going to utilize.

This latter holographic concept encompasses far more than just viewing the brain from the perspective of right brain versus left brain functioning. I believe that many of the ideas and perceptions regarding right and left brain functioning are highly simplified and overly generalized. I concur that both hemispheres of the brain must function jointly in order to process information, but the deeper levels of information emanating from the vertical unity of the entire triune brain are necessary in order to open us into the energies of our inner-directed guidance. Whenever we are operating with anything less than the whole triune brain and/or whenever the synchronization into the inner rhythm of the heart chakra is lacking, we have not completely opened into the full potentiality of the energies that exist within our inner-directed soul guidance, and we are consequently operating out of a mixture of inner and outer direction.

During the time that I was struggling with my outer mind to understand the concept of the brain as a transducer of energy that could alter perceptions of reality, I received a most enlightening image through my inner-directed guidance. It was at a time within my own journey when I was exploring the energies of crystals and other forms of gem stones and minerals as transducers of energy. The first image I received was that of the brain as a "whole crystalline structure." Prior to this time, I had always visualized the brain as being divided into two equal parts, the right and left hemispheres. Next I was shown an image of the brain as being divided into five parts, which I later understood to be the triune brain, and it was made very clear to me that this whole triune brain structure was one solid, connected mass. Many individuals with whom I was acquainted were exploring the use of crystals and minerals at the time in an attempt to heighten their own levels of energy and awareness. I was inwardly asked if, instead of exploring crystals, I would like to explore the internal crystalline structure that exists within each human being. Could I begin to perceive the human brain as a crystalline structure that could be energized, brought under the direction of the heart chakra, and then be explored in terms of the various existing vibrational frequencies? I was told that by exploring this concept, I would be able to begin living outwardly at new levels of perceptions which would parallel the inner vibrational energy that I was experiencing at that time in my meditative state.

My first reaction was one of excitement, until I began to share this vision with others and encountered their resistance to stopping their work with crystals. They had no desire to open into an inner crystalline structure that they could not see, feel, or touch. Their resistance caused me to become aware of my own doubts, and it took me several months to acknowledge the existence of this inner structure and to directly begin my exploration of the vertical unity of the whole triune brain as one crystalline structure of energy. Over the next several years I began to fully understand the ramifications and significance of exploring this "crystal" that rests atop our shoulders, inside our skull. It then took several more years before I was able to comprehend what it would mean to truly live from the energies of an inner-directed state.

During this time I was drawn to Paul MacLean's research regarding the triune brain, and I began to understand the five part system that I had initially been shown. I was led into a series of meditations and explorations through which I was shown the process of opening into the inner rhythms and perceptions of the heart chakra, and I was shown how this was related to the triune brain and its crystalline structures. As I brought this system under the volition of my own inner heart chakra rhythm, I began to see how the various parts of the triune brain were associated with the different chakras or energy centers of the body, and how this all related to the levels of perception and the quality of interactions with which we live and create.

During this same period of time in my life, I was also being led through an exploration concerning imagery and the way in which images are created within our inner and expanded inner screen. I noticed that during my own imagery exploration certain images would come forward from the top part of my inner screen and at other times they would emerge from the opposite side or from other areas. This fascinated me, and as I began to inwardly ask questions about it, I was asked to move the images about and then experience what happened within my own body as I was doing this. Although I am using the term images, I would remind you that we are exploring a much larger concept than simply a visual image. What I am referring to also includes any inner experiences or sensations that are created in conjunction with the images. As I asked the images to move from one side of my inner screen to another, I felt differing sensations within my physical body, and at times the given sensations had a different feeling tone attached to them. And when I asked these images to move into the center of my inner screen, another totally different sensation emerged. It felt as though a sudden rush of energy was moving through my entire body, which usually brought me into an inner state of unity and into a feeling of being within the energies of unconditional love. I realized that it made no difference what I was experiencing—a direct visual image, various colors, geometric symbols, symbolic events, tactile stimulation, smells, tastes, or other various sensations; regardless of the pattern that was developing and emerging, if it was created from a specific location within my expanded inner screen, I experienced a certain type of feedback and reaction in my physical body.

As I continued my explorations, I noticed that five major patterns were beginning to develop. The first pattern focused on the physical sensations and feelings from the lower right portion of my inner screen, which I would then directly experience in my physical body. The second pattern evolved from images within the lower left section of the inner screen, whereby my emotional feeling tone and memories based upon the images and feelings were heightened. The third pattern emerged from experiences within the upper left portion, which consisted of various forms of mental operations based upon intellectual memories about past experiences or upon my current attitudes and beliefs about what I could possibly do or create. When my focus shifted into my upper right quadrant, I found that I was unable to maintain any past information; instead, I would experience a stream of energy emerging that felt very comforting, loving, and nurturing. When I experienced information or sensations from this quadrant, its focus was always directed either toward a new potential for me to create or toward being able to do something with great ease. Often these sensations directed me into concepts or deeds that I had thought or felt would be impossible, or at least very difficult, to achieve. But through the levels of inner energy that would subsequently emerge, I could begin to inwardly see and feel that anything was possible. The fifth pattern was one which emerged whenever I had two similar sensations or patterns within my screen that were not related to any particular quadrant. I found that if I directed them into the middle or center point, my inner screen would automatically expand and open around me. At this moment, I would no longer feel that I was merely watching something in front of me; rather, I felt as though I had become the total experience, and that I was at the center of what was occurring. After a time, though, it became very difficult for me to direct the experiences. Finally, after several weeks of frustration, an inner voice said to me, "Why not ask the images and feelings to move when you are within the expanded space?" And when I did, I discovered that everything changed quickly and easily, without my having to exert any control.

After mapping out these inner spaces over the course of a year, I began to recognize the connection between the spaces of my inner screen, my whole triune brain, and the various chakras or energy centers of the body. Over the next three years I pursued an in-depth exploration of these ideas and concepts with various groups and individuals. This further verified the existence of the inner connections and various inner spaces within all of us. I began to realize that the expanded inner screen was similar to a control window for guiding the functions of the brain and nervous system. I discovered that when we awaken into the expanded space and heart chakra, we shift into new levels of brain functioning, whereby the brain truly becomes a messenger for the energies between the inner-directed guidance and the physical body. When this shift occurs, all of our physiological functions and perceptions begin automatically to change.

In 1985, I began consciously exploring ways to fully live within the expanded inner space while conducting the everyday events of my life. This began the next level of my exploration—that of understanding what it means to be awakened to, and to live from, the energies of my inner self while talking, walking, and interacting with others. I was thus awakening to the living aspect of one's post-biological development, and by the end of 1985 I began to understand that this constituted the next level of human development. This would awaken us into our true purpose of being human—learning to live and create from our inner self-actualizing energies and allowing a heightened level of creative functioning to emerge from within us. Therefore, since late 1985, the basic purpose of my explorations with individuals and groups has been to open them into and to explore with them the means of living naturally from the energies of our inner-awakened creative states.

As the triune brain and nervous system begin to work as one resonating unit, individuals can begin to feel and experience the subtle vibrations and pulsations that move from the inner crystalline structure. Individuals describe these sensations as similar to that of a current of electrical energy moving through them, and they begin to feel a subtle wave emanating from the heart chakra throughout the body. These are the feelings and sensations that emerge from the inner self-actualizing pulse. Regardless of what outer task I may be performing, when I am within the energies of my inner-directed guidance, these inner sensations and feelings are always present. And whenever I am in my outer mind performing a task, the inner-awarenesses and inner sensations are gone.

Rarely in my life have the inner sensations interfered with any of my physical actions. During the late fall of 1982, I experienced such a deep form of this awakening energy that, whenever I sat down, individuals around me would feel and experience the same pulsating waves of energy. At times the pulsation was so strong that other individuals were unable to get up from their chairs or even move in their chairs until I would first leave the room. On one occasion when I was conducting a group meditation, none of the participants were able to get up from the floor until I myself physically moved. During that particular week, the energy force was anything but subtle. However, this extreme level of intensity in energy has only occurred twice in the past ten years. Many times when I am seated in a chair or on the floor, or am in a lotus position, my physical body will begin to rock back and forth in a very slow and deep rhythmic vibration. Sometimes this rocking actually moves my body physically, but most often it is a sensation moving within me. Having once moved through the initial stages of fear connected with this, the movement has become one of the most nurturing and loving experiences I have ever encountered. This is not something I can by demand "turn on" or create; rather, it is something that occurs naturally several times a day.

As I have explored these subtle energy forces with others, allowing them to awaken into this rocking motion, I find that many individuals have difficulty in allowing themselves to let go and trust themselves to the energies of this inner-directed level of movement. These and other experiences are available to all human beings as they move into the energies of their inner spaces. Through the outer mind we cannot experience, or even begin to appreciate, what these experiences mean for us. And without them, we cannot fully open into the energies of our inner-directed guidance. I am sharing these personal experiences with you, in the hope that you can avoid having to go through any initial stages of fear in understanding the gentle and loving movements of your awakening self-actualizing energy.

Through these and other experiences, I was able to understand and finally accept that I could experience various levels of these heightened energies, based upon the depth of vertical unity that I could achieve within my triune brain. When I allowed my brain to shift into its role as "messenger" between my physical body and the energies of my inner-directed soul guidance, I understood and experienced things I had not thought possible. But when my brain resumed the role of being the director of my outer mind, these other perceptions and thoughts were but fleeting dreams in the night. I realized then that the difficulties that I was encountering in my life were due to the constant shifting from one state of awareness to another. So when, in late 1985, I was finally asked by my inner-directed guidance to begin to live daily from the inner state, another series of explorations opened to me in order that I could accomplish this task.

As you personally move through various explorations, your brain and nervous system will steadily begin to feel more unified and focused, while your level of concentration will automatically increase as your inner chatter decreases proportionately. Many times we are not aware of how different we will feel once we learn to live and create from the inner-directed state. The difference, for example, could be compared to one's occasionally touching the runner's high, in contrast to living in a state where the runner's high was present in many daily activities. Can you imagine how different life would be from this perspective? The difference I am describing as one moves into and lives from the energies of an inner-directed state is equally as drastic.

In our next exploration we will be using the expanded inner screen, heart chakra, and quadrants which we explored before, but we will begin an exploration into the use of colors. Colors hold certain levels of vibration, and we are going to explore the four colors of green, blue, violet, and white. You will experience for yourself how these colors interact to quiet your inner chatter and open you into your inner-directed guidance. First, read through the entire exploration. Then make a tape or have someone read the exploration to you for maximum benefit. Do EXPLORATION #5: DEEPENING THE EXPANDED INNER SCREEN, only after you have completed Exploration #2 a minimum of three times.

"Close your eyes, and ask that your inner screen expand *** bring your awareness into your unified center point *** feel that center point of your screen being focused at the heart chakra, at the center of your chest *** *** begin to feel and sense that center point deepening inside of your heart center *** *** feel into the crystalline structure of emerald green light *** sense it slowly pulsating at the center of your chest *** releasing wave upon wave of emerald green light *** feel the waves moving through your body and beyond it *** *** bring your awareness into your potential or spiritual quadrant (upper right) *** ask to feel and experience the emerald green light flowing into this quadrant *** allow the waves of emerald green light to pulsate *** **** feel it spreading into the mental quadrant (upper left) *** *** down into the emotional quadrant (lower left) *** *** into the physical body quadrant (lower right) *** *** again bring that emerald green light into the center point of your chest *** ask it to deepen *** *** ask the screen to expand *** in the potential quadrant now ask to feel and sense the color blue *** allow the waves of blue light to pulsate *** *** feel the color blue move into the mental quadrant *** *** and into the emotional quadrant *** *** feel it in the physical body quadrant *** *** ask it to move into the center point at the center of your heart chakra *** *** ask it to deepen and spread throughout your physical body and beyond *** *** ask your screen to expand *** *** in your potential quadrant ask to experience the color violet *** let the waves of violet light pulsate in this quadrant *** *** allow the color violet to move into the mental quadrant *** *** to spread into the emotional quadrant *** *** into the physical quadrant *** *** feel the color violet in the center point of your screen and in the center of your chest *** releasing wave upon wave of violet light throughout your physical body and beyond *** *** ask to expand your screen once again *** in the potential quadrant experience and feel the brilliance of white light *** allow the waves of white light to pulsate *** **** ask the brilliance of white light to move into the mental quadrant *** *** into the emotional quadrant *** *** the physical body quadrant *** *** bring the brilliance of white light into the center point of your screen and into the center of your chest *** ask it to deepen into the center of your chest *** *** releasing wave upon wave of brilliant white light throughout your body and beyond *** *** *** now ask to maintain your inner-awareness within this space *** ask that your body feel light, energized, inwardly connected and attuned to this inner-awareness *** *** ask this inner awareness to emerge as your outer awareness *** *** become aware of your body and your surroundings, move your body, and open your eyes when you are ready."

I would like, at this time, to bring forward a number of comments that are related to the five explorations you have now experienced. This information relates to comments and inquiries most often made by the many individuals with whom I have explored these processes.

Many people are initially surprised at how easy it is for them to shift into an inner awareness, and to begin experiencing the inner energetic states I have been describing. With each color, individuals feel an inner shift occurring. This is because the emerald green color, for example, opens us into both our inner world and our heart chakra. When this feeling is firmly set within us, the mental inner chatter automatically begins to neutralize. The color blue allows us to deepen and to begin to experience the first real level of inner silence, quieting the emotional inner chatter. Deepening into the color violet causes many to feel as if a "floor" or "bottom" within them has dropped. This feeling emerges very strongly and powerfully because at this point we have shifted through the body armor and are fully ready to experience the energies of the inner self-actualizing pulse or inner-directed guidance, which then emerges through the brilliance of white light. Eventually, you will be able to experience this sequence of colors in a matter of a few minutes, thus allowing your entire triune brain and nervous sytem to move into the energy of inner-directed guidance. Eventually, when you are in a meeting, driving, or performing any task, you will be able to ask your screen to expand, focus on the feeling of emerald green light, and then allow your inner space to emerge whenever you desire to shift your outer awareness.

If you have difficulty experiencing the fullness of the brilliance of white light, you are most likely stuck within some level of your inner chatter. To more fully comprehend the effectiveness of the process of color utilization, sometime after experiencing the color blue in the sequence, feel into and experience the color red or orange. You will be amazed at how quickly you move out of the quiet and back into the inner chatter. Yes, colors do produce a significant difference for us, although this is not necessarily true for the outer colors that we wear. The inner colors, though, do represent different inner rhythms or vibrations which can open us to our inner self-actualizing energies.

Many individuals sincerely doubt that they can shift easily from an outer awareness into an inner focused state. Recall, though, how quickly and easily you move into a level of fear or anger when you are confronted with a fearful or angry situation. You don't need a lot of practice to create this fear or anger, or much time to think about it; it happens easily and automatically. This same level of ease will be available for you in moving through your inner explorations. You are in the process of creating a new history of awarenesses, through which you can create and shift many of the feelings and sensations in your physical body. As your history begins to develop, you will be able to create from inner realms with the same ease and depth with which you previously reacted in fear and anger to the outer realms.

Some individuals, as they first experience the colors white and violet, feel that they are moving in and out of them, and have a difficult time maintaining the focus of the color. Until a certain level of inner restructuring is attained, maintaining this focus may be somewhat difficult; or you may notice that maintaining the focus is more difficult for you at certain times than at others. As you deepen into your inner silence, you will be surprised at how easily you move and how solid each of the inner spaces will become. If you still find yourself having difficulties after the first several explorations, just ask that your inner screen expand and deepen your inner focus at the center point and heart chakra. This will shift your inner-awareness and move you through the inner chatter, aiding you to open into your inner-directed guidance. Remember the key is for you to ask this space or these colors to emerge within you, not for you to create the color or the inner space. You can outwardly create only so much, at which point you must then ask that the energies of your inner self-actualizing pulse gently pull you along in your journey.

As individuals deepen into the inner spaces, their images will change from situation to situation. Some will no longer be as clear nor contain the same level of detail as before, while others will be very sharp and bold. As you move deeper into the various inner spaces, you will experience a feeling of vastness along with a variety of inner sensations. This feeling of vastness or the "oneness" within this inner space is what is waiting for us to explore. Sometimes an image will be created and seen very clearly, but when you try to hold onto that image, you lose it. You do not need to do anything with the image itself, but allow the "experience" to move you. The feelings, inner sensations, and knowing are the most important elements of exploring your inner images— not the images themselves.

Some individuals begin to experience a pulsation, a beating, or a racing feeling moving through them or focusing around the center of the chest. Many think this is the heart beating faster and faster. Brugh Joy talks about a number of individuals experiencing their heart chakra opening to the occasional feeling of a sharp pain in the chest region. I have known people who have felt tenderness, motion, a pulling feeling, and many other types of sensations with the opening of the heart chakra. These experiences are sometimes frightening for individuals, since they have no related history with which to compare them. As one opens into the energies of their inner-directed guidance, a new world of inner sensations, feelings, movements, and knowing emerges that was not present before. All of this is part of the next level of our human development. One cannot avoid experiencing at least some level of discomfort when bringing about a radical level of physical change. But when the outer mind realizes and accepts how normal it is for these experiences to occur, the level of discomfort becomes minimal.

I have moved through several deep awakenings of the mystical energies during the last ten years. The first two of these experiences were somewhat frightening and painful. But I have matured in my own understanding of the process of spiritual emergence, and I now know how natural it is to move into the energies of the deeper inner creative spaces. Thus, the last several deepenings were very easy and pain free. It is amazing that my own fears, coupled with an incomplete understanding of what was occurring, could have caused me such great levels of discomfort. But they did! I was the creator of the difficult situations due to the beliefs, attitudes, and experiences that I thought were real. By shifting into another belief structure, I now know that the same experiences can be fun and amazing to explore!

As your heart center deepens in its opening and you open into deeper levels of inner exploration, you will at times feel an electrical pulse running through your body or sense that some sort of current is running outside of you. Your body may experience sporadic jerking or uncontrolled movements as this energy is deepening and moving. All of this is quite normal. In order for your body to move into the deeper inner spaces that you are consciously exploring, it must also adjust and release its old tendencies to hold onto former energies, body armor, and physical habits. The more you focus on the sporadic movements or feelings of fear within you, the more intense and heightened they will become. By asking your inner screen to expand and by focusing your awareness on the heart chakra, you can move through whatever you are exploring, and this will no longer cause difficulties for you. These experiences are merely a part of the total exploration of the energetics of these spaces which you are mapping out for yourself. Just as with everything you have explored up to this point, the more you focus on worry, the crazier it becomes. Even though you may still at times be questioning things, your level of inner chatter is not the same as before. When you are in an anxious state, the level of inner chatter is very different. Also, when a sensation of movement related to your inner awakening is occurring, your body does not feel the same tension that it previously experienced with stress. This is another feedback mechanism of which you should be aware.

As you begin to explore the inner spaces, it becomes important that you not expect things to occur in the same way each time. The first time you move into your inner-directed guidance or self-actualizing energy, you have no preconceived ideas about what is supposed to happen and are therefore very open to whatever emerges during the exploration. But once you become aware and begin to expect certain things to occur, it sometimes becomes more difficult to move back into the inner-directed energies. We cannot exercise control in the inner spaces, nor are we able to demand that these spaces emerge. They are naturally present for each of us to explore and utilize, once we allow ourselves the time and space to get out of the way and allow them to emerge.

I spend time each morning, anywhere from twenty to sixty minutes, in allowing myself to be immersed in these energies. I allow the level of energy to emerge for whatever is needed for that day. I sometimes use a similar exploration to what I describe as the "harmonizing of our inner rhythms." Sometimes I receive very direct inner guidance or information during this early morning exploration. More often, though, I just allow the inner restructuring of these energies to take place. During the rest of the morning and early afternoon, I then experience a totally different awareness and perception of the situations that are occurring. I move through the day and its many events as if I understood and knew things that I earlier had not been aware of, or that I possibly had doubts about. When I occasionally neglect taking the inner time, or when I spend time trying to control certain situations, my day does not feel the same and my life no longer seem to synchronize with those things with which I am involved. At midday I also take a break in order to adjust my energies for the remainder of the day and evening.

I naturally awaken around 5:00 a.m. each morning, and work until 10:00 or 10:30 p.m. in the evening, so it usually is midnight by the time I go to bed. This schedule is the same, regardless of whether I am working and teaching with individuals and groups or whether I have time for myself and my own journey. So long as I honor my inner-directed guidance, I have an abundance of energy and strength to accomplish whatever my inner purpose designates. However, when I fail to honor my inner purpose and begin thinking that I know what to do, I become very tired, irritable, and fatigued, and any thought of creative energy is only a vision. Throughout the course of the day, I refocus into my inner space whenever I notice that my focus has restructured back into an outer mind awareness. It takes much less time and effort to refocus (a minute or two), even when I am with people and still talking, than does the consequence of shifting into a reactive energy, and then having to work to bring forth the creative energy once again.

Often individuals will lose their outer awareness of thoughts, feelings or consciousness during an exploration. Sometimes they have no recollection of an entire segment or specific part of an exploration or meditation. And when their awareness does return, they panic, fearing that they fell asleep. To the outer mind this seems to be the only explanation that makes any rational sense. Then the next time that they meditate, they are afraid that they will again fall asleep and not be able to hear and sense everything. Thus they prevent themselves from fully surrendering and letting go, and they begin to set up a level of control. Consequently they find it difficult to become as inwardly focused as they had previously been.

It is important for you to understand that there is a major difference between falling asleep and entering into a deep inner state of awareness. When you emerge from an inner experience you feel unified, energized, and focused; an inner quiet is present, and you are ready to create. When you have fallen asleep, you will have feelings similar to what you experience after awakening from a nap, and you will very seldom emerge at the end of the exploration tape. Sometimes as much as five, ten, fifteen, or more minutes will elapse before you awaken. If you have been in the energies of your inner-directed guidance, you will usually emerge at the completion of the exploration.

If you think back to the triad structure discussed previously, you will recall that when we are focused through the outer mind we have total awareness and control of what is happening. When you begin to release this outer control and shift into the energies of inner-directed guidance, you are initially not always aware of the inner experiences that are occurring. The inner spaces are not yet familiar to you, and that is why you have little or no outer awareness of what is happening. You lose outer awareness or consciousness; yet, you emerge precisely at the end of the exploration, and you have all the feelings and inner sensations of the exploration present within you. You initially lack only the outer awareness of what has transpired.

As you develop familiarity with the inner spaces, and as you deepen into the energies of your own inner-directed guidance, you will begin to move into the observer state of the experiences, a state within which you are experiencing something new and in which you have no outer control over what is emerging. Many times the deeper levels of restructuring that we are exploring occur only during such "black-out" periods. Even after having extensively explored the inner spaces of the expanded inner screen and the heart chakra since 1982, I still have many periods of black-out during my own personal inner explorations. When they occur, I know something profound has begun to awaken, and that my perceptions, feelings, and thoughts will be different so long as I allow myself to create from that moment. This is the space I earlier described as being within the now moment. It is through these same inner spaces that we can allow the feelings of the now moment to be present in our outer world. Without the black-out experiences, it becomes very difficult to truly be free of past and future awareness. We should view our experiencing of the black-out space as being the first real leap into the energies of our inner-directed soul guidance. Furthermore, I believe that from the inner spaces of the black-out periods we experience the feeling of "oneness" that allows the emergence of the inner images which bring forward the greatest levels of change in the physical, psychological, and spiritual health.

As individuals learn to surrender into the energies of their inner-directed guidance, the next question or concern always centers around the issue of control. "If our outer mind is not aware of what is happening, how do we control or bring about any level of change?" There exist two forms of control, an outer control and an inner controlling mechanism. Virtually all of our experiences from the time of birth up through the age of eighteen reinforce and explore only the outer level of control. Yet we unconsciously realize that there is another mechanism existing very deep within our hearts that has the ability to emerge from another level of understanding. This is a stage of development similar to that which many four- to seven-year-olds begin to experience when they move into a period of inner intuitive knowing. This stage usually is frightening to the adults in the child's life. This is why experiencing the runner's high is very confusing and even disturbing for many people. They are concerned about who is in control. They realize that they are not in control of themselves, yet the body is flowing along, performing at levels which they had not thought possible. Yet, when the outer mind later attempts to duplicate the performance, it becomes impossible. When we move into the energies of our inner-directed guidance, a deeper level of synthesis emerges that restructures and educates us into a new level of learning and performing. Whenever we allow this inner part to emerge, it always guides us into the highest levels of creative expression that are available for us at that particular time. This is precisely what we are exploring as the transformational journey. So this shift occurs initially in the space of black-out until we have acquired sufficient experience to move into the inner realm of unity and to be present in the observer state.

If you reach a point at which you feel stuck in your journey, the outer mind does not have the capability of taking you any further. What is necessary is to allow a deeper level of your self-actualizing pulse to emerge and to allow the direction to be brought forward through the energies of your inner directed guidance. This inner-directed guidance actually provides the creative pathway, while crisis provides the reactive pathway to opening into this inner space. Either pathway will eventually allow you to connect within, and when you do, you will once again experience the black-out period of unknowing until the observer state once again emerges, thus allowing the outer mind to be reeducated and brought into the fourth state of awareness of the heart, creating a state of inner and outer unity.

Many people become confused in an attempt to comprehend the relationships of the psychological processes of the conscious, subconscious, and unconscious minds and how they relate to the triad of Soul/Mind/Body which we are exploring. The outer mind is that part of the conscious mind or awareness that directly relies upon the information that is stored within the subconscious part of us. The subconscious consists of the entire programing of all the messages and history we have explored throughout our lifetime. This includes influence from all areas of our lives— everything from parents and other adults and children, to our religious and cultural heritage, education, morals, and geographic location. In addition, it includes all of the related experiences that have existed over the past twenty thousand years or more, which Carl Jung and others have called the collective consciousness of our species on the earth. Many of the awarenesses that cause us difficulty are often not fully rooted in or caused by direct experiences that we can consciously acknowledge. Instead, many stem from the deeper subconscious forces and experiences which each human being brings forward into his/her life. Yet each of us also holds the inner ability to transmute these perceptions into another focus for living and for understanding ourselves as human beings.

Our conscious awareness is that which we are perceiving, thinking, and feeling at any given time. We usually, however, are not aware of the extent to which all of these same experiences are simultaneously being influenced by our subconscious programs and energetic forces. When there is a discrepancy between the two, we then experience inner chatter. But each time that we move beyond the inner chatter into the energies of our inner-directed guidance, we touch the unconscious part of ourselves, and each time that we move into this inner space, we change. This is because we bring into our awareness a heightened energy, along with a new perception, hope, and feeling of becoming more. Each time that we move into the inner space, we bring forward a new awareness that then allows the subconscious part of us to be educated about new aspects of what we perceive and are capable of performing. The unconscious is the only aspect of self of which the outer mind is currently unaware. Thus, we need only to realize that whenever we feel stress, pain, or crisis in our lives, we are being asked to reach into this unconscious part of ourselves, open to the energies of our inner-directed soul guidance, and allow ourselves to experience another perception or feeling concerning whatever it is that we are encountering. This is what I mean by the statement the odyssey begins— the awakening into our human potential.

Some individuals talk about experiencing the dark side of the unconscious. Any experiences that I have encountered with the dark side have occurred when I was stuck within my outer mind as a result of the programing that was deeply lodged in my subconscious. As I begin to experience such levels of darkness or confusion, I readily forget everything that I know and have personally experienced. I begin to believe that the present experiences or information constitute the only reality that exists. Thus I ignore the inner feelings that continually urge me to move back into my inner guidance and the heightened energies of my soul. Whenever I am able to open into this inner state of awareness, I can clearly sense what is outwardly occurring. At some point in this process, I always come to the realization that the feelings of the heart chakra and the fourth state of awareness are infinitely more real than anything that I am currently experiencing, and I open once again into my inner self-actualizing energy.

I know it might be difficult for you to grasp and believe what I am saying in this regard. When you or anyone else encounters a crisis situation, all that I have written here will not help you unless you have begun to experience similar awakening feelings and concepts within yourself. When you reach this point you are developing your own inner history, and with that, you also will be able to acknowledge new concepts and allow new choices to become a part of your life. Until you actually experience this for yourself, however, nothing I am saying will be real to you. Remember that all of our information and perceptions are state-bound, so at one level of energy, one set of perceptions exists, and at another level, a totally different set exists. Both are real, and the choice is ours—to which reality do we choose to direct our focus?

Many individuals experience tears when they merge into their inner-directed state and bring their inner-awareness forward. Others experience such a profound feeling of awe or are so deeply moved that they feel inclined to cry. The level of awareness is dependent upon the depth of inner silence and synthesis that you allow to emerge as you clearly connect into your inner-directed soul guidance. When I first touched into my inner spaces, merging with the inner-directed guidance, I experienced a profound state of inner peace, and suddenly was faced with a stream of tears running down both cheeks. This startled me, because I had no reason at all to be crying like this, and my first reaction was that I should stop it immediately! After several similar occurrences, I began to realize that these tears were not the same tears I had often cried when I was emotionally hurt or afraid. These tears, once I allowed them to flow freely, actually brought me into a new level of inner restructuring and understanding. Now whenever the tears are present, I know that I once again am ready to move into a new level of guidance and into a new space of unconditional love. I know that through these tears my life will ultimately take on new depth and meaning.

Such an emergence of unexpected tears generally occurs at those times in our lives when we are ready to experience the energies of the expanded states of unconditional love and to begin the shift into our inner-awareness. Few individuals, however, realize the true significance of such events. Whenever we block the tears from emerging, we stop the natural process of deepening. Often individuals will sense these feelings emerging when they are in what they call their "non-safe places"—in the supermarket, on the job, or just basically in the presence of other people. What I have found in my own journey, is that I need to trust that there is a reason for these occurrences and that I need to allow the freedom for such feelings to be present. If I become embarrassed and stop them, I am stopping the synthesis and the subsequent emergence of new perceptions. Once I truly become comfortable with this, I no longer feel embarrassed by the emergence of the tears. I need only to learn to honor the feelings and to allow their movement through me, regardless of when or where it happens. This process plays an important role in shifting the inner self actualizing energies into one's livingness.

As you learn to refine your energies and deepen into the process of awakening, the natural feelings of unconditional love can be present without the outer process of tears. In every one of my university classes, at some point virtually all of the participants experienced similar inner spaces causing tears. Once each student learned to feel at peace with the experiences, the outer tears were greatly reduced, although a feeling of awe remained with them and, for some, even increased throughout the term. Most of us tend to fight the tears, not understanding that this level of feeling is truly of the Divine, not of human emotions. Become aware of your inner feelings when the tears are present, and then notice how different you feel after you bring your awareness back. Sense the deeper feelings that are present and the new levels of inner peace that have emerged. You may even begin to notice new perceptions of outer reality, and you will ultimately realize that each such experience is a vital step along the pathway to becoming YOU!

Another experience common to these explorations is feeling that the body has no boundaries, that it is expansive and unlimited. Some people describe this as an out-of-body experience. I explored out-of-body experiences for a number of years, and what individuals open to within the process which we are exploring is actually an expansion of consciousness that is not limited by the boundaries of the outer skin. This is very different from out-of-body travel, which carries connotations of being a paranormal experience, and is really not related to the perfectly natural phenomenon of opening directly into the expansion of energies from one's inner-directed guidance. Since the beginning in 1983 of my present phase of exploration, I have not experienced out-of-body travel and, from the expansion of my consciousness, I am now able to freely move into different levels of inner knowing and experiences, regardless of where I am or what I am doing. Within such experiences, one has a different awareness of what the body is, but yet knows that the physical body is always present within the new levels of awareness. It is difficult for individuals to finally accept and acknowledge what physics has long discussed— the fact that one's body is, in reality, a vibration; and this vibration is not limited by what we think we are perceiving.

In my university classes I explore a concept of allowing others to tap into my perceptions while I am traveling at a great distance from Fort Wayne. This process is called remote viewing, and is based upon work done at Stanford Research Lab and later documented in the book **The Mind Race**. To do this exercise, I choose a set time at which the students are to move into their expanded inner space and heart focus, allowing their consciousness to open into wherever I may be. They have no idea where I will be traveling, since I spend time on both coasts and in Mexico. They are not to try to ascertain my location so much as they are to try to become aware of my feelings, sensations, thoughts, and what I am perceiving through my various senses at that particular moment.

The last time I explored this with a group, I was in midair flying from California to New York. I decided to release an image of being at Nob Hill in San Fransisco early in the morning before sunrise, viewing San Fransisco Bay and experiencing the cable car I was riding. Individuals in the class would be tapping into this experience that evening. I found that every person in the class was able to sense different parts of what I was exploring, with many of the students actually describing most all of the sensations I was feeling. It didn't matter that they were picking up on these experiences nearly twelve hours later. Man's consciousness is capable of seemingly remarkable feats when it comes to tapping into and picking up information. No one in the group had an out-of-body experience; rather, they allowed their own consciousness to expand beyond the traditional dimensions of both time and space. I later explored with them how to effectively utilize this same process in their professional lives in the forecasting of sales trends and new product feasibility.

I would like to make just one additional observation that may be relevant in your present exploratory experiences. Some individuals become confused about distinguishing their inner right quadrants from their left quadrants. If this happens to you, just close your eyes, expand your screen, become aware of your upper right quadrant, and physically touch the side of your face where this right quadrant exists. You should have touched the right side of your face. If you did, then you are perceiving your right quadrant correctly. If you touched the left side of your face, close your eyes and ask the screen to reverse; repeat this until you touch the right quadrant and the right side of the face at the same time. I have discovered that if individuals are not receiving a clear set of information through the quadrants, it is usually due to this reversal process.

In summary then, we are viewing Transformational Psychology as the process of shifting one's awareness from the outer mind into the energies of the inner-directed soul guidance. The heart chakra is then opened and the brain is shifted into the role of "messenger," thereby allowing new perceptions of reality to emerge. The human brain is capable of more direct learning with less instinctual programing than any other species on this planet, with the possible exception of dolphins and whales. All other species seem to possess a built-in process of instincts that needs to be activated. As this takes place during the early months of life, animals learn their appropriate behavioral patterns, as well as the structures and limits for all of their behaviors. The human brain possesses very few such inherent instincts and limits for its behaviors and perceptions.

It appears that the human brain is one of the few existing brains that can actually learn to observe itself, restructure reality, and make direct conscious choices; other species can focus only upon what is currently available to the outer awareness. It is the process of observation that allows us to transform our perceptions that are based upon learned behaviors into perceptions which evolve from a process of direct inner-guidance or inner knowing. Through the shift into an inner focus the brain becomes capable of transducing a heightened level of energy, which in turn allows us the ability to take the energetic vibration into a new structure of information and sensory awareness. It is this process that enables the human species to make a quantum shift in its understanding of reality and to choose new perceptions, feelings, and sensations from which to create.

It has been found that even when entire sections of the brain are removed, individuals are able to recall information that was earlier stored in memory. If we view the brain as a storehouse of electrical circuitry which controls the biochemical and hormonal processes, then it stands to reason that it is this resonating vibration which picks up the various images that are created. When this electrical system of the brain resonates through the confusion of the outer mind, it distorts the perceptions and available information. But when this confusion moves into a state of balance, both our recall of information and our perceptions change. And eventually, as the electrical activity becomes harmonized under the energies of one's inner-directed guidance, a totally different set of structures, perceptions, and sensations will emerge naturally from an inner reality of unity. Until we begin to acknowledge the fact that the brain is actually the transducer of this electrical system of energy, however, we will be unable to comprehend that the brain, operating in conjunction with the heart chakra, can take one level of vibrational information and, by changing its resonating frequencies, can filter this vibration into the images and sensations we call our senses and perceptions. As the vibrations or resonating frequencies of the whole triune brain deepen, various filters of reality are lifted, allowing us to then perceive other inner natural states of awareness. When we no longer maintain our former level of vibrational frequency, it is as though our former perceptions either never happened or no longer seem to be real.

Whenever we experience a heightened level of energy or explore the Kundalini or mystical awakening of our inner energy, the brain and nervous system are quickly transformed into a new vibrational pattern. When this happens within a very short period of time, one's reality also changes very quickly and will soon become distorted due to the fact that the outer mind cannot comprehend, retain, and process all of the new information, sensations, and perceptions. Fears will also then arise very quickly, soon to be followed by the body's reacting in a violent way to the levels of profound and sudden change. However, if this process of change can emerge effortlessly and over a period of time that honors an inner timing process, we can understand and appreciate the different levels of reality that exist, thus eliminating most of the fear and physical discomfort. The focus of our perceptions determines and creates our reality, and we consequently find it extremely difficult to comprehend that something different can and does exist for us. Once we open into the next layers of our inner-directed guidance, however, and allow this to emerge into our outer awareness, we will then understand our next levels of inner human development— the post-biological phase.

I believe that the resonating frequencies of the triune brain, guided through the heart chakra, allow us to connect with and merge into the energies of our inner-directed soul guidance. I feel that as long as the triune brain remains separated in its various parts, and the primary focus of our awareness is through the energy centers other than the heart and/or heart-crown connection, we can receive no more than fleeting images or sensations of our true potential. Once we have experienced the feelings of unconditional love and the energies of our inner-directed soul guidance, it becomes obvious to us if we are not within that focus. I have found the process which I am herein describing to be an exciting and safe way to awaken and discover the inner creative worlds that exist as mankind's next level of human development.

CHAPTER SEVEN

AWAKENING THE TRIUNE BRAIN

Before we begin our next exploration, I would like to discuss in detail how the process of awakening the triune brain allows us to awaken into our next level of human development, the post-biological phase. Very seldom do we perceive our brain as existing as a vertical triune structure, wherein one brain is superimposed upon another. This triune structure consists of the old or reptilian brain, the mid or paleomammalian brain, and the neocortex or neomammalian brain. Most individuals perceive the brain as consisting only of the right and left hemispheres, and envision the processes of these two hemispheres in a very simple way, not being aware of the wonderful, yet complex, dance that exists within the whole triune brain and nervous system. Most people are concerned only with the lateral separation of the functioning of the right hemisphere versus the left hemisphere of one's brain. I see this as but a small part of a much larger structure. I believe the real complexity in human functioning is a result of the vertical separation between the three levels of the triune brain and the way in which each of these levels actually creates a totally different picture for us of how we perceive our world.

Each area of the triune brain utilizes a different form of imagery, thus allowing distinct forms of dreams to emerge from each respective area. The way we experience our many feelings, perceptions and sensations also varies based upon the specific area of focus within the brain. This, in turn, causes changes in our perceptions and the way we choose to interact with our outer world. With the existing split in brain functioning it becomes difficult, or virtually impossible, to experience the energies of one's inner-directed soul guidance or any profound level of inner silence. As I have directly experienced the unification of my whole triune brain into a vertical unity, I can easily bring many of the perceptions, feelings, and sensations I have inwardly explored back into my outer awareness. In this way, what we have perceived through the energies of our inner-directed guidance is brought forward and restructured within the outer mind, thus altering all of our perceptions. On the other hand, when the outer mind is in a state of confusion and creates varying levels of stress, the triune brain is functioning in a way which allows us the opportunity to easily hold onto our stressful perceptions and feelings as being real. If we are in a state of pain, the triune brain is likewise within a vibrational frequency which allows us to hold onto the focus of pain. Whatever we are experiencing, feeling, or sensing, is totally dependent upon the current level of electrochemical activity that is established within the brain as it resonates. Some areas of the brain may be resonating at one frequency, while other areas of the brain are resonating at another, thus bringing one's perceptions into a state of confusion. When this occurs, we become confused about what we are feeling or experiencing. Thus our emotions and perceptions shift and scatter in many different directions.

We sometimes forget, or never even realize, that every object in life holds a particular vibration that is unique to that object, regardless of whether it is a tree, water, a building, a chair, or even a human being. Each individual object within a particular category, such as a tree, holds a certain energy common to all trees. But an elm tree, for example, also holds yet another vibration that is unique to all elms; and an individual elm tree also holds a unique elm tree vibration of its own that distinguishes it from all other elm trees that exist. In addition to maintaining these very unique vibrations, the elm tree also interacts with the energies of every other object in its environment. Each object and structure thus holds a unique vibration or level of resonation, even though, through our various senses of sight, sound, touch, smell and taste, we interpret each one of the objects as being a solid mass.This vibratory frequency is a part of the energy or electromagnetic field that some individuals are able to visually see, directly feel, or experience through their other senses.

As I previously mentioned, by 1981 I was able to see, feel, and sense the electromagnetic field of individuals, objects, and other spaces of my outer environment. At first I thought something was wrong with my eyes, but as I explored this with my inner guidance, I soon realized that what I was perceiving was the deeper structures that exist as the living object. If an object exists within our awareness, it holds a certain vibratory frequency, which means that every existing thing is a vibrating object—even a rock. Although many individuals experience this vibratory energy around objects, it is a misconception to think that the solid object gives off the vibration. What I have discovered over the years is that the electromagnetic field is the real energy of the object and that it is moving at a higher rate of energy or vibration than is the perceived object. Some physicists describe this resonating motion as a wave-form frequency, emanating from the implicate order of energy. As an object or individual moves into a state of what we perceive as a solid mass, this wave-form vibration actually changes into another frequency, which physicists describe as a particle-form vibration, or part of the explicate order of energy. Particles of the explicate order of energy are also moving, but at a vibrational level that we perceive through our outer senses as being solid.

We sometimes forget the simple fact that no one has really ever perceived the outside world. All of the perceptions that we experience move through our various sense organs, and it is the job of our brain to interpret the varying electrical patterns through these sense organs. I, for example, may think that I am visually perceiving, touching, and smelling a tree. But my eyes, nose, and fingers are actually picking up the many vibrational frequencies of the tree, while the various areas in and around my brain are organizing and interpreting the electrochemical activities within the brain cells, sorting through all previous information about trees, specifically information about any former vibrations from this specimen of tree. This process occurs instantaneously and is fed back into the outer mind as visually seeing, feeling, and smelling a tree. Everything in life is interpreted through these same processes. Our perceptions are really very fluid, and they are constantly changing, based upon the level of activity and total functioning of the brain.

In many group sessions and university classes, I explore the processes of changing the vibrational frequencies within the brain in order to either heighten or decrease one's senses. Once participants have learned to awaken the triune brain, within a matter of minutes they can be taught to alter their sensory experiences by modulating different vibrational frequencies within specific areas of the brain. Many individuals have learned to heighten their sensory experiences to such a level that they can listen clearly to a lecture being given six classrooms away, with all doors and windows closed; furthermore, they concur as to the topic of the lecture that is being given. Many participants are able to visually read small printing on the board from across the room or they begin to perceive colors and sounds as being greatly intensified. Virtually everyone begins to experience a level of depth perception with objects and with their total outer environment that they had never dreamed existed. Even individuals with hearing aids or glasses, while within their inner focused state, are able to accomplish these same tasks. Such heightened levels of sensory perception can likewise be decreased with a similar degree of ease. In short, what we as human beings think we experience is truly but a small part of reality; a whole new world awaits us if we will but open and experience it.

As I stated before, when the brain is in a state of confusion, certain areas of the brain are vibrating at one level, while other areas are functioning at a different vibration. This interferes with the perception of what we experience as being our reality. Exploring the particle-form process of reality merely touches that 2% of reality that I have mentioned so often, while moving into experiencing and understanding the wave-form frequency of inanimate objects, of individuals, and of one's total environment will open us into the other 98% of unknown awareness. Within fifteen minutes I can usually teach individuals to begin to experience, either visually or tactically, various wave-forms of energy, although most will not have any comprehension of what this means for them in their everyday lives. Even individuals who have little or no visual perception because of blindness are still able to "perceive" through touch or through the sensations they receive from people or objects. Through the outer mind, we have learned to rely very heavily upon our sense organs for information, and we have learned to mistrust, or even deny, the existence of the much more accurate feedback of our world as it can be seen through the inner-awareness of the energetic structures or the inner vibrational sensations. These inner experiences are related to what we perceive as being the reality around us.

All of these awarenesses, as well as many more, are available to every human being. However, we must first open to an inner shift in our brain's functioning before we can open into the depth of inner knowing that emerges through one's inner-directed guidance. Focusing primarily within a certain energy center or chakra can also change the brain's interpretation of the various vibrational frequencies and thus alter its electrochemical activity. This, in turn, alters our perception of what we perceive as being real.

Perceptions emerge through a very complex process. Many factors come into play in allowing us to experience the world in the way that we do. In order to move into alternative forms of perceiving and knowing, a totally new and different process must be developed to facilitate opening into our inner world. Through biofeedback it has been shown that we can directly alter our brain wave rhythms. (I refer to these as vibrational frequencies, since they are more complex than simple brain wave processes.) I believe that initiating an awakening of the triune brain with a wave-form rhythm (or self-actualizing pulse), which emerges as we shift into our expanded inner screen and heart chakra, begins the transition from the brain as the end result and producer of consciousness to its being the messenger between the energies of our inner-directed guidance and our outer world. As we learn to maintain this inner wave-form frequency and bring our inner-awareness into the outer world, our perceptions and understanding of reality and various events will easily and quickly change. Awakening the triune brain and then moving through the process of unifying this vibration with the physical body allows us to live at our next level of human development. Without this shift, man's inner world remains very much separated from the outer world, and most individuals will be totally unaware of any real inner existence.

Many theorists believe that each stage of evolutionary history has been dependent upon a major shift in the brain and nervous system development. The present state of the physical brain and nervous system being encased and protected within a bony structure did not evolve until the advent of the fish; within this species began the evolvement of the rudimentary elements now common to man's brain and nervous system. From birth through the age of three, humans progress through a complete evolutionary cycle of brain development that is reflected in the development of the physical, emotional, spiritual, and intellectual self. At about the age of four, the physical development of the brain is complete, allowing us to interact with life over the next several years through both an inner and outer focus of awareness. Many parents, however, become frightened by their children's perception of inner intuitive information during this period of development. Due primarily to a lack of parental approval and support, these important inner processes are blocked and thus remain dormant throughout subsequent development. I believe that during the period ranging from approximately age four to age seven, the triune brain is functioning as one complete synchronized brain system. The brain wave activity of children of this age indicates a high degree of focus within all three of the levels of brain wave states. The focus of alpha and theta states allows many children an easy access to their inner world, allowing what adults call "their imagination" to structure imaginary playmates and other perceptions. Through my explorations with children, and taking adults back into these childhood periods, it appears that these structures contain the seeds of our first contact with the energies of our inner guidance. Children's perceptions within their outer world then emerge from the fact that they have instinctively learned to maintain an inner level of focus. However, rather than taking this level of inner-awareness into the next stages of development, most children close it off and progress only by means of outer information; thus, they continually feel a sense of incompleteness in their lives.

I am convinced that much of the difficulty which adolescents experience in moving through the period of identity crisis that is encountered between the ages of fifteen and eighteen is due to the fact that their development of this level of inner-awareness was arrested prior to the age of seven, thereby preventing the natural synthesis of their inner-awareness and inner guidance from emerging into their outer world structures. Since late adolescence is a time for analyzing and making sense of the outer world, most adolescents lack the inner base to support many of their emerging perceptions, feelings, ideas, and views. Since the inner spaces were denied during earlier periods of development, the only access which adolescents have to opening into the inner space is through drugs, alcohol, and sex. A great similarity can be seen in the process of development during the period from the age of four to seven, the onset of puberty, and during the period from fifteen to eighteen; these are times for structuring a new perception of life. Just as the younger child is ready to move into a state of outer learning of specifics, the late adolescent is ready to give up this process and move into an inner world of generalities that explores the "why" of the specific information he/she has been taught. Confusion results because there is no inner focus available to which adolescents can anchor their new outer perceptions of themselves and their changing world.

At about age eighteen, those that our society now calls young adults are ready to begin the next level of development; but since there is no model to follow, they must continue to use what they already know. Soon they begin to feel frustrated and confused, questioning what the real purpose is in gathering additional information without being able to apply it in a new and more productive way. Having spent eighteen years in the development of specific experiences, what is actually needed at this time is to begin the inner journey into the exploration of those structures which exist beyond all previous learning. This is the journey into the unknown awarenesses within ourselves and our world; this is the unexplored 98% of life. However, the inner journey rarely begins for individuals until later in the life cycle, in spite of the fact the period of adolescence could constitute the period of easiest access and development. I found a great similarity between my own perceptions of these developmental shifts and the work of Joseph Chilton Pearce in **Magical Child Matures**. Over the years, I have altered many of my own terminologies in describing these processes, in order to allow for a similarity of words to describe the similar processes we are exploring.

As we begin our exploration into awakening the triune brain, it is important not to get intellectually stuck in viewing this process from the "correct" physiological perceptions you might have been previously taught. The areas both within and adjacent to the brain that I will ask you to focus on do not represent the scientifically defined physiological structures of the triune brain. They do represent the initial levels of exploring our brain as an energetic structure. What becomes important is what you begin to feel, sense, and inwardly experience for yourself as you allow the levels of energetic restructuring to emerge. And it is especially important that you realize how closely the experiences that you will develop parallel those of the thousands of other individuals who have experienced a very similar process. My goal in **Awaken Your Creative Potential** is not to lay out a technical structure of physiological development; rather, it is to explore a process of allowing the individual to shift his/her focus from an outer into an inner-awareness and to learn to live from these inner states of awareness within the outer world. Here we are going to focus on the energetic properties of the triune brain and nervous system and explore the means for allowing an emergence of an inner restructuring of vibrational rhythms, a self-actualizing pulse, that will then open us into the energies of one's inner-directed soul guidance. At this time, the technical physiological process is not as important as the process of awakening, living, and creating within a new level of heightened creativity. We sometimes forget how little we truly know about the physiological structures of our brain, nervous system and body, not to mention the conflicting theories that exist regarding our inner physiological functioning.

Although I will define the structures of the triune brain in three categories— old, mid, and new or neocortex, I am referring to the structures that Pearce describes in **Magical Child Matures**, which include different levels of physiological functioning that are sometimes associated with differing areas of the triune brain. It is not important at this time to be concerned with the various functions of the nervous system and the many other physiological structures. As one moves into the inner-directed space, all related physiological functions become very automatic, just as one's breathing and heartbeat are automatic in the outer mind's focus. We will refer to these new experiences as inner pulsations that carry inner feelings and inner sensations vertically through the brain and nervous system creating a new awareness of "inner unity." Initially I like to use the analogy of a light or a dimmer switch to exemplify this. When you bring your focus forward, you will feel as if a dimmer light is slowly being turned on. As this becomes brighter and brighter it releases a stronger and brighter pulsation of color and vibration into an indicated area of the body, which then spreads throughout the entire system. As this occurs, you can actually connect your physical body into the various inner spaces we are planning to explore.

The first area of the triune brain that we are going to explore is called the old brain. What I am referring to as the old brain is the reptilian brain, that of the era of evolutionary history when the brain and nervous system first began to develop. This is the portion that governs the sense of seeing and provides control of the physical body. The old brain is connected to numerous specific outer perceptions of reality. When you fall asleep the old brain is "turned-off" to the body, and you can dream of various images and not physically react or carry out what you are dreaming. This is one level of the separation of your dreams from your outer world. If the old brain were activated while you were asleep, you could physically carry out your dreams. The old brain is connected to the motor processes, but does not hold any form of imagery or memory in the sense that we normally think of it. Reptiles do not create images or memory in the way that we do as human beings, nor as do other animals that have a mid-brain structure. Neither do they dream in terms of what we call dreams.

To physically locate the energetic structures that we will explore as the old brain, place your hands at the base of your skull where the head is attached to the top of the spinal column, and feel the two soft spots or pressure points that are located on each side of the spinal column at the base of your skull. This is the area of focus for the old brain exploration. Allow yourself to inwardly sense the old brain as resembling an inner core moving through these soft spots and extending deep inside the skull. You will feel the energy flowing through these two points and on down to the tip of the spine. This can be sensed as a single column connecting within you, extending from the very tip of your spine to a point about eighteen inches above your physical head. We will begin to focus our awareness at this point, and allow the pulsations of the four different colors, green, blue, violet, and white to initially release their pulsations within this core extending from the tip of the spine to the point above your head, and then automatically spreading throughout the entire nervous system. And as the dimmer light becomes brighter and stronger, allow this same feeling of brightness to merge throughout you. Imagine that this column is turning clockwise within you, spinning a continual flow of energy from its center throughout your nervous system and body all the way to the tips of your fingers and toes.

Next we will explore the mid-brain, which moves us into the next level of evolutionary history, the period of the development of cats, dogs, and monkeys. Through the mid-brain, we can move into more advanced forms of perceptions, which will open us into our emotions and feelings. To explore this energetic connection, I would like you to close your eyes for a moment, and pretend that you can see out the back of your head with your eyes. Allow yourself to become aware of the two areas on the back of your skull at which you are looking, and then feel and sense this area with your hands. Can you feel two bumps or points there? This is the area of focus for the energetic structure of the mid-brain. Now allow the same pulsation to emerge here as you did in the old brain, and imagine the dimmer light becoming brighter with each color. Visualize the movement of a column extending from this inner part of the brain down through the next two soft spots at the base of your skull and on down to the tip of your spine and reaching upward to that point above your head. Sense and feel the column of the old brain merging into this column, creating a single, pulsating movement.

When we talk about the right and left hemispheres of the brain, we are referring to the energetic structures of the brain, the focus of which is located at the soft spots on the top of the head. Imagine a pulsation moving from these two areas in much the same way as you did in the old and mid-brain areas. Let these two points become the outer base of a larger column, rotating in a clockwise direction and connecting with the next set of soft spots at the back of the skull. Allow this column to extend downward to the tip of the spine and upward into the space above your head. Allow this to merge with the previous columns to form one movement or pulsation.

The final area of consideration within the brain is the connective point, which is called the corpus callosum. This area will allow the integration and synchronization of the other areas into one single inner rhythm. Explore the energetic structures of this connective area which is located above your forehead at the base of your hairline. Feel this movement as a spiral turning downward in a clockwise direction, merging with the other columns and dissolving any boundaries existing between the different layers of the brain which we have been exploring. Feel and explore this as a single motion that slowly moves down through the entire head and down the spine to its tip.

Allow the entire brain structure to now move into one inner rhythm, which constitutes the essence of the triune brain exploration. Explore this through the use of the same colors as before, beginning with the color green, and proceeding through blue, violet and the brilliance of white light. This constitutes the training that is needed to help you recognize and ultimately experience the energetics of your deeper inner states. After you have done this several times, you will find that you will be able to move through the process that we have explored in just a matter of minutes, if that is what is needed; or you can deepen with it over a longer period of time if desired. Later you can eventually progress to a shortened version of the process which takes less than one minute. If we can create pain or stress, fear or anger, in less than a minute, why can't we create these inner feelings and awarenesses just as easily and quickly?

As we begin EXPLORATION #6: AWAKENING THE TRIUNE BRAIN, it is important that you open your inner awareness to the feelings and sensations that will begin to emerge as the whole triune brain comes under the direction of the inner self-actualizing rhythm of your inner expanded screen and heart chakra. You will then begin the process of deepening into the various levels of inner rhythms that will develop through the use of each color. This will allow you to begin directly experiencing your inner self-actualizing energy in a totally different way. At this point it is important that you erase from your thoughts the details of everything I have just explained. There is no need to ponder or worry about the technicalities; just allow yourself to follow the exploration into your new experiences. I merely wanted your intellect to feel somewhat satisfied in order that you do not have to continually ask yourself, "What's happening?"

"Close your eyes *** ask your inner screen to expand *** ask it to expand again, until you feel yourself back in that inner expanded space *** *** feel the center point of your expanded screen at the center of your chest *** *** ask to feel and sense the crystalline structure of emerald green light at the center of your chest *** ask it to begin pulsating wave upon wave of emerald green light *** ask that it expand and deepen at this center point *** ask the waves of pulsating energy to move throughout your body and beyond *** *** ask to once again expand your screen *** bring your focus to the old brain area located at and above the two soft spots at the base of your skull *** ask to feel a pulsation of emerald green light in the old brain *** sense that a dimmer switch is being turned on brighter and brighter, increasing the pulsation and brightness of the emerald green light *** *** feel and sense this pulsation as a single wave of rhythm emanating from the old brain, moving down to the tip of your spine and up to the point above your head *** *** feel and sense this as a single movement rotating in a clockwise direction *** *** ask this wave-form to release and to spread this vibration through your nervous system all the way to the tips of your fingers and toes *** *** allow this pulsation to

continue as you now move your awareness into the mid-brain ***
focus at the two points behind the eyes on the back of your head
*** begin the same cycle again, and move through it until you feel
the pulsation connected throughout the entire spinal column,
extending to that point above your head *** *** feel the dimmer
switch being turned on brighter and brighter *** *** feel the
vibration merging with the old brain in a single wave rhythm
rotating in a clockwise direction *** allow it to spread from the
spinal column into the nervous system and out to your fingers and
toes *** *** ask for this to be maintained *** bring your awareness
into the right hemisphere of the brain *** feel the pulsation of the
emerald green light . *** now feel the pulsation within the left
hemisphere *** feel the two areas turning as a larger column that
is connected from the tip of your spine up to the point above your
head *** *** ask it to merge with the other two areas creating one
clockwise rhythmic motion and spreading throughout your entire
nervous system *** *** ask this to be sustained *** focus at the
connective point, at the center front base of the hairline *** *** ask
the pulsation at that point to become brighter and brighter *** ask
to synchronize your whole brain into a slower inner rhythm of the
emerald green light *** *** feel that merging with the whole brain
into a single clockwise rhythm *** ask that to slowly spiral down
through your head *** down through the spinal column *** to the
tip *** and to spread throughout and beyond your body *** *** ***
ask your inner screen to expand *** feel this deepen in your heart
center *** ask to sense into the color blue *** feel the blue light
pulsating at that same area within the old brain *** be aware of this
steadier and slower pulsation *** *** continue with the same
process as before *** getting brighter and brighter *** as one
vibration through the spine and above the head *** rotating and
spreading *** *** ask it to continue *** feel the color blue pulsating
in the mid-brain *** *** continue as before until it reaches and
merges with the old brain in one inner rhythm *** *** *** ask this
rhythm to continue *** allow the blue color to pulsate simultaneously in both the right and left hemispheres *** *** merging and
spreading throughout *** *** *** ask it to continue *** now focus
at the connective point *** ask this to synchronize the whole triune
brain into yet a slower, steadier inner rhythm with the color blue
*** *** ask it to merge into one inner rhythm *** ask it to slowly
spiral down through your head *** down through the spinal
column *** to its tip *** spreading throughout and beyond your
body *** *** *** ask to expand your screen *** feel that deepening
within your heart center *** ask to feel and sense the color violet
*** feel the pulsation of that violet light in the old brain *** continue
the same process as before *** until the violet pulsation is moving

and spreading throughout the spinal column and nervous system
*** ask it to remain *** focus at the mid-brain *** proceed in the
same manner as before, until it merges and spreads *** *** *** ask
it to continue *** focus the pulsation of violet light in the right and
left hemispheres *** do the same as before *** merging into one
inner rhythm *** *** *** ask it to continue *** focus the pulsation
of violet light at the connective point *** ask it to synchronize the
whole triune brain into a slower inner rhythm within that violet
light *** *** ask it to merge into one inner rhythm *** ask it to slowly
spiral down through your head *** down through the spinal
column *** to the tip *** ask it to spread into the left side of your
nervous system first, in your hand and the tips of your fingers ***
then to the remainder of the left side, to the tips of your toes on the
left foot *** *** then ask it to spread throughout the right side of
your nervous system to the tips of your fingers and toes *** *** ask
it to spread deeper throughout and beyond your body *** *** *** ask
your screen to expand *** feel this deepening within your heart
center *** ask to open into the brilliance of white light, pulsating
a very slow, steady inner rhythm *** focus in the old brain ***
same as before *** *** *** pulsating through the mid-brain *** same
as before *** *** *** slowly pulsating in the right and left hemispheres *** pulsating that brilliance of white light as before *** ***
*** then at the connective point *** ask it to synchronize into a
slower inner rhythm than before *** *** ask it to merge into one
inner rhythm *** ask it to slowly spiral down through your head
*** down through the spinal column *** and to slowly spread from
the spinal column to the tip of your spine *** spreading that
brilliance of white light through and beyond your physical body
*** *** *** ask to expand your screen *** feel that deepening slower
rhythm of your triune brain, that brilliance of white light within
your own heart center *** feel the white crystalline structure of that
light deepening *** release that from the deepest part within your
heart, flowing through the physical nervous system, organs and
other related systems *** releasing wave upon wave throughout
your physical form *** ask it to deepen into your cellular level and
spread throughout each cell within your physical form *** *** ask
it to deepen into the atomic and subatomic levels within you ***
touching that deepest essence of your inner self-actualizing pulse
*** *** ask to synchronize this inner rhythm with your whole triune
brain *** *** bring your awareness into the potential or spiritual
quadrant, the upper right *** ask to feel and experience the
energies of unconditional love emerging in this quadrant *** ask to
maintain this inner focused state in the outer world *** *** ask
this feeling to move into the mental quadrant, the upper left *** ask
that the same feeling of unconditional love emerge *** ask to

bring your mental awareness of this inner focus into your outer world *** *** ask that feeling to move into the emotional quadrant, the lower left *** ask that same feeling of unconditional love to emerge, bringing your new emotional awareness into your outer world *** *** ask it to move into your body quadrant, the lower right *** ask the feeling of unconditional love to emerge *** ask to maintain this feeling within your physical body in your outer world *** *** bring your awareness into the center focal point of your inner screen *** ask your screen to expand *** ask to unify this feeling of unconditional love with your spiritual, mental, emotional, and physical self *** *** ask this to deepen within your heart-center *** and to spread throughout your physical form *** and beyond *** synchronizing this feeling of unconditional love and living it in your outer world...ask this to connect you to the energies through all of time *** to all of space *** ask to bring together all of the inner forces that will allow this inner rhythm of unconditional love to remain open and that will allow your outer awareness to emerge from this inner self-actualizing pulse *** *** ask that your body feel light and energized as you maintain this inner-awareness *** working as one inner team *** *** become aware of the space around you *** of your physical body *** feeling light and inner connected *** opening your eyes *** sitting up ***.

Just as we explored in the previous chapter the different sensations and feelings that may occur as one opens into an inner-awareness, many similar processes develop in the physical body each time we move into this new inner-directed space. With this exploration, a number of individuals either feel inclined to, or actually do, begin to cough. This is quite natural, since the throat chakra begins to open into a different vibration with this exploration. Learn to be comfortable with the feeling; don't try to stop it. Just ask that your screen begin to expand, and allow it to continue expanding until the coughing or tickling feeling dissipates. The more you try to stop it and focus on not coughing, the more heightened that energy becomes and the worse your coughing will become. Do the same thing with any body pain that occurs; expand your screen, and let yourself move through it. If you focus on the pain or annoyance, it becomes heightened. Whatever you focus on, regardless of whether it is beneficial or detrimental, is always created by your focus. Remember that by staying at your present level, or by lowering your energy, you will not bring about change. The change, regardless of whether it is psychological or physical, always exists at the heightened level of energy.

Through this exploration, you can begin to feel the brain being altered and brought under the energies of inner-directed guidance. Many people feel as if they had been wearing a hat that now has been removed. One common result of awakening the triune brain is a sense of an expanded feeling in the head. This is because each one of the colors will begin to represent a shift into a deeper inner rhythm, which consequently changes the resonating frequency of the brain. The color green begins to shift you into a different brain wave state, while the color blue deepens that to even steadier realms. The violet opens you into a yet deeper and slower inner rhythm, while white deepens this process further. Through biofeedback exploration, we know that as individuals move into these inner realms, the brain wave rhythms also begin to change, opening one into various levels of imagery and into different levels of inner sensations. However, the process which we are exploring is still very different from most traditional techniques of brain wave exploration that are explored within the areas of biofeedback.

When individuals move into the deeper colors of violet and/or white, it is not uncommon to experience physiological shifts. For example, in shifting through the colors many people feel a flickering movement in their eyelids. Some begin to fear that their eyes will pop open during the exploration. This will not usually happen. So just be comfortable with it and let your eyelids flicker should this tendency occur; this is merely another indication that you are moving into other levels of vibration within your brain. Within the deeper inner states associated with violet or white, many individuals notice a marked shift in their thinking. Their outer thinking stops, and they move into an inner feeling state of knowing. This shift is associated with the heart chakra and is the first level of experiencing the energies of unconditional love that I mentioned earlier. The shift into the energies of inner-directed guidance opens one into the knowing. One cannot be within this state of knowing unless there is a shift in the brain's inner rhythms. The two go hand in hand. Some people actually hear a sound, almost as if they hear the brain shifting. If you should hear such a sound, don't be frightened by it. And don't be frightened if your body begins to jerk. Remember, your body is a reflection of what is happening within your consciousness, and when you are shifting your consciousness to the level where the brain becomes the messenger, you will feel many jerks or other movements and sensations within your body. There are many layers to be released as you move into deeper inner rhythms, and with each one of the layers the body will experience subtle, and perhaps not so subtle, changes. As you move deeper into the inner states, whatever your consciousness is focused upon, you will begin to create that particular level of focus for yourself.

Notice how different your body feels. Notice how quiet it feels inside of you; sense the layers of inner silence. Silence is very easily attained once you expand and move into the energies of the inner directed space. Silence is not nearly as difficult to experience as most people proclaim it to be. However, a state of silence can be achieved neither through the intellect nor by attempting to push oneself into it. The important thing is that you allow your focus to shift and by so doing, allow your brain to move into its proper perspective of providing the intermediary process, thus becoming the messenger. Just allow the energies of your inner-directed soul guidance to begin to direct this process for you, and the inner silence then becomes automatic.

Sometimes a new form of inner chatter develops for individuals. This consists of an image or a chatter that moves into one's consciousness and then immediately moves right out again. You might have already noticed this happening. Suddenly an image or a thought comes forward, but there is no sense of needing to do anything with it. Just observing it seems to be sufficient, and then it is gone. This is because, as you begin to deepen into the inner spaces, the higher levels of energy will automatically change many perceptions without your consciously doing anything more than merely observing what is there. If, however, you should get stuck in one of these perceptions, it indicates that further exploration is needed. By merely observing the perception, you do not attach yourself to it as being real; thus, you do not start ruminating about it, thereby breaking the energetic bonds. If suddenly you do attach yourself to one of these images or thoughts, you will pull yourself out of the inner-directed space, and back into your outer mind. If you cannot allow yourself to merely observe the perceptions, they will never change. One cannot truly change anything until it has been brought under the volition of the energies of one's inner guidance. Being able to focus upon something from the observer state indicates that one is ready to allow that perception to be shifted into a creative energy. This is what the process of perceptual shifting is—being able to take any image or life situation with which you are dealing and eventually allow the energies of your self-actualizing pulse, or unconditional love, to transmute it into a new perception of unity. Saying or thinking that you accept or love some problematic part of yourself will not make it happen. You need to create an energetic space within that allows the inner-directed energy of that moment to transmute it into the heightened vibration of unity.

In EXPLORATION #7: AWAKENING THE NERVOUS SYSTEM, we will integrate many of the ideas we have explored up to this point. Our goal is first to learn how to direct the inner energy from the brain into and throughout the nervous system, and then to allow ourselves to merely ask that this energy shift. We want to note then what bodily changes occur. Lie down on a flat, firm surface, or you can do this exploration sitting upright in a chair. You may wish to try both of these postures to see if you experience any difference.

"Close your eyes *** ask that your screen expand *** focus at the center point of your inner screen and at the center of your chest *** ask that an imaginary line be drawn down through the middle of your physical body, dividing your body into two equal halves *** imagine starting at the top of your head, moving down between your eyes, dividing your nose, lips, mouth, and chin in half *** continue down through your throat, shoulders, chest, stomach, and into the pelvic area *** and continue drawing that line between your legs and feet *** now ask that no matter what your focus is, it will affect only the left side of your physical body *** no matter what you say or do, the right side of your body will remain just as it is until you remove the imaginary line *** with your awareness at the center of your chest, ask that a feeling of pulsation move only from the left side of that line, sending ripples throughout the left side of your body and beyond *** *** ask your screen to expand, but that this affect only the left side of you *** bring your awareness into the old brain *** ask the pulsation of emerald green light to awaken and pulsate down the left side of your spinal column to the tip of your spine *** ask that feeling to move back up the spinal column *** ask it to lower again to the tip on only the left side of your spinal column *** bring your awareness into the mid-brain and proceed through the same process, asking that only the left side of your spinal column be affected *** *** now focus on the right and left hemispheres and proceed through the same thing as before *** *** and now move to the connective point and ask that to move slowly down the left side of your nervous system *** *** ask to feel a continuous flow of energy moving from your brain into the left side of the brain stem, down through the left side of the spinal column to its tip *** *** ask the energy to move from the left side of your spinal column through the nervous system (NS) to the bottom of your left foot *** *** now ask it to again move through the NS to the left ankle and down through the left foot *** *** ask it to move through the NS connecting the left knee and continuing as before to the bottom of your left foot *** *** ask it to move through the NS to your left thigh and connect it downward *** *** into the left hip *** *** left buttocks and pelvic area *** *** ask it to spread through the NS on the left side of your body, through your lower abdomen and lower back *** *** through the left mid back and chest *** **** spreading through the left upper back and chest *** *** through the left shoulder *** *** down into the left arm *** *** left forearm *** *** left wrist and palm of left hand *** *** spreading out through the fingers of your left hand *** *** into the left side of your neck *** *** ask that the NS of your whole left side deepen within this feeling *** *** ask it to spread through the NS into the left jaw and left side of your face and neck *** *** left side of your lips, and into the gums and teeth in the left side of your mouth *** *** your left nostril and nose *** *** left facial cheek and left ear *** *** left eye and left side of your forehead *** *** left side of the top part of your head and down the left side of your head into the neck *** *** ask that the pulsation within the left side of your body deepen *** *** ask to expand your screen and feel into the color blue, allowing it to deepen through your NS on the left side of your body *** *** **** ask to expand your screen and to deepen into the color violet throughout the NS on the left side *** *** *** ask your screen to expand and to deepen into the brilliance of white light on the left side of your body *** *** *** now become aware of the difference between the left side of your body and the right side *** *** notice the sensations at the points of contact between your body and the chair or floor— is there a feeling of warmth and expansion? *** *** ask that the feelings and conditions of your body remain the same, still divided between the left and right sides, even as you prepare to get up to stand and walk *** *** now allow yourself to slowly stand up, still maintaining the division between the two sides of your body *** walk around the room and become aware of the difference between the right and left sides of you *** *** notice how your left foot feels in contrast to the right foot as your feet touch the floor when you are walking *** *** notice how your left arm and hand seem longer than on the right side *** notice how fluidly and easily the left side of your body moves *** *** now allow yourself to once again sit or lie down *** *** ask to open to a belief that the right side of your body can move into this same level of balance by transferring the inner energy through your nervous system, thus bringing the two sides of you into total balance *** *** ask your imaginary line to now disappear *** focus at the center point of your screen with the emerald green color and ask it to move through the entire nervous system *** *** focus on the color blue and ask it to move in the same way through your entire nervous system *** *** now the color violet *** *** and the brilliance of white light *** *** if there is any area of your body that still feels out of balance, focus at the center point of your screen and ask the energy to be directed into that particular area to bring you into a space of inner balance *** *** *** ask to maintain this inner balance and focus *** *** ask to feel light and energized *** *** and ask these feelings to emerge into your outer awareness *** ** open your eyes when you are ready."

One of the most difficult questions with which individuals struggle centers around the concept of one's inner focus and the ability to thereby change and create something new. If we were to spend time talking about how, through this exploration, you would be able to direct the movement of your focus through half of your nervous system, creating profound levels of restructuring to the point of physically dividing your body into two distinctly different halves, and then how you would ultimately be able to allow the other half of the body to move into an equal depth of change and restructuring within one tenth the time, it would be difficult for your outer mind to grasp all of this. As we are focused within the outer mind, it is difficult to really grasp an understanding of any level of change, much less grasp and accept the revolutionary concept that our solid physical body is actually very fluid. But once you have awakened the inner self-actualizing energies, this level of inner focus can and does move a solid mass into a different unified structure. At the levels of inner awakening, whatever an individual is focused upon begins to change very quickly, even to the point that when I do this exploration with large groups, individuals can physically see the changes in other people's arms and shoulders when they first get up to walk and then again at the completion of the exploration. You are the living focus of your inner consciousness, but when you are in an outer focus, you are the living structure of that focus, too.

As I first began exploring the various resonating frequencies within the brain, I reasoned that it was similar to the brain wave process that biofeedback had been exploring for the last twenty years. However, I have since come to realize that the brain wave process of exploring the four distinct brain wave rhythms associated with the beta, alpha, theta, and delta states is very limited, and merely touches the surface of man's inner realms. It fails to give any consideration to the awareness that is available to us through the energetic experiences of our inner-directed guidance. Many Eastern philosophies and mystical teachings mention the existence of some 22 major states of awareness, and I believe that biofeedback touches only the fringes of this exploration. Through my inner experiences, I have felt, sensed, and experienced spaces that went beyond the structures laid out in biofeedback and the traditional study of brain wave rhythms. It is, in truth, the inner rhythms or vibrational resonance of the brain and heart chakra that open us into the various levels of our inner-directed guidance, which we must then honor in a timely manner.

Since late 1985 I have experienced several very distinct levels of inner realms, and each successive level that I experienced possessed its own distinct quality of energetic structures, inner perceptions, sensations of knowingness, and deep levels of inner-directed guidance. My outer mind was initially not pleased with this. I had hoped to create a formula for understanding one's inner-directed guidance, and I was hoping that there existed the inner space from which to bring forward one exact and unchanging truth. Over the years, however, I have realized that while I may touch an inner space that is very deep for me, this depth is dependent upon the level of openness, synchronization, and blending of various energies and vibrations that have emerged at that particular time. If my body feels balanced with the information which comes forward, then I know it is correct for that day. If my body does not feel the balance, then I know that another inner space still exists which needs to be explored. Yesterday's information may have brought me balance yesterday, but that same information may feel different today. Thus the great insight I previously gained may no longer feel right if I have not taken the direct action that is needed based upon the inner levels of appropriate timing. The physical body's reaction to the vibration of the information becomes the feedback for knowing whether one's information is emerging from the deeper levels of inner guidance, from the outer mind, or from some blending of the two.

During this same period in time, I became aware of the need to explore the possibility of living continually from the inner realms of awareness, regardless of the outer activity in which I might be engaged. At first my outer mind reasoned that this would be an impossible task, but as I began to explore it, I found it to be easier and more peaceful to live from within the inner states than it was to be living and creating from the customary outer awareness. The explorations shared in this book have provided me with the inner training necessary to adjust into the new levels of perceptions, feelings, and sensations that I experienced in the process of bringing my inner meditative states out into the real world of living. I knew from my readings that the Zen Masters had been able to function and talk while in the theta and delta states of brain wave activity; and yet, current biofeedback and scientific research portray sleep as being a condition of the theta and delta states. But if just one individual can succeed in mastering the theta and delta states while functioning in an awakened state, then it is possible for every human being to do likewise. In one form of yoga called Karma Yoga, the focus of exploration is for individuals to be actively involved in various forms of outer activity while simultaneously maintaining an inner receptive state that is open to any and all inner levels of energetic awareness, sensation, perception or feedback. I believe that these conditions are a vital part of the unfoldment which we are exploring as we move into our post-biological development.

I would like to discuss some of the many and varied changes that can take place for us as we work through the various explorations. This includes the physical, emotional, mental, and spiritual (or potential) aspects, as well as the new unified living self, which becomes even greater than the totality of the above aspects. We will then explore how the triune brain relates to the expanded inner screen and the various quadrants. If we work from the premise that the energetic levels of brain functioning make us human, then it follows that as the brain moves into new levels of resonating frequencies, different levels of human characteristics or potential will begin to emerge. This function is analogous to what happens when the brain moves into states of resonance that create disruptions or patterns of dissonance, and thus impair the quality and level of our human functioning. As human beings we have the ability to shift into ever deepening patterns of resonating brain frequencies, and each one of the patterns will awaken us into a broader and more complete understanding of ourselves as being human. I believe this is what Maslow describes as a self-actualized person.

We have already explored the brain from the two perspectives that consciousness is contained both within the brain and beyond the brain; therefore, we can conclude that our consciousness is a direct result of our immediate focus and brain resonance. As we learn to shift the role of the brain from an outer into an inner direction, the brain becomes a transducer for the inner-directed energetic vibration that opens us into new levels of inner-awareness and human capabilities. I believe that this shifting into the perspective whereby the brain is indeed a messenger or transducer for the inner vibration takes place when the heart chakra fully opens. The awakened vibration then guides the synchronization of the triune brain into a new inner rhythm. At this point we will have fully shifted into awakening our creative potential, which will be explored in Exploration #15.

I believe that the earlier explorations begin to touch some of the deeper aspects in the awakening process, and at this point in the exploration, you will feel, sense and experience a major shift within you. This is the shift in inner perspective that results from the brain's new role, which allows you to explore the inner realms and the various levels of consciousness while in an outer awakened state. You will be able to feel this shift within your physical body, within the brain, and in the changing perceptions that will emerge from your sense organs.

You will experience various levels of physiological changes and self-regulation that will not rationally make sense within the context of traditional Western medicine or science. Many of the changes will greatly alter your physical movement, inner and outer healing abilities, and the regeneration of various physical structures, not to mention major changes in the levels of inner-awareness of the sensations and feelings which all become a part of your new capabilities as an awakened human being. The deeper inner realms of your body awareness will move beyond what most individuals will tell you is even possible, so you have to begin to believe in your own changes. When exploring these processes with individuals who are in various stages of illness, lab tests and X-rays do indeed confirm definite physical changes, although the doctors have no outer knowledge of why they occur. Upon awakening into the inner creative potential, one's physical, psychological, emotional, and spiritual livingness are no longer dependent solely upon the previous condition of one's outer organs or physical capabilities. It becomes possible to move beyond the previous levels and to open into new levels of increased human functioning.

On the emotional level, one's outer awareness is traditionally evidenced through anxiety, stress, fear, anger, shortness of temper, low self-esteem, and a host of other emotions and feelings. As we open into an inner-awareness, we begin to allow new feelings and sensations to emerge on the emotional level. We move into an emotional calm and a state of balance, and we develop a new understanding and tolerance for others and for ourselves. All of this takes place without really making any overt effort to attain it; due to the shift in brain resonance something automatically and naturally begins to emerge from within our hearts. As we move into deeper inner realms, we experience a profound feeling of well-being. Something within us knows on an emotional level that all of our perceptions and feelings have yet another possibility or perspective; we need only to avoid letting ourselves get caught in believing that what is currently happening is the only reality that exists for us. Through the emotional inner shift, we open into deeply profound feelings, and we perceptually shift our experiences into the energies of unconditional love and unity. As this opens within us, we can easily discern the feelings of personal or infatuated love from the energetic feelings of the inner heart. We begin to experience the feelings of unconditional love not just for other individuals, but for ourselves and for humanity as a whole. As this awakens within us, the state of unconditional love will become the new norm of our emotional character and will govern the way we interact and create within our world.

On the mental level we will no longer gather outer information just for the sake of acquiring additional information that is then to be used merely for rote recall. Our mental or intellectual journey up to this point in time has traditionally been focused on gathering very specific amounts of data and information that others have explored, with little or no inner-awareness of how this information fits into our own personal experiences. As we awaken into an inner mental awareness, we begin to gather only that information which we can directly apply and experience ourselves. Many, if not eventually all, of our previous attitudes, beliefs, and perceptions about ourselves, our reality, and our world, will begin to change as we personally experience new areas within our lives. We will no longer be continually in an active search for outer information; rather, as we move into a passive state allowing information that emerges from our inner guidance to be directed into our outer environment, we will actually be taking on a very active role in our learning process. No longer will time be needed to ponder, as in the past; time will be needed only for inner quiet in order that an inner synthesis may then emerge very naturally. This will often occur even as we are speaking or discussing things with someone else and consequently a totally different understanding of what is being explored right at that moment can develop. This is a part of those earlier experiences that I referred to as living in the "now moment." A sharp increase in memory and recall abilities will be noticed, as well as new depths of deductive reasoning. As the process deepens, we move into an inner knowing of information and events regarding ourselves and others. This knowing emerges naturally from within, so long as the levels of inner silence are maintained. This constitutes the restructuring of one's outer mind into an inner-awareness that is guided by the energies of one's inner-directed soul guidance.

On a spiritual or divine level, the potential for new information, capabilities, and creative pursuits will begin to evolve. No longer will we feel limited in our perception of what is possible for us, and within the newly emerging structures we can begin to experience a broader perspective in understanding the human journey. This then opens us into new levels of security because we realize that we are never alone, and we can both feel and see the synchronization of inner and outer events in our lives. As the inner knowing deepens, we spend less time talking and thinking, and much more time in our creative pursuits of living. We recognize our own particular purpose, and begin the unraveling of our purpose as human beings. We seldom question or doubt our own abilities or those of humanity as a whole. Life begins to take on a mystical or transpersonal quality that extends beyond any outer form of religion, and we clearly sense the connectedness of all human beings and their unity with all other forms of life. Transcendent experiences become the norm of living, and yet we come to realize that even greater awarenesses exist.

Our unified living self then allows us to bring the new inner-awarenesses of all of these aspects directly into the outer world. We can learn to live at what once was our meditative states, which will in turn open us into yet deeper inner states. And eventually, the new inner states of awareness will become our outer reality. Thus the cyclic journey continues.

None of these experiences can exist for us unless the brain and heart chakra shift into new patterns of resonance. Many individuals, and scientists in particular, do not even acknowledge these inner spaces as being real, only theoretical at best. But when any of these doubting or unknowing individuals begins to experience the shifts in vibrational patterns within their own brain and heart, a whole new world opens even unto them. No matter who we are, explorations into the brain, nervous system, and heart chakra open us into the world of our dreams, and subsequently allow us to create those dreams in our newly emerging world.

I have found Paul MacLean's work with the triune brain to be quite exciting because it parallels many of my own experiences in inner guidance exploration. One basic premise of the theory of the triune brain is that it views human beings as possessing three separate levels of brain functioning. Each level or area of the brain also represents a distinct stage within man's evolutionary process. Although each of the separate parts of the human brain bears a similarity to the physiological functioning of other groups of species, when the triune brain in the human being is unified, it no longer operates as three isolated systems. Although man may exhibit a similarity in behavioral or processing patterns to other species, he is not limited to animalistic behaviors or tendencies. The new level of integration that separates man from other species, with the exception of the dolphin and the whale, is the neocortex. This area of the brain allows man to have naturally emerged as a human being, not as an evolvement from a lower species. Man's triune brain contains a vast amount of unused neocortex space, with more than 90% of it not presently being utilized. I believe it is the development of the neocortex portion of the brain that allows us to emerge into our heightened levels of creative functioning. And it is this area of functioning which allows us to be different from all other species. Why then do we not utilize more of the brain functioning process which ultimately allows us to become and be who we are?

Today many individuals in the various scientific disciplines are discovering that within the area of neocortex brain activity lies the unknown inner creative potential that will allow us as human beings to become more than we ever thought we were capable of becoming. Further, I believe that the opening of the heart chakra and its inner awakening self-actualizing energies constitutes a vital step in utilizing this area of the brain. Explorations #6 and #7, which we explored in this chapter, allow us first to find the balance that currently exists within the brain and nervous system by dissolving any existing vertical blockages and then to open the channel for the development of new inner communication patterns. I believe that the vertical blockages between the separate aspects of the triune brain are as serious a problem for man's survival and further development as a species, as the various blockages within the physical heart are to determining either an individual's physical survival or, at the very least, the available quality of life.

However, the real exploration begins from the balanced state that evolves as the energies awaken one's inner creative potential or guidance, as we will discover through a group of explorations in subsequent chapters. This will allow us to take the next leap into the unknown awareness of our selves. As I have stated previously, I believe that the awakening of the heart chakra and the unifying of the triune brain will open us into the unexplored areas of the neocortex, thus allowing us to explore that 98% of our unknown awareness that Buckminster Fuller described. However, before proceeding with the next explorations, I would like to discuss the various functions of the triune brain and their relationship to the expanded inner screen and quadrants.

Each time that we unify the triune brain we move ourselves out of our current levels of functioning as a human being, thereby opening into new levels of creative energy. Through the vertical separation of the triune brain, our perceptions of our world become organized through a dissonant pattern. Due to this separation, we are not able to fully channel the heightened creative energies, thereby limiting us in achieving a balanced state and, most likely, causing us to create through a reactive process. Consider, for example, a situation in which we are confronted with an issue of jealousy regarding a spouse or lover. Our emotional (or dissonant response) is to inwardly, and sometimes outwardly, totally lose control. Anger, rage and hurt instantly begin to emerge, our thoughts turn to revenge, and before we know it we are in the midst of creating a plan of action that may be totally unrelated to the outer events which initially began the sequence. But within the outer mind, our current perceptions and feelings are so real that we are not even aware of the possibility that another perception might be available; nor are we aware of the possibility that our original perceptions may have been initially misperceived. Because we are stuck within a logically-illogical part of ourselves, we take actions which actually deepen the frustrating feelings, the perceptions of hopelessness, and the belief that the situation will never change. In such states the triune brain is functioning from a very strong and dominant energy localized in the old and mid-brain areas; high emotion is being explored out of the mid-brain while physical security, survival, and reaction needs are being dealt with out of the old brain. Very little information is emerging from the neocortex, the area of the brain which could afford one the ability to observe an alternative to what is occurring. We could choose to unify the whole triune brain and thus allow the energies of inner guidance to emerge, which would provide insight for seeking some deeper pattern that might be causing the inter-action and for observing how both parties involved actually are jointly creating the conflict. By utilizing this heightened energy of inner guidance, no one becomes a victim and no one is to blame. So long as there is a victim in any given situation, nothing really changes. You may choose to leave the relationship, but have you noticed that whatever relationship you then enter into, be it a personal or a job-related relationship, it opens you to again feeling like a victim.

It is vital to realize that no one ever pushes us into a victim's role. To be a victim requires that we ourselves cooperate in accepting the perceptions of victimization as being correct and real; and, because of the manner in which the brain is functioning, our worst fears and perceptions of self consequently emerge. Many of the resulting perceptions and fears actually do not have any probable cause for existence based upon the given current situation. If the brain becomes unified, however, we cannot be caught up in such a reactive energy; we will be inwardly focused and calm, and will open to the emergence of the energies of an inner feeling of quiet. Through this quiet, the reactivate energies will shift into creative energies and new solutions, perceptions, and possibilities will continually emerge. And from this inner space, no one will be to blame—neither you nor the other person. You will be able to see the situation for what it has to offer and new solutions will emerge, allowing a new inner peace to come forth as you act upon the new solutions. And be assured that you will have available all the energy needed for carrying out these changes.

Thus, as you can see, we have available at least two totally different outcomes for the same given conflict or outer situation. The difference lies within the integration and unification of the triune brain—in other words, choosing unification instead of a reactive dissonance. The choice is always ours! To live as our potential heritage is evolving, we must choose the unified vertical approach. By continuing to live at our current level of human functioning, we will persist in believing that our present perceptions are real and will therefore continue to create by merely reacting to life.

I would like to discuss further the structures of the triune brain. The old or reptilian brain determines our state of arousal, attention, and awareness. It monitors and controls all motor functions within the body, as well as the automatic responses necessary for our physical survival and well-being. Many of our obsessive compulsive behaviors, along with our automatic responses to ritualistic movements and behaviors, have as their source of creation the misdirected energies of the old brain. Some individuals believe that the old brain allows us to maintain a sense of order and stability within our changing world, but I believe this to be the case only when the higher processes associated with the neocortex are involved.

The mid-brain is often referred to as the limbic system or the "paleomammalian brain." This part of the brain is the control center for emotional development, nurturance, and bonding. It is very much connected with mood altering abilities, and allows us to respond with the diverse, primitive, and vivid emotions for which we humans are noted— everything from rage, fear, and panic to pleasure, bliss, and love. It is through the inner processes of this portion of the brain, which some brain researchers call the visceral brain, that our emotions directly respond to our physical body. This is related to the process whereby thoughts and feelings alter our physiological processes and, conversely, perceptions of external states and conditions alter our internal functioning. This is the manner through which the outer mind, via the functioning of our autonomic nervous system, can directly affect the physical body. However, when we are receiving our direction from an inner guidance, this same brain process allows us to just as quickly alter to new levels of perception. As the mid-brain develops, the activities connected with the old brain also change and evolve. We can see this in early mammal development, as mammals are dependent upon all fours legs for movement, but their bellies no longer drag on the ground as is the case with reptiles. Then if we consider the early monkeys, we see that there is direct availability, and necessity at times, for only two legs to be used for movement. Early monkeys also exhibit a different leg and arm coordination in climbing movements, and utilize a much more refined motor activity. This is easily visible in the development of the great ape, where the option to stand on two legs is available, but all four legs are still used for rapid movement. A finely tuned muscle coordination is also present, as well as powerfulness in gross motor activity and strength. Also evident is massive body development and an increase in spinal structures.

Another name for the neocortex is "neomammalian brain," which refers to that portion of the brain that is often referred to as gray matter. This part of the brain allows for a yet more heightened order of functioning, moving into the abstract and cognitive areas. It allows us to perceive and learn about the world as being comprised of separate identities. It provides the capabilities for remembering the past, evaluating the present, and anticipating future events. There is also involvement with the specific develop- ment of complex language structure, conscious thinking, and voluntary movements and actions. This is where much of the exploration of right and left hemispheric functions is focused. Study of this area of the brain is based primarily on the existence of a horizontal split, ignoring the vertical separation, which I feel is much more important to mankind's survival and evolution. We present-day human beings are very different from our early human ancestors, and I believe that the potential, or superhuman being of the future will act and behave just as differently from us today as we currently differ from early man. I do not believe that the shift we are presently beginning to experience is going to entail a drastic outer physical change, but rather an inner awakening and a new perceptual functioning in understanding ourselves and our world.

There is also an area of the brain called the "corpus callosum," which is a bridge of connecting nerves that allows for direct communication between the right and left hemispheres of the brain. It is interesting to note that this area of the brain does not begin to develop until around the first year of life, and does not finish in its development until sometime in the fourth year. At this time the brain is outwardly complete in its development, and the child between the ages of four and seven then experiences a whole new world of perceptions, feelings, sensations, and information. With the completion of the development of the corpus callosum comes the ability to begin to separate one's perceptions from self and to thus develop a unique identity. This is the age at which children open directly into their energies of inner guidance and perceive the world for what it truly is. Unfortunately, as I stated before, most children quickly begin to close off their perceptive ability due to the lack of outer model approval. And because of this, they may then have difficulty in understanding their inner or divine nature throughout the ensuing years of their lives.

The exploration of the inner screen quadrants and the shifting of feelings, awarenesses, or perceptions within the quadrant is directly integrated with the triune brain structure. From one perspective, each area of the brain functions as a separate form of energy or vibration, and as this occurs a separateness and dissonance is created. As we move, however, into the expanded inner screen and the opening of the heart chakra, we actually set in motion the transition of a particle-based form of energy into a wave-form of energy, thereby allowing each area of the brain to shift its own resonant structures. This shift is what allows us to begin to perceive new information and sensations and/or to perceive old information and perceptions in new ways.

The physical quadrant relates directly to the transformation within the old brain, changing it from the particle-form of energy into a wave-form of energy. This allows us to understand both our body sensations and our awarenesses from a totally different perspective, and also to move into a different form of potential for body movement and healing. The emotional quadrant is directly linked to the transformation of the mid-brain area and creates the shift of our human primitive emotions (including our concept of personal love and personal power) into the energetic feeling state of unconditional love. Through an inner emotional feeling state, we are then able to respond to ourselves, to others, and to the world from an inner presence that is capable of changing all things. I believe that the implicate order, or the beginning of the wave-form energy, initiates in the mid-brain and then spreads throughout the neocortex. Superquantum waves emerge only when the brain is allowed to shift into its role as messenger, which occurs once the triune brain is synchronized with the inner vibration of one's heart chakra and inner self-actualizing pulse. The mental quadrant transforms the energy of the neocortex in a manner that allows us to cease focusing primarily through the processes of concrete thinking and logic, through which our focus centers on abstract and creative processes that are based upon outer information. Instead, we can focus from a restructured inner-awareness and see ourselves as an extension of a creative energy that creates through its own presence as well as through the presence that it brings forward in each object and activity that is seen and performed. The potential or spiritual quadrant allows for the transformation of the connective point of the brain, or the corpus callosum, which deepens the awareness of our inner potential. Typically the corpus callosum directs the information created by all areas of the whole brain guided by and based upon one's outer awareness and function. But as the brain shifts into a new wave of potential energy, it begins to direct and synthesize the information as it emerges from the energies of one's inner-directed soul guidance. This allows the restructuring of the outer mind to take place.

Focusing upon the center point of one's screen, and deepening this with the heart chakra energies, allows one's inner-directed soul guidance to merge with the physical body. This forms the direct link, as mentioned earlier, whereby the body is directly integrated with the energies of one's soul, and yet still maintains its physical form. The deeper connection at the center point of the expanded screen and its relationship with the heart chakra allow for the transformation of the energy throughout the physical body, and one is then able to maintain the new vibration as it moves directly from the inner self-actualizing pulse into the typical outer events of daily life. Without this synthesis, one cannot bring the energy and deeper awarenesses of the meditative states into the outer everyday world. I see this process as the awakening of one's creative potential, and feel that it is the real beginning of our next level of human development. I believe that this is the process that David Bohm calls the "generative order" of energy.

Each area of the triune brain is independent and can function at an autonomous level. Each area of the triune brain has its own desires and motivations, memory capabilities, and differing forms of imagery, wherein dreams are created differently and problems are solved through diverse means. But when the triune brain functions as one entity, something very different occurs that separates us as human beings from the other species of the earth. And when we choose to expand our inner screen and initiate the opening of our heart chakra, we then begin our odyssey into a new level of human development; we move into the unknown awarenesses of ourselves and allow the unknown parts of who we are to be activated and to emerge within our outer world. This is our odyssey in the awakening of mankind's individual and collective creative potential!

CHAPTER EIGHT

EXPLORING INNER-
DIRECTED IMAGERY

One of the first techniques I learned to utilize during late 1977 was the process of guided imagery or visualization. The first phase in my process explored the active role of guiding a series of images through a specific situation that I wanted to actually be created. These situations would focus on health, money, relationships, jobs, and so forth. The process involved creating as clear an image as possible of whatever I desired to see accomplished or created in my life. In the second phase of my imagery process I played a more passive role, allowing myself to move into the role of observer and having another person (or a tape) guide me through a series of images. I always followed a certain progression, and at some point I would ask for specific information to emerge, often from a wise old person or a guide. As I watched a solution or information come forward, I would then guide the images into an area of resolution. It was great! These two processes of imagery were as revolutionary and exciting to me as if I had just experienced the invention of the wheel. At last I had found a way of controlling life and directing it in any way that I desired. It was at this point that I thought I comprehended the statement "that you create your own reality."

Approximately six months later another form of imagery spontaneously began to come forth. This was emerging from a very deep inner space; I was neither creating it nor directing it. The images spontaneously emerged out of a focused, heightened inner energetic state, with the focus of the images being quite different than what I was expecting. Through this form of inner-directed imagery, I was brought into levels of awareness and was exposed to levels of information that my outer mind had never even thought could be possible. This was part of the process that began with the restructuring of my physical body in 1978. I found that when I allowed myself to take direct action based upon the inner-directed images, I would automatically begin to feel a new sense of inner calm and peace, and my outer life would begin to change without my trying to push or control anything.

Several years later, I encountered some research from the Menninger Foundation which described a process of imagery called hypnagogic imagery, or a creative reverie state. I initially thought that their process was synonymous with the form of imagery through which my life had begun to change. I later realized that although what was occurring for me was similar to what occurred through their process, it was also noticeably different due to the awakening energies I experienced in 1978.

When I myself directed and created the images based upon how I thought my life should move, very little real change took place. Sure, some things did begin to change as a result of my outer directed imagery process, but I often then seemed prone to quickly create something else that moved in an opposite direction. I very seldom experienced any prolonged periods of inner silence or calmness while I explored the outer directed process of imagery.

It was during this same period of time that I first began to explore the process of imagery with cancer patients through the local Cancer Society. Over the course of the next six years these cancer patients truly taught me about living, dying, and transformation. By exploring different forms of imagery with them, using pre-recorded tapes along with my own explorations, I became aware that the aggressive images which the tapes utilized were initially very useful in allowing a reactionary form of change to take place. But I found that as individuals continued visualizing the aggressive images of their cancer being attacked and killed, they were not able to maintain the same results as they had initially achieved. And very few of them ever attained any inner level of peace or quiet in their lives. They were continually concerned that their next cold or flu might be related to the cancer, or they worried incessantly about when the cancer would return. It was extremely difficult, if not impossible, to achieve any level of true transformative change through the outer directed imagery processes.

By 1982 I had become capable of detecting the subtle changes that occur in a person's energy or electromagnetic field. I was able to observe the direct effects that imagery and other techniques have on an individual's energy field. I began to notice that at certain times during an imagery session an individual's energy field or aura would automatically undergo a major shift in the flow of energies. The energy field would become lighter and fuller, and would exhibit a certain distinguishable quality or depth. Following such an experience, I would inquire of the individual as to whether anything different had happened at a given point during their imagery process. A consistent pattern began to emerge. The visible shifts seemed to correspond to a spontaneous shift in the images that were manifesting within the individuals. At the point when the change occurred, they had felt that they themselves were no longer directing the images; instead, a spontaneous image or series of related images seemed to emerge from within, automatically moving them into a deeper inner state of awareness. They related that all of their spontaneous images had a spiritual or mystical quality to them. Some individuals' images focused on traditional figures or symbols of major religions, while others simply experienced an inner peace and calmness, a knowing that something was going to change. This was usually triggered by a white, gold, or emerald green light, or by some form of geometric pattern. Many individuals reported having experienced a series of spontaneous images which emerged prior to any major changes that occurred in their illness and in their lives in general. I discovered that many individuals had previously experienced these images during our explorations, but they had never mentioned them because they felt that it was unimportant or that they were being distracted due to not having followed the directions of the exploration. They had had no previous exposure to such occurrences through the books they had read, because the only focus they had been taught had been one of directing images into changes of health. Furthermore, what most individuals perceived as health seldom was a level of health that would take them into a new direction in their lives. Generally their images of health directed them back into their past, to a time in life that they perceived as having been healthy and happy. They had failed to comprehend the fact that these were really the times when they had needed to make a major change in their lives, and that they had actually had a choice whereby they could have accomplished the change without the reactive energies of illness. Few individuals had ever been able to perceive and experience themselves as becoming radically different in their beliefs, attitudes, perceptions, relationships, or in dealing with life in general. Yet, their cancer was now saying, "a radical change is upon you!" Only through the inner-directed spontaneous images were individuals at last able to glimpse their first view of themselves as being radically different and alive.

As I then looked back and reviewed my own past, I began to realize that the major changes that had occurred for me had all been directed by the inner spontaneous process. I had rarely consciously thought about the changes beforehand, and in most cases, even as the spontaneous images were occurring, a part of me was feeling that what I was imaging would be impossible to achieve. I recall that when I brought this forward into the energies of my inner guidance to receive further clarification regarding the deeper meaning as to what was truly happening, I was shown the process through which the outer mind operates as a very powerful director of energy. Whenever the mind begins to direct us in a certain direction, corresponding changes usually occur. The difficulties arise in that the mind is not always aware of the real inner-direction that is needed. Problems result due to the confusion of the outer mind taking charge and creating one direction, while the deeper inner-directed energies of one's soul need to go in a totally different direction. Although at times they may both achieve the same outer results, the inner-directed process will produce a very different form of creation, whereby an individual is gently pulled toward the needed goal. I now understand that the basic problem with most imagery processes is that they are very much outer mind directed and do not honor the direction or awareness of the energies of one's inner soul guidance.

During one of my meditations in 1982, I was asked if I would like to explore a totally different process of imagery— one that would be inwardly directed and that would allow each person the total inner freedom (even within a group) to search out and be guided into what was needed for their particular personal growth. Included in this exploration would be a process of directly experiencing the new heightened energy of transmutation for change, since an energy always precedes the creation of an inner image. Of course I consented; and I felt a strong desire to be enlightened at that very moment. I was told, however, that this could not be directly brought forward; rather, I was first to explore the process myself, and was to then work with a small group of individuals who would come forward wanting to explore this form of inner soul directed imagery with me. Gradually I was to become aware of the differences involved with the emergence of the inner images, the level and quality of energy that was involved, how it felt within my own body, and the changes that could occur in my life as the energies of the inner-directed images emerged.

As I explored this process over the course of the next six months, I experienced a number of subtle, yet powerful changes. During a meditation one morning in early 1983, I suddenly realized that I was actually exploring, within myself and with others, a totally different process of imagery— a soul-directed process. Since that morning, the process has been greatly refined as a result of learning to allow the level of inner direction to emerge as a heightened, refined level of energy. Through the emergence of this heightened energy, a series of events capable of changing and altering the direction of an individual's life can automatically be set in motion, manifesting in the areas of health, physical body changes, employment, personal relationships, and in many other circumstances of life.

At this point I realized that the soul-directed imagery process fulfilled everything I had read concerning the Tibetan process of transmutation, and yet it was focused within the concepts and philosophies of our modern western culture. Nowhere, however, had I ever been able to find in written form exactly how one was to allow the process of transmutation to take place. Through my own personal exploration and through explorations with various groups of individuals (now totaling some several thousand persons), this has developed into the exploration of awakening one's creative potential and is the form of imagery that we are exploring together in this book.

Imagery communicates to us on a variety of levels. Some individuals will actually see very vivid pictures, situations, and patterns being created within their inner screen. These images will seem so real that it is difficult to differentiate them from actual outer events. Other individuals who utilize the imagery process will visually see nothing. This does not constitute failure, for the "visual" pictures have nothing to do with direct visual seeing. Rather, what actually is happening is that individuals have tapped into the most important element in imagery—the energy of the feelings and inner sensations that emerge from within—and are learning to interpret this inner form of communication or knowing.

All outer perceptions are interpreted by the brain through sensations, patterns, or vibrations, and are then created as outer senses, which we in turn interpret as being physically real. Likewise, the inner feelings and sensations will be interpreted as images that also seem to be physically real. In order to interpret the inner images, individuals need to be focused within their own inner-awareness and need to be experiencing the various levels of inner silence that are available. When a great amount of stress or inner chatter exists, the interpretation of the inner sensations and feelings is very limited or even distorted. This is a phenomenon similar to that of white noise in blocking out various forms of sound.

Since the inner images can be interpreted through a process of inner knowing, they can emerge from any or all of our senses. Smell, taste, touch, sound and/or sight can be the channel for allowing the inner representation to emerge. When I personally connect with my inner guidance, I sometimes hear a very distinct voice, but more often I receive a series of feelings and inner sensations that are automatically translated or impressed into my consciousness as words, similar to a process of hearing audible sounds. You may become very frustrated in your own inner journey because you do not directly "see" or "hear" anything similar to outer sight or sound. But if you can deepen and allow the inner silence to emerge, and can begin to trust the inner sense of what you felt you saw or heard, you will be surprised at how accurate these feelings of information will become. Some individuals see colors, while others inwardly see images in black and white. The process of inner-directed soul imagery can encompass all of these things, as well as many more.

It is important to realize that whatever is created within our inner screen is always significant, for it is the direct result of some inner process that is emerging. Some individuals feel that images, or even dreams, are a random process of recall that have very little to do with current events in our outer lives. I totally disagree with this. Through my personal experiences and with what others have shared with me, I realize that each image or dream has a very specific correlation to an outer event in life. It is as if some inner force is stimulating a set of images or events in an attempt to communicate with us about our outer events. In my exploration with individuals regarding their dreams, I find that most people are able to begin experiencing a strong correlation between their dream states and the images and feelings that emerge in the events of daily life. They are able to connect today's events with tonight's dreams and vice versa. Many have chosen to maintain such levels of connection for months on end, thus understanding the continuation of experiences throughout both the sleep and awake states.

Both our inner images and our dreams may be represented by various forms of geometric shapes, colors, or patterns. Our inner images may also contain direct psychological information through the playing out of a spontaneous sequence of events that actually did occur, or of a sequence in which we now image an altered situation or different ending. Symbolic images may be created from our own individual subconscious process or we can tap into the collective unconscious process of humanity, where various forms and images are created through mythology or archetypal events and patterns. It is also possible to tap images that are representative of highly transcendent or transpersonal realms of experience which bring forward the mystical or spiritual natures within us. There are no limits to what can emerge from within the heightened creative areas of our inner world.

During my meditations in 1985 I began to experience a series of images that appeared as cartoon characters and played out situations that lasted for an hour or more. The cartoon characters portrayed ways for me to resolve various situations and conflicts in my personal life. Now when I find myself experiencing images in the form of cartoons characters, it seems to be at a time when I am taking life too seriously, and an inner part is showing me ways to lighten up and have fun. The characters seem to be telling me that nothing in life is as serious as I think it is! Some individuals become aware of a process of imagery that seems to be holographic. Such images, sensed either visually or by means of a full level of inner sensations, harbor a certain depth and quality that are projected within the inner screen, creating a sensation similar to viewing a 3-D movie. The process of imagery that we are exploring allows this depth perception of images to become a normal part of life. I first began to experience this process in 1983, and over the last several years, as I have learned to maintain an inner focused state, I find that I can view 3-D movies at the theater and actually see things clearly without the 3-D glasses. Since 1982 I have been able to perceive and sense different forms and movements of energies with my eyes open. And just within this past year I have moved into a process of observing another form of imagery whereby I simultaneously perceive what is being created within my inner screen of images (movements, geometric designs, or pictures), and at the same time can open my eyes and continue to see the inner images projected into the spaces in front of me, viewing the same colors and movements. I am able to easily move with my eyes closed or open and still maintain the same images; and it makes no difference whether I am in a dark room or whether I am outside on a bright sunny day. The more clearly we can perceive and maintain an inner focus of such sensations and feelings, the more easily our own life patterns and our physical bodies can begin to change. This is commonly referred to as focus or as a "level of inner concentration." There are many exercises that teach individuals how to focus and develop clear concentration and a steadiness in the imagery process, but few explore the process of deepening into the inner silence and allowing the images to emerge naturally. Thus the labels or terms that are used may be expected to vary, because we are just now awakening into the processes that are available to all of us for understanding what inner-directed soul imagery is capable of bringing forward.

In Chapter Three we explored the process of Physiological Self-Regulation and the ease with which we are able to create physical changes through shifts in our inner consciousness. Sometimes in group work I explore the process of creating stressful images so that the participants will realize how easily and quickly stressful feelings can shift them out of an inner focused state and back into an outer awareness. Many individuals, once they have shifted from an inner focus into an outer focus of stress, then have trouble letting go of the stressful feelings and find it difficult to move back into their previous state of inner-awareness, relaxation, and calm.

Individuals who experience this difficulty also usually find it difficult to let go of the things in life that become upsetting to them. Does this statement describe you? Once you become tense and angry, for example, do you tend to hold on to the tension and anger?

I often ask individuals to regress into their childhood or adolescent years to exemplify one of the most dramatic means for understanding this level of mind focus. Even though an incident may date back some forty years or more, individuals are invariably able to experience it with the same level of stress, pain, or joy as if it had just happened yesterday! With some groups I explore the re-creation of an old injury or physical trauma. Within a matter of minutes individuals are able to restructure the old patterns of pain, discomfort levels, and actual lack of physical movement. I ask them to stand and move around in order to fully grasp the power of what can be created by a focused mind and to understand that all perceptions, including physical injuries, are still stored within a part of one's consciousness. Thus it can clearly be seen that by focusing one's concentration on past patterns, everything returns to its previous state or condition. But within a few minutes of shifting into an inner-directed focus, one can again return to the previous levels of balance. Before I explore this with a group, however, I make sure that the participants have already learned to hold a certain level of mastery of inner-directed focus. Thus they will no longer react with fear or get stuck ruminating in their old habits or thoughts, at least not while they are present within the group. For if individuals get stuck in their old forms of perceiving and feeling, they may have greater difficulty in releasing the past perceptions and thus once again maintain a part of the difficulty. In any of the situations which I explore through this approach, participants never leave the room and no one talks directly to or directly guides any participant into a past experience. It all emerges naturally through their own quality of focus. From my perspective, if you have the ability to focus and bring forward pain and suffering, you have equal strengths and capabilities for bringing about other change. If you have the ability to create or notice differences in your physical or mental/emotional self, no matter how minute, you also have available to you the ability to explore and create an inner state of unity. The greater and more pronounced one's reactive energy or crisis, the greater is one's opportunity to transform into the inner creative potential. The two, crisis and opportunity, always go hand in hand.

The important concept I want you to grasp as a result of this discussion is that of the enormous potential of a focused mind. Regardless of whether the mind is focused on stress, anger, joy, love, excitement or whatever, the power of one's mind cannot be underestimated. It always creates its present focus. If the mind becomes locked into a state of confusion, the only thing it will perceive, feel, and experience is confusion, and the decisions that will subsequently be made will be a reaction to the confusion. If the mind is brought under the direction of one's inner-directed guidance, the decisions and perceptions will be made through the energies of creation, and will thus move the individual in a totally different direction. The real choice that we have in any situation is dependent upon the state and focus of the mind, be it outer directed or inner guided. Whatever we say, or however we choose to interact and create with others is always dependent upon our choice of focus.

Over the years I have been able to perceive a step-by-step process that occurs as individuals shift their focus from inner-awareness into outer stress. Each individual moves through this process; sometimes it happens within seconds, and at other times it takes weeks or months. But whenever perceptions change from a creative inner-directed energy into a crisis or reactive form of energy, a predictable pattern emerges. This is the process called projection. Likewise, there is a similar process that allows the outer mind to shift its projection into that inner creative energy which emerges from one's inner-directed soul guidance. This is the process called transmutation that we have previously discussed.

Both of the aforementioned processes deal with a concept called Mind-Set, which refers to the specific beliefs, attitudes, and expectations we hold concerning ourselves, others, and life in general. These expectations are the direct result of our years of learning, coupled with the direct life experiences we have encountered. Each human being also carries within them a unique inner history that consists of a series of collective awarenesses that has evolved directly from various religious and cultural time periods throughout history. This collective group of perceptions is also a part of one's Mind-Set. It is under the full direction of the mind that one's nature of reality is constructed; so our individual Mind-Set becomes the base camp with which we compare all outer perceptions. What we perceive as our base camp, also is in the process of changing as we add new inner and outer experiences.

Each of us also has a Perception of Reality through which we perceive a given situation or from which we react. When our Perception of Reality matches our Mind-Set, we are able to create and move easily through life. We have no new awarenesses coming into play, and we are creating from a balanced creative energy. However, if our Perception of Reality, the second awareness, does not match our Mind-Set, we begin to create the first levels of a reactive energy that is actually asking us to evaluate our current perception or projection of reality. Such dissonance can emerge for a variety of reasons, but as long as one continues to focus upon the why or what of the problem, nothing will change.

The third step in the total process is the one whereby we begin to choose a direct path from which to create. Either we believe that our projection is correct and thus move into the first levels of inner chatter and reactive energy, or we allow a heightened energy to emerge and explore the process of transmutation and inner-directed guidance as they evolve from our creative energies. In either case, the choice is always ours.

If we choose to remain with the projection, then the fourth step is that of Mental Inner Chatter. At this point we begin to hear a critical inner voice talking to us. This voice does not focus on anything constructive nor does it focus on ways to bring about integrated change; instead, it either maintains a focus on what cannot or will not happen or it begins to recall all of the related past experiences one has encountered. When the Mental Inner Chatter is present, it becomes more difficult to remain focused, and one's ability to concentrate begins to decrease. These are the first signs of outer mind confusion.

The Mental Inner Chatter can easily shift into the fifth step of Emotional Inner Chatter, where feelings of fear, worry, doubt, frustration, anger, and confusion begin to emerge along with the critical inner voice. It is at the level of Emotional Inner Chatter that the confusion deepens and we begin to emotionally react to situations in inappropriate ways. Our feelings begin to dominate our perceptions, which serves only to deepen the reactive energies.

This quickly evolves into the sixth step, the creation of Inner Images and Physical Levels of Inner Chatter (or stress and tension), which causes physiological changes in the body. At this level, the Inner Images that portray our worst fears and difficulties begin to emerge, and as a result our perceptions become distorted and it becomes difficult to separate them from our outer reality. Due to an increased energy being focused upon these Inner Images, the physical body begins to change by mirroring the Inner Images in its physical form. This constitutes the Physical Inner Chatter, which causes the body to hold a certain level of movement or body armoring as its new physical structure, thereby further reinforcing the perceptions! As a result, we finally move into such a powerful state of outer focus that we are ruminating continually about the given situation or problem. The only things we can think, feel, or talk about are the levels of the problem, and therefore, our Mind's Confusion, the seventh step, becomes our reality.

You clearly know when you are in this seventh state because the only focus you are capable of maintaining is that of your problem, and you also begin to move other people's conversations into the focus of your problem. Even when alone, you continue to focus on the problem with great intensity. It is as though there is nothing that can sway the direction of your focus. Your Mind's Confusion is very real, and the longer you remain within this reactive focus the tighter you lock yourself into believing that the reality of your perceptions from within your Mind's Confusion is indeed real. As a result, you move so deeply into the seventh step that you become 100% Logical within the Illogical Perceptions of Your Mind's Confusion. At this level of perception, you know that you are Logically Correct in your thinking. If someone attempts to point out your faulty perceptions, you can readily prove them wrong, and just as easily prove yourself to be correct in what you are feeling, seeing, and thinking. In your own eyes you are being Logical; to everyone else's perceptions you are Illogically focused within your own Mind's Confusion!

It is at this level of awareness that projection is firmly locked in as your reality, and every decision that you make is based upon the illogical information which you unquestionably know to be true. Your decisions and conversations are usually either very emotionally based or completely void of any emotion or feeling. As you stay focused within the reactive phase of Illogical-Logical Thinking, you begin to experience a decrease in the amount of energy that is available to you. This causes you to move even more deeply into the structures of duality in your thinking and subsequently causes you to experience deep and unsettling emotional feelings about life in general.

This decrease in energy creates what I refer to as Mind Confusion. This constitutes the final step in the process, and yet it is the beginning of the process, for it starts the cycle all over again. The next perception that emerges takes on the same energy of projection and becomes increasingly more difficult to transmute. Can you begin to see what role this cycle of creating projections plays in your own life? Hopefully you can begin to understand that all projections are created by you yourself in conjunction with the direction of your Mind's focus. When you can grasp and acknowledge this fact, you can then choose to transmute the projections into an inner creative energy.

The process of transmutation allows us to clearly perceive a problem or a situation in reality and to experience the energy that is being configured at that level. We then can allow ourselves to open into the intensity of an energy which emanates from the heightened and more expanded awareness of one's own inner-directed soul guidance. This can both change the perceptions we hold and also allow the energy to emerge into our daily lives. This allows us to interact, create, and live differently with the people and events in our world. The process of transmutation is always a creative choice which we can utilize by allowing our perceptions to shift into the fourth level of awareness, that of the heart chakra. As I have stated previously, only by means of an energetic emergence through the heart center can the shift in awareness emerge.

To achieve this we must begin at the third step of the process I have just set forth. We must first realize that there is an imbalance between our Mind-Set and our Perception of Reality and must then determine that this time we are going to choose to explore through the creative energy of transmutation. With an awareness and acceptance of the fact that all perceptions are transitory and that our condition of nonbalance is occurring in order to allow a new perception and energy to emerge, we will be guided into another level of understanding ourselves.

The first level of transmutation involves exploring the Expanded Inner Screen and Heart Chakra. By immediately choosing to expand the inner screen and open into the heart chakra, we automatically shift into balance. The perceptions which one currently holds cannot be sustained once the inner screen is expanded and the heart center energies are allowed to emerge. The next level is comprised of a process for deepening the energies and perceptions by means of focusing upon the Inner Quadrants, recalling a past experience of unity, and allowing the inner sensations of a profound love or peace to emerge. From this point one begins to Awaken the Triune Brain and it moves into new levels of inner harmony and synchronicity. Once this is attained, the shift into the heightened energies of one's inner-directed soul guidance has been activated. As these heightened, focused energies are released, they are then Harmonized throughout the Nervous System, allowing us to synthesize our physical, emotional, mental, and spiritual energies. Through the heightening of our inner-awareness, we can then explore the individual Subtle Energy Bodies as they relate to each of these levels, observing what is currently being created. We then allow the energy of the heart chakra to transform the Subtle Energy Bodies into a new level of energy at the fourth state of awareness— the unity of unconditional love. From this new level of energy, we can explore the Living Unified Self in order to perceive how we will experience, feel, and live within the new and heightened expanded state of energy. At this point we can then allow ourselves to move into the energy of Coexistence and can live from the inner soul-directed space while simultaneously living and interacting within our outer world. This process of allowing the heightened aspect of consciousness to transmute the lower energies that exist at the level of the problem constitutes the process of transmutation.

Some people view this process as a monumental undertaking and feel that accomplishing it would require entirely too much time and effort. True, any new exploration does require an initial investment of both time and inner desire. However, I have found in my own experiences that it also takes considerable time and great amounts of energy to exist in a state of being "stuck" in one's projections and states of mind confusion. If I am inwardly open to change and am willing to move in whatever direction is needed, I find that the process actually moves very quickly and naturally. I am able to experience levels of change regardless of what I am physically doing or saying at the time. It does not work, however, if there is any part of my consciousness that does not really desire the change or that feels the change must be directed in a specific way. Change always stops at the level at which I lose my willingness to move and be openly flexible.

Frances Horn has a wonderful book entitled **I Want One Thing**. The focus of the book stresses how we are often willing to change everything in our lives except for "one thing"; and it is usually due to this one thing that we find ourselves "blocked." Until we are willing to change this one thing into "whatever," nothing will work for us. We remain at a level of awareness of feeling stuck until we either go deeper into our rumination and projection, or until we can allow a more focused and heightened energy to emerge. The longer one explores living from the inner-directed soul guidance and moving into transmutation, the more easily one can awaken into the inner levels of creative potential by merely asking the changed and heightened energy to emerge. Only a heightened and focused heart energy will shift a blockage, and this is always available through the simple process of intent and asking. The inner spaces we are exploring are not created by you, me, or any other human being. They already exist within each of our hearts and merely await our opening to them. Each shift of an outer perception requires an attunement into a new inner vibration. The brain and heart chakra become the transducers for converting this vibration into the new perception of reality.

I would like you to once again do Exploration #4 on page 67, but this time it will be called EXPLORATION #8: MIND-BODY EDUCATION: INNER-DIRECTED. This time I want you to move physically only when you measure the distance which you initially are capable of reaching to the right and then to the left. Then allow yourself to move into the deeper inner expanded space we explored in the last exploration and, through your physical body quadrant (your lower right), ask to sense, feel, and allow an inner image/sense to emerge throughout the remainder of the exploration. Allow yourself to inwardly complete the sequence of movements to the right, and after you have experienced that sequence, go directly into the left sequence. DO NOT PHYSICALLY MOVE UNTIL THE END! Whenever I ask you to measure, allow only your inner movement to extend more fully in that given direction, without any outer movement. Continue the inner exploration throughout the entire exercise, and allow yourself to outwardly move again only when you measure at the end of the exploration. Allow yourself the time to tape Exploration #4. This will aid you in deepening within this exploration.

Hopefully you not only experienced a great flexibility in your movements and a number of physical changes within your body, but were able throughout the exploration to also allow an inner sense to emerge, as if you were actually physically moving. Some individuals even begin to feel dizzy or disoriented because this experience feels so real. It is real. That is why the changes occur! What you are beginning to sense are the first levels of exploration with your subtle energy bodies— in this case, your subtle physical energy body. In Chapter Ten we will continue with this deeper level of inner energy body exploration.

For now, are you at least beginning to understand that your focus does indeed create a reality for you? If you were to sit back and intellectually think about creating this type of movement through the process of your outer mind, nothing would change— the only thing you might possibly experience is a level of added stress and stiffness due to your spending so much time thinking about it happening. As you open into and are able to allow your inner self-actualizing energy to guide you, change will take place quickly and easily, and your outer mind will feel comfortable with the level of awareness. If you had difficulty with the exploration, just allow your inner screen to keep expanding and make no effort to create the images; rather, allow an emergence of an inner sense or feeling that the movement is being created within you. This is initially a subtle awareness, but once you awaken into it, it will no longer maintain a subtle identity.

I remember the first time that I experienced the depth of the inner space that is called the void. I felt awed, excited, and frightened. By focusing on the level of fear and continuing to think about what had occurred, my outer mind took charge and I moved away from the inner-awareness of feeling awed and excited, and moved into an uncomfortable feeling of uneasiness. As I tried to verbally describe what had happened and what I was then feeling, I realized how difficult it was to describe something that a few hours before had seemed very clear and real to me. The harder I tried to remember and describe what had transpired, the more directly I moved into a panic reaction state. And when I again wanted to move back into the inner spaces, my focus moved back into the fears and uneasiness related to what had previously occurred. As a result I became more cautious, which only served to increase the difficulty. I have found similar experiences to be quite common for other individuals who have explored these inner spaces. When one experiences the inner depths and then afterward persists in holding onto a perception or feeling of difficulty, it is due entirely to the outer mind and its focus, although one's intellect will swear that something else must be occurring.

Each individual describes the inner space or void within them in their own, unique way. "A part of me wants to jump right in, while another part of me feels lost and overwhelmed." "To be in the void means to be nothing." "Open ended—that is not always very exciting!" "I lose my intellect, and most of the time that does not excite me." "It is a space so peaceful and loving that I could never experience it without being this inwardly connected." "So full of feelings. I try not to think—just allow myself to feel." "I sense it as a bottomless pit." "I know something is there; it feels like an all encompassing shadow. That doesn't always feel good." "The void is a place of change, and the level of my excitement within the void varies depending upon whether I am wanting to change or not." "The void is continuous, and with that comes a whole new definition of what change really means." "It represents a continuous process of change, rather than an isolated change of just one small part." "An unformed energy, sometimes exciting, sometimes not." These reactions are typical of what individuals begin to experience as they move into the deeper inner realms of the 98% of the unknown awareness. But once they understand the safety and love that can be experienced within the void, individuals desire to live at the levels of coexistence.

Earlier I discussed the various levels of inner chatter—mental, emotional, and physical. When we reach into the level of spiritual inner chatter, we are touching what surrounds the area of the void and what constitutes our approach into and through the deepest levels of our inner space. It is impossible to allow the heightened level of creative energy to emerge into our new levels of outer awareness without first merging into the levels of our inner realms. Over the years I have realized for myself, and have seen with others, that what prevents us from allowing transformative changes is our reaction to and perception of what the void truly is. The void is a space and time within which no outer communication can occur, although something very profound and important does indeed happen. Within the void, individuals sometimes experience the feeling of falling asleep, but emerge at the end of the experience feeling great and experiencing everything around them as being very different. Once we have moved through the space of this black-out, nothing will ever be the same for us.

For me, exploring the void or black-out period has a very definite structure. In fact, it is the only area of life wherein true structure always exists. What I mean by this is that when I lack the knowledge of how to do something or when something is not working out very well and I need additional information, there is but one place where that necessary information always exists— within the deeper levels of my own inner guidance, or in that inner space of the void. To truly find change, you must tap into a part of you that already knows what is needed. Do not become lost in the outer aspect of yourself that may not be aware of the needed information. The outer mind usually constitutes one of those spaces which lacks the desired information and which actually needs the self-actualizing energy in order to create a new level of awareness. These become the levels of reeducation that cannot take place without our moving into and through the inner space of the void. Yes, there is another way of exploring the unknown awareness. You can explore it with your intellect and try to analyze it. You can intellectually arrive at a particular determination, but then another option always arises. And this will continue to be the case with any intellectual choice that you make. The more you try to think about what to do, the more you create an endless progression of available options. With each option you can see even more possibilities. So how can you know which choice to make? And yet we view utilizing the outer mind as a safe and secure process of problem solving!

As you move into your own inner guidance and allow the self-actualizing energy to emerge, a new synthesis of information begins. But this level of synthesis can only exist at a level of heightened energy, from which the process of transmutation then evolves. For this to happen, you will need to experience the period of black-out in order that the inner synthesis may begin. The black-out occurs due to the fact that the outer mind has no current level of information regarding what is occurring, so it cannot relate any direct visual experiences to your brain. As you begin to accumulate more inner experiences, you will begin to create a more direct access to your inner sensations and awarenesses. This in turn, will allow the outer mind to feel more comfortable in exploring the inner realms.

Individuals sometimes feel that the void has no boundaries. Through my own personal explorations, I know that boundaries do indeed exist, especially if we are to view this space as being safe and secure. Recall the observer effect of quantum physics that we discussed, and realize that the key word is focus. Whatever you maintain as your focus formulates the rules by which you play. This does not imply that you should fervently hope for something to exist, but rather that you should allow yourself to know and feel that it already does exist.

On several occasions during the last ten years I have spent as much as a week at a time moving and exploring within the inner spaces while maintaining an outer structure of reality. On those occasions when I moved into a space where I sensed distinct boundaries, I inwardly perceived a transparent boundary as if made of glass, which I was unable to penetrate; yet, I could see through it and know that still other levels of inner space did exist. Whenever it was time for me to move into a deeper level, I would feel and sense the boundary being removed and would feel myself being gently moved into a new inner situation or space, ready to explore a new depth and a heightened level of energy within my creative journey.

I have come to realize that there are rules to follow within one's inner space, just as there are rules that we follow in our outer awareness. These rules always evolve as we need them. The way our bodies feel and the various levels of inner silence are the feedback for us as to the accuracy of the rules from which we are creating. Do your rules allow you to experience the levels of inner space as a loving, gentle, nurturing process? What is your definition of the void and the various levels of inner space? Your answers will give you a clue as to your own feelings and the level of ease with which your inner movements will flow.

In the transformation process, as you begin to explore or change even one small part of your life, you will find that everything else also begins to change. All of life exists within a synchronization or flow that allows the pieces to fit together like a large jigsaw puzzle. If we remove or alter one piece, everything else then needs to be redefined. Our intellect usually cannot handle such an all-encompassing shift in movement. So from the perspective of the outer mind, we traditionally attempt to alter only one piece, attempting to hold everything else the same. However, this rarely is effective. Even when we explore the process of imagery and try to create the changes we think are needed, something always seems to happen that moves us into the unknown areas of our awareness. But through the inner awakening of the energies in the black-out space, a natural synthesis occurs that will "pull" us along into a new level of awareness and into a new flow of outer events. This direction may be drastically different than that upon which one had previously been focused .

As you experience the inner spaces of the void, you may not be aware of the various levels of change that I have been describing. But you will sense and move with a new level of inner sensation, feeling, and energy. As you are able to allow these energies to remain within you, they will eventually create a series of inner perceptions regarding what you should do. Or you may emerge from the void feeling very different than you did before. When you are then faced with a particular outer situation, you will be surprised at how easily and differently you react. Initially you may not even understand why you react in the way that you do, but it will feel as though this is the only choice available to you. This actually constitutes that process of reeducation that I mentioned earlier. Through the process of living differently and by remaining with a feeling of the inner creative space, you will interact with all of life from a new perspective. This is the livingness of one's post-biological phase.

The best way to move into the inner space is to allow yourself to "free-fall" each day into your inner self-actualizing pulse. Exploration #16 will later become the base exploration into this inner awareness. As I allow this space to emerge in my own personal explorations, I ask my inner guidance to naturally adjust my levels of energies to whatever level I need for that day or for whatever period of time I am exploring. Through this level of inner adjustment, I then allow the energies to remain, merge into, and become my outer awareness. In this way I am able to create with life from a totally new and exciting perspective. If I sense myself shifting into an area of reaction, I ask my inner energies to shift back into the unity and allow a new perception or understanding to emerge. Through new levels of heightened energies, I can then move into new levels of creative functioning in my lectures, writings, business decisions, sports and other physical activities, personal relationships, and all other areas of my life. I need only to choose to allow my inner-awareness to be my guide. Thus, this is not a process of false trust or hope, but rather, one of knowing. All individuals have the capability of sensing and feeling these same levels of energies as they emerge.

Remember, there are two major ways to explore the process of imagery. The first process centers around the outer mind guiding the images in a certain predetermined direction. The second process evolves from the inner-directed guidance and allows a new level of heightened inner energy to naturally emerge into a nondetermined focus. This energy is understood through a process of knowing and is experienced as various levels of inner sensations, feelings, or visual perceptions. Both processes of imagery emerge from the same brain and nervous system. The difference between the two is the level of vibrational resonation and unity within the brain. This determines the role that the brain will play in the gathering and structuring of information.

I will be guiding you through a process in the next chapter that allows you to shift the focus of your brain from its outer perspective into one of being the messenger between the inner-awareness and the new perceptions of outer reality. In this process, I will not be teaching you how to become creative or how to outwardly think differently. Rather, we will explore a process which allows the unity of the brain to emerge. From this perspective, you will be introduced to a totally new way to live and you will be able to explore new means of processing information and of channeling it into a new order of creative functioning.

CHAPTER NINE

AWAKENING YOUR
CREATIVE POTENTIAL

Before we begin EXPLORATION #9: DEEPENING THE TRIUNE BRAIN, be sure you have completed Exploration #6 a minimum of three times and Exploration #7 at least twice. This will give you the foundation necessary to deepen with the next set of explorations. In Exploration #9 we are going to work with the use of colors once again, but this time you will awaken each area of the triune brain and shift the vibration of each separate area until you have reached your synchronized inner-directed space. This will allow you to move directly into your inner-directed guidance energies in a matter of just a few minutes. Now lie down on a flat surface or sit in an upright position with your back straight.

"Close your eyes *** ask that your screen expand *** ask it to expand again *** bring your awareness into the center point of your screen *** feel this at the center of your chest, at your heart center *** *** ask the pulsation of the crystalline structure of emerald green light to emerge *** ask it to deepen at the center of your chest and to move throughout your body and beyond *** *** bring your awareness into your old brain at the two soft spots at the base of your skull *** ask to feel and experience the color emerald green at these points *** feel the emerald green color turning on, releasing its pulsation throughout the old brain and connecting into the column of energy that extends from the tip of your spine to a point about 18 inches above your head *** *** ask this to spread throughout your nervous system *** ask this to take place automatically every time you feel inwardly set with your column of energy *** *** now ask to shift into the color blue, and slowly allow it to turn on while still focusing at your old brain *** *** as you will do with each consecutive color, allow the pulsation to automatically move into the column of energy *** feel it spreading throughout your nervous system *** *** *** ask it to change into the color violet and 'turn on' *** *** *** *** ask that to change into the brilliance of white light and turn on *** *** *** *** now bring your awareness into the mid-brain *** ask your screen to expand *** feel and experience the color emerald green at the soft spots on the back of your head *** *** *** *** shift into the color blue *** *** *** *** shift into the color violet *** *** *** *** shift into the brilliance of white light *** *** *** feel that deepen throughout your column of energy *** now shift your awareness simultaneously into the right and left hemispheres *** ask that your screen expand *** ask for the pulsation of the color green *** *** *** feel that deepen into your column of energy *** shift into the color blue *** *** *** *** shift into the pulsation of violet light *** *** *** **** shift into the pulsation of the brilliance of white light *** *** *** ask that to deepen into the column of energy *** and to slowly move through your nervous system *** *** focus at the connective point *** ask your screen to expand *** feel into the pulsation of emerald green light *** *** ask this to synchronize your whole triune brain *** ask it to move through your column of energy and throughout your nervous system *** *** ask to feel into the pulsation of the color blue *** *** ask that to synchronize your whole triune brain *** ask it to move through your column of energy and throughout your nervous system *** *** feel into the pulsation of violet light *** *** ask that to synchronize your whole triune brain *** ask it to move through your column of energy and through the nervous system *** *** feel into the pulsation of the brilliance of white light *** *** ask that to slowly synchronize your whole triune brain *** ask it to move through your column of energy and nervous system *** *** ask the screen to expand *** bring your focus into the center point *** ask this to unify the potential or spiritual part of your being *** the mental part of you *** the emotional part of you *** the physical part of you *** ask this to deepen through your heart center *** *** ask this new inner rhythm to pulsate throughout and beyond your physical form *** *** bring your awareness into the body quadrant *** ask to feel and experience the palm and fingers of your right hand as being extremely warm, even hot *** *** image a feeling similar to your earlier dimmer switch turning on the heat in your right hand *** *** ask your right hand to deepen in its extreme warmth and ask that pulsation of heat in your hand to deepen *** *** your right hand is extremely warm *** bring your right hand to your face and become aware of how it feels touching your cheek *** bring your left hand to your face and become aware of the difference you feel between the touch of the right hand and the touch of the left hand *** lower your hands *** ask your screen to expand *** ask that same pulsation and feeling of heat to be present in both of your hands *** *** feel both hands and all of your fingers pulsating this warmth *** *** feel and sense both hands turning on warmer and warmer *** *** both hands and fingers are extremely warm *** bring both hands to your face and become aware of how they feel *** *** then rest your hands at your side *** feel and sense that your feet, from the bottoms of your feet up to your ankles, are being turned on *** *** feel and sense your feet absorbing and pulsating with this level of heat *** *** both feet are extremely hot *** *** sense how hot your feet are *** now feel the pulsation of heat moving from the bottoms of your feet through your toes and ankles, spreading up into the calves of both of your legs *** *** as the pulsation is moving through this area, sense that the heat is releasing a glow *** *** feel the pulsation rising into your knees *** and into your thighs *** *** feel the heat pulsating into your pelvic area and into your hip joints *** your legs, feet and hip joints are extremely warm *** now feel the pulsation spreading through your buttocks and pelvic areas *** *** rising up into your lower abdomen and lower back *** feel the heat pulsating through this area *** become aware of the difference in temperature between your upper torso and the lower portion of your body *** *** feel this heat pulsating up past the navel into the center of your chest and mid-back area *** *** pulsating heat *** ask it to move higher into the shoulders, upper back and upper chest *** continue the pulsation of heat *** *** feel this pulsation of heat move into the neck, and then through both shoulders down into the elbows, forearms, wrists, palms, and fingers of both hands *** *** feel the continual pulsation of heat deepening in these areas *** *** and then throughout your entire body from the neck down *** ask to feel a glowing of heat pulsating from your body *** *** ask to expand your screen *** move into the center point *** ask that the temperature automatically adjust throughout your entire body to a level of comfort *** feel the changes and adjustments that are taking place throughout your nervous system as you adjust to this level of comfort *** *** now ask that your body feel light *** alert and energized *** and that it maintain this profoundly relaxed physical state *** *** and ask to bring your awareness back *** ask to maintain the inner focus in your outer awareness *** become aware of your physical body *** open your eyes when you are ready *** slowly move your body *** and bring the awareness fully into your outer world."

As we have been deepening with these explorations, are you beginning to feel layers opening within you? Most individuals are surprised at how easily they feel and sense the temperature changes throughout the body. Many begin to grasp an understanding of how one's inner focus of awareness is capable of shifting every physiological structure in the body, and how the structures can be repeatedly altered by moving through an endless succession of inner levels. The body responds to internal images, regardless of whether they are being created by the outer mind or by the inner-directed soul guidance. It requires more time, however, for the outer mind's images to direct the physical body, even though it may be in a state of great stress or tension. If this were not the case, and if every inner thought or feeling upon which one's outer mind focused was then physically created, can you imagine the roller coaster ride that the physical body would continually experience? On the other hand, as you open into your inner-directed guidance, the body quickly and easily responds to internal directions and restructures into whatever is being called for at that particular time. The same process of focus is also responsible for creating the tension and stress which you experience when the outer mind takes charge and cuts off the energies of inner guidance.

This entire process involves a direct change in the vibrational level of your energy. As a result of the inner guidance which emerges with this exploration, you begin to shift naturally from the particle flow of energy into the wave flow of energy, thus allowing a new structure to emerge. As the new structure deepens within you and you emerge from the exploration, you will feel different because a new particle form of energy or inner vibration has been created. If you felt that you missed a certain part of the exploration or experienced a black-out period, this is quite normal. Remember, the important element is how you feel after you have brought your awareness back—not that you remember and do everything exactly as instructed. Our goal is to allow an inner part of you to bring forward the change, rather than having you or your outer mind doing the changing. Thus, losing the outer consciousness during this type of exploration is quite normal, and you may notice it happening with increasing frequency as we continue our exploration of the brain and nervous system.

As you begin to deepen and synchronize the triune brain, a new quality of vibration or energy emerges, which is your inner guidance. This vibration opens you into sensing an inner quiet and profound peace. As your inner sensations and feelings deepen, you will no longer feel the separateness within your brain, and you will realize that each area of the brain has the potential to change and to interact with the others as a new unified whole. With this shift in your inner-awareness and feelings you will be able to understand why your perceptions begin to change. You will find that at certain times you are able to feel and act outwardly in a manner consistent with what you are feeling and doing in your explorations. At other times it will seem that from moment to moment you are moving into diverse directions or feelings. If, for example, you are creating irrational or compulsive behavior patterns, become aware that this indicates that your old brain is not functioning from within an inner-directed rhythm. If you are experiencing massive amounts of irrational fears, this signals the fact that your mid-brain is not synchronized with the other aspects of your inner guidance. Such behaviors and feelings are the direct result of the outer mind's confusion. But all such experiences can be easily changed once you open into the inner-directed guidance of your heart and allow that rhythm to move into your triune brain structure.

Hopefully you can begin to see that the inner vibrational levels (the resonating frequency of the brain) determine how we interpret our outer perceptions and what reality we will experience. Merely thinking about being rational and nonfearful rarely changes the vibration. This is why many verbal·or cognitive forms of therapy cannot maintain the needed inner change. Behavior modification programs can create a change within the outer mind, but very seldom do they open one into an inner-directed guidance, whereby a new perception or direction in one's life can be effected. Behavior modification therapy merely allows individuals to cope with the same traditional 2% of reality with which they are already familiar, rarely opening anyone into the 98% of unknown awareness. Opening into the previously unknown area of awareness can occur only through an influx of a heightened energy or vibration that is directed by one's own inner guidance.

It is possible for another individual to balance your energies for you or to induct you into a heightened state of energy. However, if you yourself do not open into a heightened level of inner guidance and allow that to synthesize and emerge in your physical body, once you leave the group or the presence of the individual(s) that opened you into the heightened energy state, you will be unable to maintain the changes that were explored. This is what occurs in instances of faith healing. In the excitement and conviction present within a group of individuals who are opened into a very heightened energetic state, individuals may indeed shift both physical and emotional structures. But once they return to their homes and shift back into a level of energy that they themselves usually maintain, no longer being in the heightened energy state, the original illness or psychological structure may again manifest within a few days. It is not a case of never having experienced the change. It indeed did occur. But the individual failed to allow the new energy to be brought into the physical body and to then allow the physical body to change sufficiently to alter its vibration into the new awareness.

In the process of learning to transfer energy from one person to another, the entire physiological system of both of the individuals involved is drastically altered into new levels of heightened creative functioning. The new levels affect every physical, emotional, mental, and spiritual perception or organization maintained by the individual. Brain waves are altered; electrical, biochemical and hormonal levels are restructured; the nervous system, muscles, and related organs undergo drastic changes; and the composition of the blood is altered, allowing the immune system to begin functioning in a way that accesses new levels of inner healing potential. All such changes can occur without ever directly thinking or asking for them; it is necessary only to be open to one's inner intent and to believe that the changes are possible through the transfer of energy. Individuals who can perceive changes in the electromagnetic field of others notice, within seconds of when the process of energy transfer begins, that an individual's field has been brought into new levels of balance. However, these levels are very seldom sustained due to the fact that the consciousness of the individual who is receiving the energy is not focused within his/her own inner self-actualizing energy. Just as the outer awareness shifts from focus to focus, so also does the maintained level of energy shift. In many cases, even after an hour of energy transfer work, an individual may reconfigurate their consciousness back to the old perceptions within a matter of a few minutes.

The explorations in **Awaken Your Creative Potential** will allow you to open into the levels of inner change. It becomes a process of energy transfer, with the energy emanating from one's own source of inner soul guidance and shifting the outer mind, the emotions, and the body. I perceive this process as being one of the greatest gifts in our understanding of new heightened levels of creative functioning. If you are interested in exploring the energy transfer process in greater depth, I highly recommend the process Brugh Joy describes in **Joy's Way**.

Individuals who have mastered the initial levels of exploring their own self-actualizing energy sometimes feel that they are cheating when they create things from the heightened levels of energy. They feel that they themselves are not the ones really doing the creating, since at an outer focus level of energy their perceptions and capabilities are able to produce or understand things only at a certain level of awareness. At a heightened level of energy, however, they can understand and produce things that were previously not even available. This is the case in the process of igniting one's own inner healing abilities, as well as in the areas of artistic expression, writing, music, lecturing, sports, or any other area of living. Most individuals ignore the fact that moving into the inner levels of self-actualizing energies constitutes a level of accomplishment in and of itself. It takes a certain level of trust to shift into one's inner process and observe life through the energies of coexistence. And it is indeed an accomplishment to learn to open into these levels consistently, first within the process of inner exploration, and then in the process of living life.

In the total process of awakening, it eventually becomes easy to open into and bring forward an inner level of perception and heightened creative energy; but the focus of the journey must at some point shift away from focusing predominantly upon how much one can produce or upon how the end result is observed. We ultimately must focus on the process of effortlessly maintaining the inner levels of creative energies and of readily shifting back into them when we realize that we are not operating or living from the inner spaces. This, in and of itself, can provide sufficient exploration to keep one from becoming bored for quite some time. Most individuals can easily tap into the inner heightened levels of creative energy, but few have the inner trust and desire to explore a livingness and consistency of creation through their new inner-awareness.

The heightening of one's inner energy constitutes the process of transmutation, but if an individual is unable to transform into a new physical body structure, it will become difficult to maintain the energetic configuration because it always returns to the level which the body is comfortable in handling. This involves the deeper levels of body armoring which I discussed earlier. Most individuals feel comfortable enough within a heightened group energy to acknowledge new awarenesses, but most have not yet allowed the energy to restructure them into a new physical form that sustains the capability to maintain such levels of perception on their own. Once individuals experience a heightened state of energy, they have the full potential at that moment to allow the change to emerge. This is truly the goal of all of these explorations— to allow a heightened energy to emerge from your inner-directed soul guidance, and to then allow the restructuring of your outer mind and physical body so that the change can be maintained and lived in your everyday life. Without restructuring these two areas, nothing really changes, and when the old vibration returns, all of the old habitual structures also return. Your mental, emotional, physical, and spiritual selves are all energetic vibrations that structure you into a certain pattern of living. And changing that pattern becomes the process of transmutation— allowing a more heightened energy to emerge from your inner-directed soul guidance and thereby altering your pattern of living.

In this chapter you are beginning the restructuring of your energies into a new heightened vibration which will allow you to transmute whatever perception you are exploring at the moment. If you are not able to bring your new heightened energy or vibration back into the physical body, chances are that your change will not hold for more than a few hours, or several days at most. Throughout the remainder of the book I will be discussing the process of bringing the heightened energy into the physical body and thus maintaining change.

I would like to reiterate how each of the quadrants interacts with the areas of the triune brain that we are exploring. As I explained in previous chapters, the physical quadrant interacts with the old brain, the emotional quadrant with the mid-brain, the mental quadrant with the right and left hemispheres, and the potential or spiritual quadrant with the connective point of the brain. The center point of the inner screen then unifies and merges one's inner-directed guidance into the unified living state. As you awaken the separate areas of the triune brain, become aware of the new feelings and energetic sensations that are moving from within each of these inner spaces. Allow the awarenesses to expand into each one of the quadrants as you focus on the respective triune brain structures. You can very easily handle both experiences simultaneously if you have awakened into your expanded inner screen and heart chakra.

Exploration #10 explores an acceleration of this process, whereby the vibration directly opens you into the energies of your inner-directed guidance in a matter of a few minutes. Eventually you will be able to bring this process forward in about thirty seconds, provided that you have not moved completely out of your inner-directed awareness. If any level of inner-awareness or coexistence is maintained, the restructuring takes place quickly and easily. In this exploration we are going to again utilize the dimmer switch concept, but we will move much more rapidly through the emerald green, blue, and violet colors, and into the brilliance of white light, exploring the colors in each area of the triune brain structure. Open yourself to believing that this accelerated process is possible, and that it will happen for you.

You are now ready to explore EXPLORATION #10: DIRECT ACCESS INTO YOUR INNER-DIRECTED GUIDANCE. Remember, do not dwell upon the mechanics of how you are to do it and do not try to make logical sense out of what is being explored. Just ask, and open into trusting that it will happen for you, and see what transpires. This exercise is to be explored in either a sitting or a standing position, so do not lie down.

"Ask to expand your screen ** ask it to expand again ** experience the simultaneous pulsation of the crystalline structure of emerald green light moving through your chest and throughout your physical from *** bring your focus into the old brain and into the column of energy that expands through your nervous system— green * blue * violet * white *** mid-brain * green * blue * violet * white *** right and left hemispheres * green * blue * violet * white *** connective point * green * blue * violet * white *** ask to expand your screen *** center point, unify and merge into your spiritual quadrant * mental * emotional * physical *** ask to expand your screen and float within this space *** *** *** bring your awareness into the spiritual or potential quadrant *** ask the state of unconditional love to emerge *** ask that to remain and deepen *** bring your awareness to the mental quadrant and ask it to deepen *** and ask that to emerge into the emotional quadrant *** ask it to deepen *** to emerge into the physical quadrant *** to emerge and unify at the center point and to awaken your inner guidance *** ask that to move and pulsate throughout your physical form and beyond *** ask to maintain this pulsation, this inner feeling and rhythm *** ask your outer mind to restructure and connect to the inner rhythm and allow this to emerge *** and now open your eyes."

After creating with this exploration several times, ask to feel that each time you move into a quadrant and are allowing that part of your brain to shift into an inner-directed vibration, you are automatically opening into the energies of unconditional love. By combining these two aspects in one exploration, you will be able to bring forward the depth in a matter of a minute or less.

My initial exposure to explorations that moved from the focus of the heart chakra was in Brugh Joy's book, **Joy's Way**. His book contains a series of explorations that all begin with the focus of energies being within the heart chakra, which also includes the spiral meditation. EXPLORATION #11: EXPLORING THE ENER-GIES OF UNCONDITIONAL LOVE originates in part from the work of Brugh Joy, but also includes many of the ideas we are exploring within the journey of this book. We will be using the whole triune brain as we did in Exploration #10, and you will begin to under-stand the concept that one's being is comprised of an energy that is not limited by the boundaries of the skin. Near the end of many of our exploration exercises, I have asked you to allow the vibration to move beyond your physical form. This next exploration will exemplify exactly what I have meant by that statement. The exercise will move you into a deeper understanding of yourself and will allow you to awaken into the deeper feelings and sensations of unconditional love, which is the base camp for the awakening of one's heightened creative potential. Without the presence of the energetic vibration of unconditional love, we lack the fuel that is necessary to propel us into the unknown awarenesses of ourselves and to then carry those awarenesses forward into our outer reality.

Exploration #11 requires a partner. If you have been reading this book in conjunction with someone else, ask them to participate in this exploration with you. If this is not the case, but if you know someone who might be interested, it would suffice for them to move through Explorations #1 and #2 and for you to then explain to them some of the words and terms I commonly use. Thereafter, you can explore this exercise with them. (If you have no one to assist you as a partner, just sit back and move through the exploration several times on your own, and by the time we move into Exploration #13 you will never know the difference.)

Sit close enough to your partner that you can easily hold hands, but do not connect hands just yet. We are going to bring the feeling of the energy you have been experiencing within the heart chakra into the palms of your hands; and then you are going to allow the energy to move through your hands and into your partner's hands, creating a resonance between your hands and those of your partner. Then we are going to focus on the energy you have been experiencing at the center of your chest, that of the crystalline structure of emerald green light, and feel it leaving the center of the chest and moving directly into the center of your partner's chest or heart chakra. You are going to then experience your partner's heart energy moving into your heart chakra. You will thus be beginning the exploration of a heart-to-heart chakra connection of energy which is moving from your heart chakra into your partner's, and from your partner's heart chakra into yours, thus allowing a natural continual exchange of heart energy between you and your partner. Let's begin.

"Close your eyes *** ask your screen to expand *** feel that energy moving into the center of your chest *** experience the crystalline structure of emerald green light *** bring your awareness into your old brain and physical quadrant *** experience the colors 'turning on' and moving from green * to blue * violet * brilliance of white light * and experience this movement through that column of energy extending from the base of the spine to above your head *** and ask it to move through your nervous system *** focus into the mid-brain and emotional quadrant *** green * blue * violet * white *** into the right and left hemispheres and mental quadrant *** green * blue * violet * white *** focus at the connective point and potential quadrant *** green * blue * violet * white *** ask your screen to expand and deepen the focus of your awareness at the center point of your screen and at the center of your heart chakra *** *** feel into the brilliance of white light moving through the center of your chest *** ask that feeling to pulsate into your right shoulder *** down into your right elbow *** right wrist *** into the palm of your right hand *** and to move out through the palms of your right hand and fingers *** while maintaining the movement of that pulsation, simultaneously start another pulsation of brilliant white light moving and pulsating from the center of your chest into your left shoulder *** down to the left elbow *** to your left wrist *** into the palm and fingers of your left hand *** and moving on out of your left hand *** *** maintaining this focus of pulsation through both hands, reach out with your eyes closed and hold hands with your partner, feeling the pulsation of that rhythm moving from your left hand into your partner's right hand, and from your partner's left hand into your right hand *** ask that one unified pulsation and rhythm merge between your hands and your partner's *** *** ask your screen to expand *** ask that pulsation to deepen at the heart chakra *** do not ponder what I am saying—just ask that energy to now exit from the center of your heart chakra and connect into your partner's heart chakra *** *** creating an arc of energy between you and your partner *** feel this energy being released from your heart center into your partner's heart center and that it is continuing on its own *** ask it to deepen and move without you directing it *** allow yourself to move into the observer state *** feel into the words, 'I give love' *** 'I receive love' *** 'I am love manifesting' *** ask that your screen expand and deepen within your heart-to-heart, hand-to-hand exploration of unconditional love *** *** *** *** *** *** *** *** *** *** *** *** (five minutes or so) *** ask that your energy field blend with that of your partner *** going beyond the heart and hand energies *** just ask and allow it to happen, as the inner guidance knows what to do *** *** creating a field of energy with one pulsation, the two of you becoming one rhythm *** *** *** if you feel a tendency for your body to rock back and forth, allow it to do so *** honor your inner feelings *** *** ask your energies to extend beyond you as a couple and to spread throughout the room *** and if there are others in the room, blending with them; if by yourselves, expanding to the limits of the room *** *** *** now ask that energy to return to you and your partner as a couple *** separating you from the group, if there is one *** ask that you and your partner's energies separate except for the heart and hand exchange *** *** now ask your energy to return from your partner's heart chakra into your own *** ask the energies to move from your hands back into your heart chakra *** *** release your partner's hands *** ask your screen to expand *** deepen that energy within your own heart chakra *** *** and ask to maintain the inner connection and to bring it into your outer awareness ***** ***** open your eyes when you are ready ******* give your partner a hug for what you have just shared with one another."

As you blended your energies with those of your partner, did you notice how easily the two of you moved into one single inner rhythm? You were opening into the wave-form of energy which I previously discussed with you. Now you can begin to experience how it feels to connect at this level with another human being, or even with an object, and how the energy can be allowed to blend into a new rhythm shared by the two of you. Recall how easily that rhythm expanded even beyond the two of you, encompassing the entire group or flowing throughout the entire room. Recognize that the focus of your consciousness, while you are within this inner space, automatically changes the rhythm of the particular person, object, or space upon which you are focused, and that its energy also moves into a wave-form of energy. Everything that is brought into that focus subsequently becomes a part of that one pulsation or inner rhythm. This difference may only become noticeable to you at the point when you begin to separate your energies from those of your partner. This doesn't matter. What is important is that you understand how very real your energies are and realize the depth at which they exist even beyond the boundaries of your skin. Your energies move and restructure very easily, depending upon the focus of your consciousness. These energies are always there, although they usually are beyond the scope of most individuals' awareness. This is because the outer mind cannot experience any of this; it can only open to us as we move into the beginning levels of our own inner space.

Many individuals are surprised how quickly and easily they feel the energy pulsating through them and how natural it feels to be aware of it moving through them. Occasionally after an experience like this, the outer mind begins to question what has occurred. I have known individuals to share in a seminar what they have experienced during an exploration, but later in the week call me to say that nothing is happening. When I remind them of what they shared in the previous week's class, they have no recollection of sharing or feeling any of it. When I give them a tape recording containing their own voice sharing their experiences with the group, they are shocked. But as they allow the outer mind to release their current feelings, they begin to remember what they had shared earlier. This phenomenon is called state-bound consciousness. One can only recall or remember things that are bound in the energies of the focus within which they were initially created. Thus, when the energies become more outer mind focused, it is as though the earlier inner experiences never occurred. By listening to the tape and hearing themselves talking about their earlier explorations, individuals open back into the energies of the experience and can thus allow themselves to recall what transpired. This same thing happens at all levels of awareness, ranging from those of the most deeply focused inner states to those of the high levels of stress and outer mind perception.

Many people feel a deep warmth beginning to ignite within them when they move into the inner spaces, especially as they move into the wave-form of energy. As the wave-form of energy emerges, the vibration is quickened and the warmth begins to undulate. This warmth is different, however, than the feeling of warmth that results from an outer heat blowing on you. This compares more to the analogy of a potato in a microwave oven, as it heats and is cooked from the inside out. What happens is that you are bringing the quickening vibration of the wave-form of energy into your particle form of energy, which begins automatically to transform everything it touches and becomes aware of, regardless of whether that awareness exists outside of you or within you. In order to observe the perceptions that you are feeling, your awareness must convert to a wave-form of energy, and this is what causes you to feel the inner heat. You are actually beginning to sense and feel the first stages of what can be achieved when the particle mass of the brain shifts into a synchronized wave-form and takes on the role of messenger.

Without experiencing such an inner energetic shift, you would have no concept of what I am describing or of what other people generally experience during this exploration process. The mind contained within the brain at its basic level of awareness cannot experience any of this, thus explaining why many individuals refuse to believe that the inner states of awareness are real. And in a sense, they are correct; to them, personally, the inner levels of awareness are not real. However, this does not mean that they are not real to those who have directly experienced the shifting of their consciousness into an inner-directed space.

The spaces that we are exploring are attainable only when the consciousness is focused from the heart chakra. If the consciousness is focused out of some other chakra, a different set of experiences will emerge. This can provide a viable feedback system, for when you are allowing yourself to be inner-directed through your heart you will be experiencing the expansive feelings of unconditional love throughout your being. As you have discovered by merely experiencing the previous exploration, the feeling state of unconditional love is not something that the outer mind can manufacture or pretend exists. Either it is present, and you are focused from your inner-awareness through the heart, or it is not.

Thus you possess a natural safeguard system to provide you feedback as to the level and quality of your inner information. Of course, this feedback can only be effective if you choose to allow it to be present in the first place and if you learn to cease whatever it is you are creating at times when it is not present.

Before we can continue and eventually move into deeper explorations, we must first explore the subtle energy bodies. Although the next chapter deals specifically with this subject, I need to introduce the basic concept and conduct a "mini" exploration at this point so that your inner-awareness can deepen. Very few of us are consciously aware of our physical body until a level of discomfort or pain begins to emerge. You may be inclined to contradict this statement, reasoning that you know very well when you are hungry or when you are experiencing sexual feelings. I would question even this, since most individuals rarely eat when they are hungry, choosing instead to eat based upon an outer time schedule that neglects any level of inner-awareness. And when we begin to look clearly at our sexual energy, we realize that it rarely has anything to do with true sexual needs that are shared in a loving way. Usually other types of feelings, desires, and motivations enter into play. Most individuals operate from one extreme or the other; they either use the physical acting out of their sexual feelings as a distraction from what they should be doing with their lives or they spend their time and energy wishing they had someone with whom they could be sexually involved, and since they don't have, they mope around and feel continually depressed. Most sexual feelings are actually misdirected energies that are wanting to be channeled into other aspects of life. But that could become another book in and of itself!

For now, let's assume that most human beings are not basically aware of their physical bodies and are even much less aware of the fact that they also have a series of subtle energy bodies which directly influence what the physical body can or cannot create. One's emotional energy, for example, also contains a subtle body of energy that interacts with the physical energy, not to mention the subtle energy bodies for the mental self, the potential or spiritual self, and for the synthesis of the unified living self that combines the other four energies into what I ultimately view as the state of being human. In Chapter 10 we will explore this in greater detail so that you'll know through your own explorations that these energy bodies are just as real as what you perceive your physical body as being. For purposes of our current discussion, and in order that you may begin to understand and experience this concept for yourself, we are going to do a "mini" exploration involving only the physical energy body.

During the course of the exercise I will be describing certain physical movements, and I will then want you to slowly move your physical form through those particular movements. Next I will ask you to explore your physical energy body by utilizing that exact same movement, but without any actual physical body movement. We will then rotate back and forth between the physical body movement and the energy body movement. As you will recall, in Explorations #4 and #8 many individuals experienced the energy body moving while they were exploring the inner-directed imagery of hand movement. In the present exploration we will be deepening this focus within our inner-directed guidance and will be allowing it to actually direct the movement. This will become more obvious to you as we move into the exploration. So let's prepare to begin EXPLORATION #12: ENERGY BODY AWARENESS: PHYSICAL LEVEL. You should be sitting for this exploration.

"Close your eyes *** and move yourself into the full inner space within the heart chakra and the triune brain *** allow yourself a minute to move into your inner-awareness *** *** *** ask your screen to expand again *** take your physical right arm and hand and make an infinity sign in the air in front of you *** become aware of how your whole body moves, although you are making the sign only with your arm and hand *** notice how everything moves when you do this *** now put your physical arm and hand down *** bring your inner-awareness into your physical quadrant *** ask your energy body right hand to rise up in front of you *** ask it to make that same type of infinity movement *** allow yourself to feel the same areas of the body moving as you did before, but this time through the movement of your physical energy body *** ask to expand the screen and maintain your awareness within the physical quadrant *** you should begin to feel a full sensation of the physical body moving *** *** now perform the same movement with your physical right hand, but somewhat more slowly *** bring your physical hand down, and now repeat the motion with your physical energy body, using the same slow movement *** *** ask the right hand energy form to enter back into your physical right hand *** now with your left arm and hand go through the same movement *** become aware of how the whole body moves with this *** rest your physical left arm and hand, and ask your physical energy body arm and hand to perform the same whole body movement of the infinity sign *** let your energy body arm and hand reenter your physical form *** raise both of your physical arms and hands making an infinity sign, and become aware of how that feels throughout your whole body *** lower the physical, and now with your physical energy body arms and hands perform the same movements *** *** lower your energy body arms and hands

*** raise both physical arms above your head, and become aware of how this feels *** lower both physical arms *** raise both physical arms *** now as you lower your physical arms, ask your energy body arms to rise at the same time *** passing one another at midpoint *** lower the energy body arms and raise the physical arms *** become aware of how this feels *** lower the physical arms and raise the energy body arms *** now lower the energy body arms, allowing them to reenter into the physical, and become aware of how this feels *** *** now ask your physical energy body to step outside of you *** as if you were getting up *** ask your energy body to sit back down inside of you *** some people experience a body twitch or jerk as the energy body reenters *** ask your energy body to again stand up in front of you *** become aware of how this feels *** ask your energy body to turn around in a small circle in front of you *** now have the energy body come back and sit down inside of you *** ask your screen to expand *** become aware of how your body feels *** then open your eyes."

Individuals are always amazed at how real the physical energy body feels to them. Those individuals who regularly create very strong feelings with imagery, especially in the areas of sports, physical therapy, or body restructuring, experience such feelings very naturally because of having previously touched into an inner sense of their physical energy form. In the next chapter we will continue exploring not only the physical energy body, but also the emotional energy body, mental energy body, spiritual energy body and the living energy body. Each one of these will produce a different set of feelings and sensations, and some will inherently create more movement than others. When individuals are capable of experiencing equally full, clear feelings and sensations with all of their energy bodies, change can take place very easily. This is especially obvious in the area of sports. When an individual has difficulty performing a specific movement or position in some sport, it is most always an indication that a clear energy body movement does not exist. Even though the sport may be physical, and the physical energy body may be very clear, the block can be occurring at one of the other levels. We truly experience a mastery of life when there is a clarity within all of our energy bodies.

The exploration with the energy bodies awakens many neurological connections and, once achieved through a certain level of inner mastery, can produce the same or even stronger wave patterns and electrochemical activities within the brain as does the physical movement itself. The stronger the inner physiological changes become through the energy body exploration, the easier and more complete the actual movement will be in outer life. Recall how clear your awareness felt as a result of the actual physical movements of your entire body and also how clear it felt with the energy body movement of your whole body. The energy body awareness should be as clear, and sometimes will be even clearer, than is your actual physical awareness. In the next chapter you will become aware of the fact that your energy body is representative of what you really feel and sense inside. You cannot lie to yourself. You can pretend with your outer mind that something can change, or you can actually physically perform something, but your energy body will always represent the real status of what is possible at any given time. Our basic purpose then is to allow the energy body to become fluid in its movement or process of change, which will then allow us to easily carry out and achieve our desired outer goals.

We are now ready for EXPLORATION #13: EXPERIENCING UNCONDITIONAL LOVE THROUGH THE ENERGIES OF OUR INNER GUIDANCE. This exploration is similar to number ten, the one in which you shared the heart-to-heart energies with another person. This time, however, you will be sharing and experiencing the energies moving between yourself and your energy body. We are going to be exploring the potential or spiritual energy body and will be focused within the potential quadrant. Once you bring forward your potential energy body, you will physically connect with the energy body through your hands and heart. You will have a feeling similar to, if not stronger than, what you experienced in the similar exchange of energy with your partner.

Utilizing this process becomes an effective means of developing a true inner sense of love and peace within yourself. Such an inner love and peace constitutes the essence of true self love. It is not a love reflected in the inflation of one's ego, but rather a true change in allowing oneself to carry and emanate a presence of inner love. This is not loving what you will become or what you have accomplished; unconditional love is the essence of energy that loves you for being who you are right now. It means ultimately experiencing a love for every thought, feeling, behavior, action, and physical part of you that comprises your being. It means not continually searching for another individual to bring this love forward or to be convincing you that you are worthwhile as a human being. You will always have yourself, no matter where you are or what you are doing!

The exploration we are about to do will begin to bring you more fully into the heightened energy we have already been exploring, and it will eventually allow a change within the energy body that will permit you to carry out your outer goals. For this exploration you should be in a sitting position, so just make yourself comfortable. If you need back and/or head support, find a place that will provide this so that you will not need to be shifting or moving your physical body during the exploration.

"Close your eyes *** ask that your inner screen expand *** ask to bring your awareness into the center of your chest *** *** bring your focus into the old brain and into the column of energy that expands through your nervous system— green * blue * violet * white *** mid-brain * green * blue * violet * white *** right and left hemispheres * green * blue * violet * white *** connective point * green * blue * violet * white *** ask to expand your screen *** center point, unify and merge into your spiritual quadrant * mental * emotional * physical *** ask to expand your screen and float within this space *** *** *** bring your awareness into the spiritual or potential quadrant *** ask the state of unconditional love to emerge *** ask that to remain and deepen *** bring your awareness to the mental quadrant and ask it to deepen *** and ask that to emerge into the emotional quadrant *** ask it to deepen *** to emerge into the physical quadrant *** to emerge and unify at the center point and to awaken your inner guidance *** ask to deepen at the center point of your chest into the brilliance of white light, and feel it expanding through and beyond your physical form *** *** bring your awareness into your potential and spiritual quadrant, the upper right *** ask your potential energy body to step outside of you and to sit down in front of you *** activate your heart energy into the palms of your hands *** ask your potential energy body hands to hold your physical hands, similar to what you did in the earlier exploration *** begin the exchange of energy between your physical hands and your potential energy body hands *** ask that a stream of energy flow from the center of your chest, your heart chakra, into your potential energy body chest *** feel the same connection of energy coming back to you from your potential energy body *** and allow the hand-to-hand, heart-to-heart con-nection to deepen between you and your potential energy body self *** *** feel that exchange of unconditional love between you and your energy body self *** feel the words, 'I give love' *** 'I receive love' *** 'I am love manifesting' *** ask it to deepen *** *** *** ask your screen to expand *** *** *** *** *** *** *** *** *** now ask the potential energy body to reenter your physical form through your chest or heart center *** ask it to gently merge with your physical form until you feel the completion within you *** *** sense and know what it feels like to be loved unconditionally by YOU, by that inner-directed guidance *** *** ask the awareness to deepen and to spread throughout your heart, your physical form, and beyond *** *** ask that you feel light, energized, and complete within your inner self *** ask that connection to remain within you *** allow it to emerge into your outer awareness *** open your eyes when you are ready."

As you feel the exchange and inner movement during this exploration, you will begin to understand what self-love is and what it really means to feel unconditional love from someone else. When someone loves you unconditionally, this is how it will feel; and when you love someone else unconditionally, you will feel the same love for them regardless of their actions and behaviors. Neither words nor the outer mind can create this heightened energy or any comparable experience. Saying "I accept you" to someone just does not have or create the same feeling. Most individuals find it is easier to allow the exchange of unconditional love with someone else than with themselves. We can love virtually anyone else, and can forgive or rationalize any of their behaviors, but seldom do we allow this same compassion for ourselves. And we are even less apt to "love ourselves" with an unconditional level of energy. But until we open to our inner self from the depths of this unconditional energy, regardless of what we may say or do, we will never feel complete.

I personally believe that these are the beginning levels of feelings that are ready to open in all of us between approximately the age of fifteen and eighteen, but that are never actualized. This accounts for that inner sensing of something wonderful being about to occur that never actually materializes. Thus our search for love has and does continue throughout our lives, and we seldom feel complete, regardless of how many relationships we experience. This is because anything outside of us will seem superficial in comparison to what inherently exists within our hearts. This level of energy, the energy of unconditional love, becomes the base camp out of which all relationships are formed—romantic, work, social, friendships, and all others. However, allowing oneself to create from the inner space and inner direction is one of the most difficult tasks that any human being faces; and yet, without this inner movement, we just will not change as we progress through life.

Many individuals, as they move into the heightened states of energies, begin to fear that their egos or personalities are going to be destroyed or annihilated. Many books dictate that a process of annihilation of the ego is necessary in order to experience one's inner-directed soul guidance. In my own journey, and from what I have observed with others, the ego is never destroyed. What transpires is that the ego shifts into a new awareness of itself. I consider the ego to be that part of one's personality which is focused within the outer world and which is reflected in the structures of the physical body. The goal in Transformational

Psychology is not to destroy the outer mind, but rather to restructure and reeducate the outer mind to reflect a different fluidity in the physical body. This emerges through the direct inner guidance of one's own soul energies. Through this process, the ego is in a constant state of change, thereby allowing us to continually bring forward into the outer world a new level of self. This level of self is therefore in a state of continual change and will never be complete. Even when the self reaches what we might term as being the highest level of mastery, there are always other awarenesses and levels of understanding that exist within yet deeper parts of one's self that will be emerging. Within this basic framework, the exploration of life can be exciting and fun as we allow the new aspects of self to emerge and begin to experience how differently we can perceive our outer reality.

The powerful energy of unconditional love that you began to feel in Explorations #11 and #13 is the force that will allow change or transformation in your life. Anything less than this level of energy, or feeling state of unconditional love, will not allow the heightened energy to fully transmute the lower energy of the problem. With anything less, you will remain stuck within some level of the intellect or of a primitive human emotion, and the full impact of change will not be present. Without bringing forward the energy or feelings that we explored in Exploration #13 your new perceptions of change will not be complete. Think back through your life and try to ascertain how many times you have allowed this type of unified energy to emerge as a vital element of change. Sometimes individuals experience a feeling of being overwhelmed when they move into directly experiencing this heightened energy. They begin to question how much deeper they can possibly blend with their energy or with the energy of another person. Remember that I earlier talked about the "pull" and about how you should allow the energy itself to take you or pull you through the vibration until you reach the inner state of being complete. What typically happens is that we succumb to an automatic tendency to stop and we thus limit the experience, rather than moving through it and allowing the synthesis to be completed naturally. Thus, we actually stop the experience because we feel overwhelmed.

As mentioned before, when I am transferring energy in a group or am working with someone on a one-to-one basis, I can see an individual's energy field become unified within the first few seconds of the energetic connection. I often, however, soon experience their energies reconfigurating right back to the previous levels. Sometimes this configuration stops at the previous level, or, if the person has become frightened by what they felt, it may even reconfigurate back to a lesser state of vibration than what they had initially exhibited. As I maintain an energetic connection, the individual's energy will continue to move back and forth until they allow their inner-awareness to become comfortable with whatever the new unified state of balance is that they have attained. This continues until either they allow an inner direction to stabilize the energy at that unified state or until they stop it themselves at a given level and choose not to continue. If they allow the inner aspect of self to be the regulator, tears often begin to spill from their eyes and they experience a profound inner state of love. This brings us to what we will next be exploring—learning to be able to stay and live at the new level of unconditional love, or at the unified energetic state of being. This allows the higher energies of transformation to emerge that permit change to occur naturally.

In the summer of 1987, just prior to starting the present edition of this book, I began to experience another major shift in my own awakening energies. I was in California conducting a series of explorations, and I was to begin a two day seminar the next morning. All day I had had an inner sense of the very familiar feeling that something wonderful was once again about to emerge from within me. My perceptions of my life at that time and of the individuals with whom I was connecting continually brought forth tears, representing some of the most powerful feelings I had ever encountered. My outer mind convinced me that what I was feeling was merely related to the present trip, and that I was just preparing myself for the weekend's explorations. At dinner, however, I began to shift into a much more heightened energy and I realized that my awareness was changing. As the energy increased, my inner-directed soul guidance kept repeating to me, "You have a choice—this can shift easily and be completed by morning, or it can take days or even weeks for completion, and it will be necessary to cancel the remainder of your trip. The choice is yours." I remember that all through dinner and during the walk about town on the way back to our hotel, I kept refocusing and allowing myself to go deeper and deeper into the "pull" of the newly awakening energies. I continued to receive inner-direction as to how I could move through the present inner awakening shift without difficulty, so long as I continued to choose the path of no drama. Throughout the next several hours I experienced new dimensions of my own inner explorations and a new set of wonderful experiences. At around one o'clock in the morning the shift was finally complete, and I at last fell asleep.

Previously, a change such as this one would have taken me weeks to move through and complete, and I would have experienced at least some bodily and psychological discomfort. However, the next morning I felt wonderful, and until I began my two day seminar I actually questioned whether anything had truly changed. My wife and several friends from Fort Wayne were with me, and over the next two days there emerged a totally new synthesis of information, startling new perceptions, and a level of energy that neither they nor I had ever before experienced. The seminar participants moved personally into new directions and vistas, and my friends also experienced a totally new dimension in the level of energy and information that was emerging. All of this transpired without any prior thinking on my part and without any attempt to create something new through my outer mind. The heightened energies of the previous night had opened me into a new synthesis and a new level of understanding, and through this understanding emerged an exciting two days of previously non-experienced insights, feelings, and energies. I, like everyone else, was wondering what might emerge next!

I am sharing this with you so that you can begin to realize that the process of transmutation occurs as one moves into a state of heightened energy, and does not take place merely as a result of exploring problems or of moving through a crisis situation. For transmutation to evolve one opens to allow an inner change to occur that will facilitate a new awareness of one's self, thus eliminating having to spend a great amount of outer time trying to do or create the change. To achieve these heightened states of awareness, a new level of human feelings called unconditional love needs to be present.

In my university classes, where I work with the first levels of this process, I explore the development of an inner self-confidence and how to apply this in a job interview or to one's present employment situation. When students begin the subtle energy body explorations and allow themselves to change due to the inner presence of self-love, their job interviews and other job related situations change drastically. In the subsequent interview process many of the students received feedback relating to their level of self-confidence. Employers were surprised to be interviewing prospective employees who felt so good about themselves, and the students were equally surprised by the fact that throughout the interview they experienced very little, if any, of their typical inner chatter or stress. The students had not spent any time trying to psyche themselves up for the interview; rather, as they had deepened within the energy body explorations, a new level of inner confidence had emerged very naturally. Most individuals related that they possessed similar confidence and self-assurance when presenting speeches and writing reports in other classes. As they began to acknowledge and accept the new aspect that was emerging within them, it also became very natural to acknowledge and verbalize the things they were feeling. They were not being pretentious; in reality, they were expressing natural feelings and perceptions that were emerging from within their being.

Many of the individuals who did ultimately secure jobs were told by the employers that they had sensed their confidence and felt that they would be able to handle any new situation that might arise. The employees had not stated that their confidence was based upon past accomplishments; they had simply felt confident in knowing what they could do now and/or in the future. This confidence flows from that knowing part of us that emerges in the now moment and assures us that we will move with whatever needs to happen. Thinking cannot create this type of confidence. These students had learned to distinguish when they were operating from within their inner space and when they were operating from their outer mind. Thus it was easy for them to allow the inner focus to once again emerge if they slipped into an outer mind focus. They were pleasantly surprised at how easily they could shift; they needed to do nothing more than make the choice to allow the change to emerge. This is a part of the process of ego shifting. It allows a new aspect of self to emerge into one's physical form, which will in turn change the outer mind and the ways one interacts and creates within the outer world.

Before we move into EXPLORATION #15: AWAKENING YOUR CREATIVE POTENTIAL, I would like to develop a synthesis of the ideas that originate in child development, brain physiology, yogic psychology, physics, Eastern philosophy and the expanded screen and quadrants. This synthesis will be a model of human development that will aid in understanding how the various forms of science and mysticism do indeed begin to overlap and integrate into an understanding of man as a human energy system. Understanding human development based upon the concept of man being a human energy system summarizes the last eight years of my own odyssey. These ideas are not merely theoretically based; they also incorporate my own journey of development and the development that I have perceived in thousands of other human beings.

In previous chapters I began to lay a foundation by first looking at the structures of the triune brain, the evolutionary history of the brain, and how I see this relating to the various quadrants and expanded inner screen. We also have explored the shifting nature of the brain and its role as a transducer of energy that alters one's perceptions of reality. We have discussed and explored how, through an inner shift, we move into a wave-form of energy that allows us to experience various perceptions, feelings, and sensations within the physical, emotional, mental, spiritual, and a unified living self. In the remaining section of this chapter we will explore the deepening aspects of adult development, the chakra or energy centers and how they relate to the various aspects of the triune brain and inner quadrants, and how to focus on the chakras in order to deepen into one's inner creative potential. The following chapter will discuss the various subtle energy bodies, yogic psychology, and layers of energy; how I perceive the physicist Bohm's conceptualization of the various orders of energy through the holomovement; and how we move through a subtle part of this journey each time we shift into the energies of our inner-directed guidance.

The purpose of my own exploration has been to develop an understanding of man as a human energy system and to explore a synthesis of human development that incorporates all aspects of living. This includes the 2% of traditional outer reality as well as the additional 98% comprised of exploring man's unknown awareness, and any other realms relating to who we are and what reality truly is. My personal journey has incorporated the biological, psychological, and spiritual natures of myself and others as human beings. Through this journey I have awakened into the next level of inner human exploration which Joseph Pearce calls our post-biological phase. As I stated previously, most human beings are actually ready to awaken into their inner journey by about the age of eighteen, but due to man's shortsightedness in understanding the importance of one's inner nature, few individuals awaken into the journey without first creating a major transformative crisis in their lives. Yes, we can begin to awaken our creative potential through the crisis process of transformation. But as a species, we can no longer afford the time lost in passively waiting and creating out of levels of personal or global crisis in order to bring about our natural levels of transformative change.

The model of development formulated in this book explores the awakening of the inner creative energy (one's self-actualizing force) and looks at how the various forms of science and mysticism synthesize this information into a working model. The explorations in this book guide one in the practical ways of exploring inner silence and the awakening that naturally occurs as our inner creative potential, without the need of crisis or of what I term the reactive pathway. However, even though reactive energies may be the initial stimulant for an awakening, one can still choose a creative path for deepening the odyssey into the inner-directed energies of one's soul. Through this odyssey, life becomes the living aspect of one's inner creative expression. We no longer need to search for an outer expression of creative energy, nor do we need to believe that an outside source or other medium through which to channel our creative expression is necessary.

Artists in the various creative fields can sometimes touch the inner creative power through their artistic medium, but they may still be unable to bring the same levels of perception and action into their personal lives. This same process is also evident in the area of sports. On the playing field, individuals consistently exhibit levels of performance and potential that stretch them even as players, but their personal lives may resemble a roller coaster. In the areas of science, all of those who develop major scientific breakthroughs are individuals who have awakened into some level of their inner energies; but how are they functioning in those areas of life that are not related to their professional field? As increasing numbers of individuals move into exploring the inner realms, new heights of performance will begin to become the norm or standard form of operation. Individuals will find it increasingly difficult to continue performing at one level in their chosen professional field of exploration and at another level in their personal lives. We actually are meant to first live from the inner levels of creative energies within our personal lives, and to then move this into the explorations within our chosen field. Very few individuals, however, choose this form of exploration. But if meaningful changes are to take place in the way we live and interact within our world, this process must become a top priority in the years to come.

When we begin to live through our creative expression, we will be creating from an inner level of peace and presence. Thus, when we feel inwardly moved to channel the creative energy through outer creative acts, the avenues of expression will automatically emerge. I believe that all jobs, relationships, sports, activities, and literally all other outer events and situations can be brought forward from the inner creative energy. In this model of development, individuals will likely first open into the inner creative energies in a chosen field of exploration— possibly in art, music, science, or sports. As the inner capabilities begin to develop, time will also be spent incorporating this into their personal lives. As this deepens within their personalities, they will then see new avenues opening in their professional lives, and the dance will thus continue, back and forth. In this way, no one aspect of life is either overly developed or sacrificed in order to develop one's level of inner purpose.

I have experienced in my own journey that my levels of information in teaching and my sharing of the inner spaces with groups can move only to a certain point before I must create a focus for also bringing that same level of energy into my personal life and relationships. This automatically opens my teaching into yet other new levels of understanding and energetic structures. Likewise, the dance continually flows through my personal relationship with myself, my relationship with my wife and friends, and then with my personal work and the development of others in their work. Since my exploration had never included conferences that extended over periods of several weeks, I was initially forced to develop an awareness of everything I needed in order to live at any given moment, and this was necessarily based upon my own level of interacting, teaching, and exploring with others. My life today is comprised of a continuous dance between all spaces of life, with no distinct separation between personal, professional, or social time. This is achieved by listening to my own inner guidance and knowing when to shift gears, regardless of whether that means taking several weeks off or working many "extra weeks" in a particular month. If I remain true to the flow of the inner dance, I always find sufficient energy and time to accomplish the needed tasks. Yet, few individuals even realize that such potential exists. Many sense that something is missing in their lives, but they have no clue as to how to release the deeper inner feelings or even that this is what is needed. Since I have experienced an awakening and the ensuing dance in my own life, and since I have observed the same awakening and dance in the lives of others, it affords me the belief and optimism that over the next twenty-five years human beings can and will evolve into a living system of this next exploration of human potential.

The next level in our evolutionary cycle is not dependent upon any major outer physical or biological changes in the species. Rather, its sole focus will be on the level of consciousness that is evolving in each human being and on the understanding of how consciousness is very much interwoven with the interpretation and creation of reality. We will no longer see ourselves as isolated from our outer environment, for we are the co-creators of our perceptions of outer reality.

I do not mean that we can choose randomly what and how we will create and interact with life. Exploring the process of co-creation means that we have a responsibility to become aware of the inner understanding that is inherently locked within each of us as human beings. When the inner energy is released, we then awaken the inner blueprint for our outer potential. Until we awaken to the inner energy of our development, we will continue to move through life just like everyone else—feeling, thinking, and struggling with the questions of what life is really all about. But as we awaken, we soon find answers to these questions. The role we play within the purpose of co-creation necessitates that we learn how to open into and to follow our inner blueprint in creating an outer world or reality that runs parallel to the inner world—the reality of the heart. To believe that we can randomly choose to create as our outer mind dictates and still find an inner peace and creative energy, is a misconception. Our choice is whether we will open and create from an inner creative potential, allowing the inner peace and movement that we truly inwardly desire, or whether we will create from a reactive energy and explore life through that process. I perceive human beings as truly having choices. Even for myself, the outer mind sometimes gets in the way and I mistakenly think that I am choosing my inner creative path, not understanding the subtleties of the shift that has occurred. As one's awakening energies increase, it becomes more obvious as to what choices truly do exist, and for me this means that I must keep choosing, to the best of my ability, my own inner-directed soul path.

I would like to undertake a brief discussion and exploration of how I perceive the whole triune brain and its interaction with the chakras or energy centers of the body. In the next chapter I will then integrate this with the triune brain and the expanded inner screen, yogic psychology of energy bodies, and Bohm's exploration of the various orders of energy. It is important that you sense and feel your energy connections. This enables you to consciously know that the inner energetic explorations you undertake actually do change the physical brain, and subsequently, as you already have explored, that the physical brain does change one's body and outer perceptions.

For our purposes here the terms "chakras" and "energy centers" are synonymous. Although many books describe chakras as being specific places on the physical body, the chakras are actually an opening of energies within one's electromagnetic field that exist throughout the layers of the subtle energy bodies. What we experience as our physical body and our physical world is the direct result of the vibrational quality of these specific energy centers. As the energy centers shift in vibration, we experience varying levels of sensations, feelings, perceptions, and bodily changes.

As we explore the old brain, together with the brain stem and the spinal column, we are exploring the chakras of the root and lower abdominal (or sexual) center. The root center is located at the very tip of the spine and the energy moves outward from the body at a forty-five degree angle. The lower abdominal or sexual center is located over the pubic bone. The mid-brain connects with the energy centers of the solar plexus, the spleen, and the heart. The solar plexus is located at a point about one to two inches above the navel. The spleen is at the base of the rib cage on the left side of the chest. The heart chakra, as we have been exploring, is located at the center of the chest, about one inch above the point where the ribs are joined together. The neocortex, the right and left hemispheres of the brain, interact with the throat chakra and the third eye. The throat center is located at the junction above the collarbones and is connected into the right hemisphere of the brain; the left hemisphere is connected with the third eye, which is located above the eyebrows at the center of the forehead. The crown chakra, located at the top of the skull, is connected with the area of the brain known as the corpus callosum, a point of energy focus located at the hairline, just above the forehead in the center of the head. The final energy center is explored when we are focused at the center point of the expanded inner screen. This connects with what is called the transpersonal point, which is a ball of energy located 18 to 24 inches above the top of the head. As we explore the whole triune brain, we are automatically shifting each of the specific energy centers into a changed vibrational frequency, and as we explore each of the individual chakras, we are likewise shifting the frequency of the whole triune brain as it exists as a unified entity.

When individuals first begin to directly explore the chakras or energy centers, it is difficult for them to sense the subtle awarenesses. Through my personal explorations of these connections over the course of the last five years, I have found that once the whole triune brain is unified and brought under the direction of the heart chakra, it is quite easy to experience the subtle aspects of the energies and the awarenesses that emerge. As was evidenced in our earlier explorations, the brain is a natural crystalline structure or transducer of higher energy, and once the brain is unified and focused, one's awareness evolves naturally into awakening the inner sensations of the subtle energy bodies. This constitutes the deepening of the interplay between the physical body, the physiological processes, and the chakras or energy centers, allowing us to experience ourselves as an interactive human energy system.

Some individuals become adept at scanning the various energy centers of other people and by so doing can learn a great deal about the other person's psychological and emotional functioning. An energy center that is balanced produces a vibration and feeling that is different than what is experienced when the individual is blocked, anxious, or feeling withdrawn. It is generally difficult to differentiate the exact emotion or feeling an individual is experiencing, but the average person can determine when an individual is balanced and moving from within an inner-directed guidance in contrast to when an individual is blocking or denying feelings. The deep and subtle movements of energy can be sensed or visually perceived, and this can provide a great deal of information about what is currently happening for another individual at a given moment in time.

I was very startled by my own levels of ease and accuracy in sensing these deeper psychological patterns with individuals as I began to explore the process in late 1982. Often the perceptions I gained as a result of exploring the energies were actually more accurate than what the individual was sharing with me verbally. This exemplifies the profound and direct effect that our consciousness has upon our psychological and physical functioning as human beings. Today, I rarely need to visually or tactically scan one's energy centers to understand these deeper dynamics. The process has become an automatic process of inner-directed guidance that allows me to move into an inner space of <u>knowing</u> whatever it is that I need to be experiencing and bringing that forward for each individual with whom I interact.

As we begin to explore the deeper feeling states of unconditional love and learn to keep all of our energy centers moving under the direction of the heart chakra, we are truly experiencing and living from a unified state. When we are focused from the heart, our feelings and perceptions are totally changed, and the whole triune brain functions in a different manner. The deeper the unified state of the whole triune brain, the more open one becomes to the subtle awarenesses.

Let us now move into EXPLORATION #14: EXPLORING THE BRAIN/CHAKRA CONNECTION, where we will directly experience the interplay I have been describing. Lie down and relax as we prepare to move into the exploration.

"Close your eyes *** ask your screen to expand *** bring your awareness into your heart center *** *** allow your awareness to shift into your old brain *** focus with the color emerald green *** become aware of your two lower energy centers, at the root and in the lower abdominal area above the pubic bone *** *** continuing with your focus in the old brain, move with the color blue *** *** with the color violet *** *** notice what is occurring in these two energy centers *** also become aware of how the other centers are subtly changing, although not with the same intensity as the first two *** sense into the brilliance of white light *** *** notice the direct link between the two lower centers and the old brain *** *** now bring your awareness into the mid-brain, and become aware of the solar plexus a few inches above your navel, the spleen below the rib cage on the left side, and the heart center at the center of your chest *** focus on the color green and become aware of what happens in these energy centers *** *** the color blue *** *** notice how these centers feel heightened while the other centers are more subtle *** the color violet *** *** the brilliance of white light *** notice what is happening and what this feels like *** *** shift your awareness into your right brain hemisphere and notice the connection at the throat center *** the color emerald green *** **** blue *** *** violet *** *** the brilliance of white light *** notice the changes in the throat chakra *** *** shift into the left hemisphere and focus on the third eye above and between the eyebrows *** the emerald green color *** *** notice what begins to occur within the third eye *** *** blue *** *** violet *** *** the brilliance of white light *** *** focus at the point of the corpus callosum at the hairline, the halfway point between the crown and third eye *** focus on the emerald green color *** notice what begins to happen at the crown chakra at the top of the head *** blue *** *** violet *** *** the brilliance of white light *** *** ask to bring your point of focus to the center of your expanded inner screen *** ask it to expand *** become aware of what you experience at the center of your chest and at the transpersonal point located approximately 18 inches above your head *** focus on emerald green *** *** blue *** *** violet *** *** the brilliance of white light *** *** ask that feeling to unify into a vibration that will be comfortable *** ask to maintain this inner connection in your outer awareness *** ask your body to feel light *** to feel energized *** open your eyes and sit up when you are ready."

All of the body's energy centers are in a constant and continual state of motion, but as you shift your focus from one area of the brain to another, a different focus of energy moves through the centers related to each respective area of the brain. Each color then allows you to experience a more deeply balanced and unified feeling as the particular color deepens. Notice what a different balance or fullness occurs naturally as you synchronize the awareness of your chakras and of your whole triune brain. Just through exploring this process you will notice a deepening of all of your inner sensations, as well as an increase in and sharper awareness of your outer sensations. This is because you are experiencing the observer effect, and what you observe greatly affects what is occurring; and allowing a deepening of the connection from the physical structures of the brain into the subtle areas of your energy will open you to observe and experience brand new worlds of exploration. Many individuals experience a deepening of colors and a natural shifting and blending from one color to another. Some sense an expansion of the inner space into a more pronounced holographic image. People often have a feeling of being bathed in light as they move into the crown and transpersonal points; such sensations of being bathed in light, provide an initial feedback that is important to knowing that these areas are now open for you.

At this point in our explorations we are still experiencing the balance point, but as we move into Exploration #15 we will begin deepening the inner structures into the energies of unity. However, I would like you to deepen your heart-to-heart exploration as we did in Exploration #13 before moving into Exploration #15. It is important that you begin to feel a completeness within the energies, so do this on your own or by utilizing one of the two former explorations. It may take an additional 20 minutes or so to complete. Deepening is important at this point for it will allow you to experience something very different during the awakening exploration.

We are now ready for EXPLORATION #15: AWAKENING YOUR CREATIVE POTENTIAL, which will allow you to move into the inner space of awakening your creative potential. In this exploration, you will now move beyond the state of balance that you have been experiencing within your inner-directed space. You will begin the journey of transmutation to a more heightened, focused energy, and will then allow it to transmute a lower focused energy. This is the direct opening into the inner-directed guidance of your soul's energies. I will be incorporating Brugh Joy's "spiral meditation" within this exploration. Now, make yourself comfortable either by lying down or sitting up in a comfortable chair.

"Close your eyes *** bring your awareness into the center of your chest *** ask your screen to expand *** let your awareness just deepen at the center point of your screen *** deepening through your heart chakra *** ask that feeling to slowly move as a wave from the center of your chest *** feel the waves moving in all directions as an emerald green light *** *** bring your awareness into your old brain and feel it connected into the physical quadrant *** allow that core of energy extending from above your head to the tip of your spine to be stimulated *** as you feel that rotating movement, allow the colors to blend from emerald green *** to blue *** to violet *** to the brilliance of white light *** and allow that feeling to spread throughout your whole nervous system *** *** *** bring your awareness into the emotional quadrant and the mid-brain *** feel that core of energy rotating and allow the colors to blend from emerald green *** to blue *** violet *** the brilliance of white light *** allow the two cores of energy to blend and feel that spreading throughout your entire nervous system *** *** *** bring your awareness into the mental quadrant, awakening both right and left hemispheres simultaneously *** feel that core of energy rotating and allow the colors to blend *** *** *** *** allow the three cores of energy to blend and move throughout your system *** *** bring your awareness into the spiritual quadrant and the connective point of the corpus callosum *** allow yourself to blend through the colors *** *** ask that feeling to unify and begin a slow spiral down to the tip of your spine, encompassing the entire physical form *** asking that to deepen throughout the nervous system *** *** *** bring your awareness into the center point and ask to expand your screen *** feel that descending into your heart chakra *** ask it to deepen *** bring your focus once again into the potential or spiritual quadrant and feel this new potential energy resonating through the connective point and slowly spiralling down to the tip of the spine and automatically spreading throughout your entire nervous system *** *** ask it to descend into the mental quadrant *** deepening that core of rotating energy *** *** to descend into the emotional quadrant *** *** have it descend into the body quadrant *** *** ask it to refocus back at the center point and at your heart chakra *** ask it to deepen into your center point and into your heart center *** *** penetrating into the deepest inner part *** ask your heart chakra to open and to begin to feel the pulsation of unconditional love *** *** allow this stream of energy to move very deeply within you *** allow it to begin to spiral into the solar plexus *** restructuring the solar plexus with the heart energy *** allow the heart pulsation to move that energy in a spiral pattern, connecting it up into the upper heart (several inches above the heart center) *** allow that to move down to the spleen center *** allowing the heart pulsation to blend with that center *** ask it to move into the lower abdomen or sexual center *** rising again into the throat *** let the pulsation of the heart energy move down into the root *** feeling the next pulsation of the heart rising into the third eye*** feeling the next pulsation moving into the left elbow *** to both knees *** the right elbow *** asking it to rise into the crown *** asking it to move into the palm of your left hand*** both feet *** the palm of your right hand *** and ask it to rise into the transpersonal point *** ask your screen to expand and bring that focus deeper into the heart *** *** *** *** ask the crown energy to descend and slowly spiral into the heart *** *** *** from the heart let it slowly continue to spiral down to the bottom of your feet *** *** focusing at your heart, have it rise again to the crown *** *** deepening the connection between the heart and crown centers *** *** *** (allow yourself to float in this space as long as your time allows, or until your awareness begins to shift) *** *** ask your screen to expand *** ask that energy of unconditional love to come forward into the spiritual quadrant and focus at the connective point *** feel that spiralling through the entire triune brain *** spinal column *** nervous system *** ask that feeling of unconditional love to descend into the mental quadrant *** moving that deeper inner core of energy *** *** ask it to descend into the emotional quadrant *** *** *** to descend into the physical quadrant *** *** *** ask your inner screen to expand as you focus on the center point and heart chakra *** *** *** ask that each energy center move into your 'new living vibration' *** allow that energy to be focused at each energy center starting at the transpersonal point *** palm of right hand *** both feet *** palm of your left hand *** crown *** right elbow *** both knees *** left elbow *** third eye *** root *** throat *** lower abdomen *** spleen *** upper heart *** solar plexus *** heart chakra *** ask it to expand and deepen *** *** ask that vibration to slowly descend into the cellular level throughout your physical form *** *** to descend into your subatomic levels, deepening your connection with your self-actualizing pulse *** *** ask the vibration to slowly move from this inner level throughout your physical form and beyond *** nurturing you with the deep and profound feelings of unconditional love *** *** *** ask it to move you throughout all of time and all of space *** *** allowing you to become your creative potential *** *** *** ask that your fully unified spirit, mind, emotion, and body move into your living vibration *** ask that you remain inwardly focused and allow this inner connection to be your outer awareness as you live the presence of who you are *** *** and whenever you're ready, bring your full awareness back *** with this new part of you fully anchored within your physical form *** allow your body to move and open your eyes."

Do not go on to Chapter Ten until you have explored this exercise several times. This will become the basic exploration for the remainder of our journey, and your level of comfort and personal attunement with this exploration will determine the effectiveness of the rest of your experiences.

PERCEPTUAL SHIFTING AND THE SUBTLE ENERGY BODIES

I would like to begin this chapter with a brief summary of the last nine chapters. As you have been exploring the exchange of energy either from your inner-directed guidance or from another individual, you have begun to experience how such an exchange of energy can directly affect the physical body, as well as alter one's inner perceptions, feelings, and thoughts. Through the same processes of energy exchange, a person can induct another individual or a group of individuals into a similar state of heightened, expanded and focused inner-awareness. In so doing, any areas of imbalance that might exist begin to move into a new state of balance or unity; or, at the very least, the areas of imbalance begin either to be dissipated or greatly reduced. This automatically allows individuals a choice to explore life from a new perspective.

There are many physiological mechanisms that can be measured when a heightened energy begins the restructuring of the body and psychological energies. Individuals show changes in heart rate, breathing, brain waves, and biochemical balances within the brain and body, to mention but a few of the many possible physiological changes. Research has proven over and over again that a heightened focused energy can alter both the physical structure and the mental and emotional structures of an individual. This is the essence of **Awaken Your Creative Potential**. It entails learning how to shift one's inner consciousness through the process of energy exchange or transmutation, whereby a heightened and focused energy can begin to emerge and alter one's outer perception into an inner-awareness. Through this process of awakening, a creative energy is released which can be channeled in such a way that man can live from a new potential of human development. Thus begins the journey into Fuller's 98% of unknown awareness.

Many individuals attempt to explore the process of change through their intellect, thinking and/or talking about what they will change in their lives. But talking and thinking do not create enough energy to change anything. In most cases, they actually disperse the energies that currently exist and keep us stuck within our more primitive outer human emotions. Once we open into the primitive levels of emotion, we begin to lose all clarity and any convictions that we initially had about desiring to change; and eventually the primitive emotions "motivate" us not to change at all or to change into a direction that no longer follows our inner creative path. Can you imagine what life would be like if every inner thought or feeling that you had was actually created? I mean every one, be it positive or negative. Energy is just energy, and it does not differentiate between positive and negative; it just exists and creates whatever is within its focus.

When we need to change, the outer mind has no idea or comprehension of the full ramifications of what that needed level of change is all about. We may think we know what is ultimately going to happen, but once we begin to take direct action, we may suddenly feel that we have opened Pandora's box as a multitude of different awarenesses begin to emerge. We perceive and feel such varied things that we may then decide we are losing control and can no longer predict through our outer mind what will happen. And whenever the outer mind (or intellect) does attempt to create what it thinks the new image is going to be, it becomes extremely difficult for anything new or creative to emerge. Every human being has the potential to open and to allow the emergence of their own level of inner guidance coupled with a heightened and more highly refined focused energy. However, few individuals are aware of or can trust this option. Most struggle with trying to comprehend or understand something that actually cannot be comprehended until it has been first experienced and felt within. Transmutation is the only process that actually allows our inner perceptions to emerge and become our outer reality. But instead of following this very natural pathway, the majority of us live life through the reverse of the process, allowing our outer reality to become what we think really exists inside of us. Thus most of us are usually afraid to change anything at all, much less feel free to live out our true inner potentials!

Through the process of utilizing the expanded inner screen, we can begin to separate and directly experience the distinct layers of energies that yogic psychology brings forward—the spiritual, mental, emotional, physical, and what I call a unified, living structure. In this chapter we are going to explore the process of the subtle energy bodies, whereby you will be able to directly feel, sense, and experience the similarities and differences between the five layers of energy.

Let's first explore the concept that each of the five subtle energy bodies maintains a distinct vibration that allows us to experience a given situation from a perspective that is totally different from the perspective of the other subtle energy bodies. However, the blending together of these distinct energies into one's living self ultimately determines how and what we feel, sense, think and experience as our reality. For example, on an emotional and intellectual level we may be ready to begin a new exercise program. When we think about it or talk with someone about what we are going to do, we are very convincing. But as we physically begin to exercise, we find that our motivation suddenly disappears. What has happened? Did we just lie to ourselves about being sincere in our intentions in the first place? Or is there some other reason that we once again fail? By exploring the differences between each of our distinct energy bodies, we can determine exactly how we feel and what we really believe about any given situation in life. Through this process we can discover what actually happened regarding our intentions and beliefs about our exercise program. One possible scenario might be that we were truly ready to begin an exercise program from a spiritual, emotional, and intellectual level; however, the physical level of energy may have been so far out of balance with the rest of our energies, that when the physical commitment was required in order to actually begin, we lost all motivation, and this in turn interfered with our desire. Often in this scenario individuals then try to "push" themselves into exercising. If this is the case, the body will very quickly provide direct feedback that says, "No" by becoming physically injured or hurt! Tapping into our true levels of creative functioning requires the cooperation and synthesis of all aspects of self working together as a unified team. We will explore this in greater detail throughout the chapter.

Earlier we discussed David Bohm's ideas about creativity and the process of creation through the various orders of energy that move from what he calls the holomovement. The process of transmutation which we are exploring integrates with his ideas of the various layers of energy through which the creative process moves. The generative order of energy contains within it the totality of all creative possibilities. Bohm describes the generative order as a superquantum wave of energy that exists and moves through the inner-awareness of every aspect of life, including human beings. As we open into the process of transmutation, I believe we allow the heightened level of energy from the generative order to emerge into our electromagnetic field, or what he calls the implicate order. If you recall, he describes the implicate level of energy as a subtle wave-form whereby the wave is manifested into a particle-form of energy, or what is termed the explicate level of reality. This explicate level of reality is what we traditionally describe as the solid mass which comprises our outer world. Yet, each solid mass (the human body included) is composed of a subtle layer of energetic vibrations called particles. Our potential energy for a heightened order of creativity always emerges from the fourth state of awareness that we have been exploring as unconditional love. And through these levels of inner-awareness, our self-actualizing energy will always create our new levels and perceptions of outer reality. One can view the fourth state of reality that emerges from the heart chakra as being composed of an infinite energy that is capable of creating a unified perception of reality, which in turn can begin the synchronization of the vertical dimensions of the triune brain into a single system. The human brain thereby becomes the messenger for the continual flow of a heightened level of creative energy. Through the neocortex area of the brain we begin to step this energy down and awaken the inner areas of our potential, or the inherent blueprint of what we can become and do. This is then stepped down into the mid-brain area, allowing a subtle wave-form of energy to take the inner blueprints, or potential energies, and translate them into various forms of inner sensations, feelings, movements, and perceptions. This in turn is translated to the old brain, which ultimately allows us to perceive and interact with reality from a new perspective, since we are then able to perceive and experience things in ways that were not available to us before. Since our perceptions are changed, we can make different choices for ourselves regarding what we will be doing or creating. And through this process, the physical body changes naturally and becomes a wonderful feedback mechanism for us to differentiate the various states of our awareness. This is all part of the total reeducation process that I have been describing.

The exploration of the subtle energy bodies comes into play by letting us tap into the level of the generative order of energy in a way that allows us to change each distinct layer of ourselves into new perceptions. This directly affects our spiritual or potential perceptions of what we can create for ourselves, and it also allows us to alter our mental attitudes, beliefs, and perceptions of what we think and what we can intellectually understand. This in turn opens us to being able to convert our more primitive human emotions into the inner feeling state of unconditional love, and moves us into a knowingness that whatever it is we inwardly can experience, we are also capable of creating. We can then allow the body to shift into being able to physically hold a more refined energetic vibration and at the same time possess the physical capabilities necessary to carry out in direct ways the levels of new creative functions. The living, unified self is the aspect that has moved into the process of coexistence, remaining inwardly connected to the flow of inner energies, thus experiencing the inner perceptions, while simultaneously living and interacting in the outer world. This allows us the capability to perceptually shift and to know that various choices do indeed exist for us as we carry out whatever tasks in life we may encounter.

Try to remember that what we perceive as our outer reality comes through the explicate order of energy, and that underneath this order of energy exist both the wave-forms of the implicate order and the inner energies of creativity from the generative order. Both of these structures of energies exist at some level regardless of what one is creating. This then constitutes the structure that exists as reality. Most individuals are only aware of the explicate structure, the 2% that Fuller terms as known awareness. The explicate order of outer reality is but one of the many possible outcomes or sequences of events that can naturally emerge from the vaster realm of inner-awareness. Where we err and create confusion is in our belief that the reality which we are currently experiencing is the only reality possible. The more we can relax into the idea that our present perception of outer reality is but one of many possible choices of reality, the more clearly we will understand why the process of transmutation and movement into a heart-centered focus and the inner self-actualizing energies is so important. Merging with the inner level of the generative order of energy allows us to truly create something that is new.

As we move out of our habitual structures of living and into the process of transmutation, we are able to directly experience new forms of inner reality, and new levels of creativity begin to emerge. At this phase of our process we will experience many levels of change which our outer mind has difficulty perceiving. This is due to the transition phase that we are currently experiencing as we move into the new renaissance, at which time we will be able to explore and live life from a new plateau of inner-awareness. At this level of awareness, we will explore being able to create and live from a host of new perceptions in understanding the next phase of human development.

The process or order that I am describing implies a successive movement from the outer reality, or explicate forms of manifestation, into the inner realms of heightened creative energies. I believe that "reality" is comprised of a succession of specific levels of energies, from which we are able to perceive the outer layer of reality as the obvious or normal. Each level holds a specific form of energy or vibrational movement. As we move through the various levels of energy, we can experience a more powerful and heightened wave-form of energy which holds together a parallel reality at a lower vibration level. This comprises the particle-form of energy that is called the explicate level. Through this inner-ordering process, we can begin to understand how these levels hold the key to our further inner-creative growth, both as a species and as a planet. This becomes the process of our post-biological development as compared to what we have experienced as normal development and change within the explicate structures of reality. The generative order allows us to experience a heightened, expanded, and focused energy. Through the process of transmutation, the heightened energy naturally emerges into the lesser forms and creates a totally new structure and perception of what life is. I believe that this generative structure of energy is what we experience as the creative pulse of unconditional love as it travels through all forms of reality, regardless of the dimensions of time and space.

Through the restructuring force of one's self-actualizing energy, each area of the triune brain moves into a new level of interpretation and expression of creative energy. As we explore the process of inner-directed imagery, we can sense different experiences from each distinct area of the brain. The old brain is responsible for our sensory material, and the images we experience here emerge in the form of various patterns and movements that can be processed through our visual, auditory, or kinesthetic modes. When the mid-brain comes into play with the old brain, we move into various forms of psychological processes that are organized into meaningful events from our own history. As the new brain or neocortex is incorporated into this process, we can move into the symbolic and abstract levels of various images and events that possess personal meaning and significance, but that also move us beyond the personal levels of direct learning.

We will also move into new levels of synchronization of events that are vastly different from those associated with the old or mid-brain processes. The latter are focused on the outer structures of both space and time, thus allowing certain events to be created only from a specific perspective. For example, the mid-brain experiences a different level or sense of time than does the old brain, and the neocortex moves at yet another level in experiencing the space/time continuum. As the whole triune brain moves into an inner level of synchronization and allows the brain to become a messenger for the heightened levels of energy, we move into still another continuum of space and time. And through this inner dimension, we experience the superquantum pulse of generative energy that allows one's self-actualizing pulse to begin its emergence, initiating what some individuals interpret as a "spiritual emergence." At this point we awaken the spiritual, mystical inner guiding forces of energy and experience a level of energy that is so powerful that it can, within a matter of minutes, actually shift all current perceptions of reality into a totally new form of understanding. This new perspective of understanding is one that transcends the obvious or outer consensus reality as we know it. One's inner guiding force awakens areas which actualize one's true inner creative potential.

The inner self-actualizing force first emerges as an energy that stimulates new areas of sensory processes and inner sensations throughout the brain, nervous system and physical body. Once this level begins to awaken and is directly stimulating the synchronized triune brain, we begin to discern new psychological structures and feelings that are capable of moving us into a totally different perception of creative functioning. With the heart chakra as the major focus of the inner awakening energy, we can move beyond the confines of duality, and into an inner force of energy that will emerge through our perceptions as unity. We then have the opportunity to perceive this unity in all areas of life. An awakening through the heart allows us to experience not merely our own inner psychological structures, but also the means whereby these structures begin to relate within the collective levels of our consciousness. We will thus be able to experience the unity that can be created with those around us and will eventually be able to experience this on a planetary level. However, without the presence of the heightened energy moving us through the process of transmutation, we will be unable to move into this new avenue of being. Or, if we focus our awareness through any other center than the heart or heart-crown connection, the heightened energy will move us into other inner spaces of duality.

Present-day concepts of both time and space become very altered as we move into, explore, and learn to live from the inner-awareness states. By moving into the inner silence and allowing an inner process to emerge, one can greatly increase the rate of thought or the subjective experiences that are possible, thus creating from various levels of new inner sensations and images. When one is focused on the physical body having to achieve the outer processes of speech, writing, movement or performance, the learning process initially takes longer in terms of our outer structure of time. But once the inner dimensions have emerged, one's inner guiding force can educate the outer part of linear reality and guide it into an inner synchronization. This creates the capability for learning new types of physical movements, changing outer behaviors, perceiving information differently, and moving into a level of artistic creation that is totally different than what it was mere moments before. This is the process whereby the inner dimensions of time and space can restructure our outer reality and the levels from which we create. Just as one's outer form of thought and imagery is not bound to the outer constraints of time, the awakening energies of the self-actualizing force are even less bound by such constraints.

Now, forget about the structures and the summary that you have just read, and let's directly experience what it means to allow yourself to perceptually shift your focus of reality and open into the subtle energy body explorations. To begin EXPLORATION #16: EXPLORING THE ESSENCE OF UNITY, make yourself comfortable, either sitting or lying down, and close your eyes.

"Ask your inner screen to expand *** continue to ask it to expand until you reach that inner level *** *** feel that inner pulsation, that inner sensation, moving through your heart, and then moving throughout your body *** allow the feeling to deepen *** bring your awareness into the old brain *** ask it to feel a profound level of inner peace within this energy *** ask it to move up to the point above your head and then down to the tip of your spine *** ask to feel the color green pulsating through that column of energy *** slowly turning clockwise *** allowing you to deepen within the inner space *** change into blue *** violet *** the brilliance of white light *** *** now feel the focus in the mid-brain *** ask to experience a column of energy *** pulsating and turning with an emerald green light *** with blue *** violet *** and the brilliance of white light *** *** now the neocortex *** the right and left hemispheres *** the column of energy *** green *** blue *** violet *** brilliance of white light *** *** the connective point *** focusing the energy and feeling it change colors *** into green *** blue *** violet *** and the brilliance of white light *** and feel that extending up into the crown chakra *** on up into the transpersonal center *** ask this to deepen *** ask this energy to begin to spiral downward through the major chakras until it reaches the heart *** *** *** and then from the heart deepening to the bottom of the spine *** *** and moving from the tip of the spine down to the feet *** *** ask your screen to expand *** and bringing your focus into the heart *** feel this deepen within you *** through the physical body *** down into the cellular level *** down into the subatomic and quantum levels within you *** and ask this energy to begin to move in a spiral pattern *** from the heart down into the solar plexus *** moving up into the upper heart *** down into the spleen *** into the lower abdomen *** up to the throat *** the root *** the third eye *** the left elbow *** both knees *** the right elbow *** crown *** palm of your left hand *** both feet *** palm of your right hand *** the transpersonal point *** and ask that the energy deepen within you

*** and now ask your inner essence to step outside of your physical body *** ask it to sit in front of you *** ask it to touch your head or your face, so that you can know its familiar feeling *** experience its familiar sensation *** ask to hold hands, and allow a flow of energy to move from your hands into and through your essence and back to you *** ask to open and to feel the heart-to-heart connection *** ask to deepen into this feeling of unity *** now begin to move into a combined spiral while maintaining each one of the previous connections *** feel the connection of solar plexus-to-solar plexus *** upper heart-to-upper heart *** spleen-to-spleen *** lower abdomen-to-lower abdomen *** throat-to-throat *** root-to-root *** third eye-to-third eye *** elbow-to-elbow *** knees-to-knees *** right elbow-to-right elbow *** crown-to-crown *** left hand-to-left hand *** both feet-to-both feet *** right hand-to-right hand *** transpersonal-to-transpersonal *** and ask this exchange of unconditional love to deepen *** *** ask your screen to expand and deepen once again *** and ask your essence to merge with your physical body through each one of the energy connections *** starting with your heart *** and then simultaneously with all of the energy centers *** *** *** ask to unify within this aspect of unity *** you becoming one with the essence of your being *** if you feel the body tending to slowly rock or needing to jerk, just allow it *** this is just the adjustment of the physical structure expanding *** *** *** bring your awareness to your potential quadrant, the upper right *** and ask that potential energy to unify and merge *** ask to bring forth and unify this new energy as your natural vibration in living *** ask this to move into the mental quadrant, bringing forward your new beliefs, your new perceptions, and your new attitudes about what this unity is and who you are and what you are becoming *** *** ask it to emerge into the emotional quadrant *** and ask this deeper unity of unconditional love to become your natural state of awareness, and to deepen as your primary emotion *** *** then ask this to deepen into the body quadrant, and to integrate and become one with your physical structure *** ask that it flow freely through your brain and nervous system, and all related organs and muscles *** *** bring your awareness to the center point and ask that point to deepen within your heart *** and as we focus on each chakra, ask the inner part of your guidance to adjust your energy to your new living vibration *** transpersonal *** right hand *** both feet *** left hand *** crown *** right elbow *** both knees *** left elbow *** third eye *** root *** throat *** lower abdomen *** spleen *** upper heart *** solar plexus *** heart center *** ask your new inner wave pattern to be released *** allow the pulsation from that deepest part within you to move throughout your physical body and beyond *** to unify you with all of time and all of space *** and ask this deepest aspect, if you wish, to remain inwardly connected and allow this energy focus to become your outer awareness *** ask your body to feel light, unified, and energized with this vibration *** and ask this energy to begin to emerge *** remaining as the inner connection to your outer awareness *** allow your awareness to drift back into your physical structure *** feeling and sensing the movement of your body *** and then open your eyes and sit up when you are ready."

This exercise evolved as a result of some difficult times I was experiencing in 1983. One day as I was lying on the floor in meditation, I began to spontaneously feel an energetic balancing of my various chakras or energy centers taking place. At one point in the process I opened my eyes to see who was there, only to find the room void of any physical human beings. My first reaction was one of surprise. But then a quickening of the same energy moved me into a focused, heightened energy, and I came to understand that my own inner guidance, or what I call "essence" in this exploration, was balancing me! I found this process to be extremely nurturing as well as very enlightening in regard to my inner capabilities for maintaining a state of unity. As I deepened with the exploration of the subtle energy bodies, I began to incorporate this exploration in my group work. Each time that you move through this exploration, allow yourself to move more deeply into the observer state; just allow the process to unfold for you. It may require several explorations before this occurs, but once it does, you will have moved into a new level of understanding and of experiencing the multidimensional aspects of yourself.

Henceforth I will not be devoting much time to discussing the explorations that we experience. Each one will continue to allow you to deepen and open into your own essence or self-actualizing pulse. Thus you can begin to feel comfortable and nurtured while exploring the unknown inner-awarenesses of yourself, and, at the same time, can allow yourself to awaken into your heightened creative energies.

In EXPLORATION #17: KNOWING VERSUS THINKING, I will explore an experience similar to that which we have previously shared. However, I want to point out that in this exploration I am bringing you into your inner-awareness through a different process; become aware of the various feelings and inner sensations that will emerge as we explore a different focus. Notice how important one's focus is in setting the stage or the intent for what is to be explored and how the heightened energies are felt, experienced, and eventually interpreted. These structures take us back into the area of quantum mechanics and into the observer effect. Do this exploration with a partner, or even with a group of individuals if they are available. Sit close enough to your partner that you can hold hands, but begin the exploration without touching.

"Close your eyes *** ask your screen to expand *** feel the waves of energy moving at the center of your chest *** experience the crystalline structure of emerald green light *** bring your awareness into your spiritual or potential quadrant, the upper right, and ask for the energies, feelings, and sensations to emerge that can move you into your self-actualizing pulse within two minutes or less *** allow your focus to shift into your mental quadrant, upper left, and allow the energies, feelings, and sensations to emerge that will allow you to move into your self-actualizing pulse *** allow it to emerge into your emotional quadrant and let your feelings shift into the heart *** to the physical quadrant, allowing your body to experience those inner vibrations *** move to the center point of your screen and ask it to expand; unify your awareness into this inner self-actualizing pulse *** allow yourself to experience the colors 'turning on' and moving at the center of your expanded screen from green * to blue * violet * white * and experience this movement through your column of energy moving from the base of the spine to above your head *** and ask it to move through your entire nervous system *** ask your screen to expand and deepen the focus of your awareness at the center point of your screen and at the center of your heart chakra *** *** feel into the brilliance of white light moving through the center of your chest *** ask that feeling to move as a pulsation into both shoulders *** down into both elbows *** both wrists *** into the palms of both hands *** allowing the energy to move out through the palms of your hands and fingers *** *** maintaining this focus of pulsation through both hands, reach out with your eyes closed and hold hands with your partner, feeling the rhythm of that pulsation moving from your left hand into your partner's right hand, and from your partner's left hand into your right hand *** ask that the pulsations and rhythms between your hands and those of your partner become one *** *** ask your screen to expand *** *** *** this becomes the first level of movement from the explicate energy into the implicate, sensing and experiencing the pulsation of the inner waves *** ask that pulsation to deepen at the heart chakra *** do not ponder what I am saying—just ask this energy to now exit at the center of your heart chakra and to connect into your partner's heart chakra *** *** creating an arc of energy between you and your partner *** feel that this energy is being released from your heart center into your partner's heart center and that it is continuing to flow on its own ***** ask it to deepen and to move without your having to direct it ***** allow yourself to move into the observer state ***** this becomes the deepening of the implicate order ***** feel into the words, 'I give love' ***** 'I receive love' ***** 'I am love manifesting' ***** ask for your screen to expand and deepen within your heart-to-heart, hand-to-hand exploration of unconditional love ***** ***** ***** (several minutes or so) ***** ask that your energy field expand, blend, and merge with that of your partner ***** extending beyond the heart and hands energies ***** just ask and allow it to happen— the inner guidance knows what to do ***** ***** ask your energies to blend into a unified field of energy with one pulsation, the two energies becoming one rhythm ***** ***** if you feel that your body needs to rock back and forth, allow it to do so ***** honor your inner feelings and physical movements ***** ***** this opens you into the fourth level of awareness, the state of unity ***** ask your energies to go beyond you as a couple (or group) and to spread throughout the room ***** if there are others in the room, blending with them; if by yourself, expanding to the limits of the room ***** ***** this is the space of "knowing," and when you desire inner information, you will experience something similar to this inner space along with the feelings and sensations that are moving within you ***** ***** shift your focus now to thinking about cleaning your home or about what you need to buy at the store for dinner ***** notice how the space has changed, and be aware of what occurs with the inner feelings and sensations ***** ask to let it go and to return to the inner space of knowing ***** ***** allow yourself to feel and experience what these words mean: 'I am love manifesting' ***** ask those same words to be felt and inwardly repeated to you from your inner guidance: 'I am love manifesting' ***** ***** now ask the energy to move back to encompass just you and your partner as a couple, separating yourselves from the group if there is one ***** ask that you and your partner separate except for the heart and hand exchange ***** ***** now ask your energy to return from your partner's heart chakra into your own ***** ask the energies to move from your hands back into your heart chakra ***** ***** release your partner's hands ***** ask your screen to expand ***** deepen that energy within your own heart chakra ***** ***** and ask to remain inner connected and to bring these inner feelings, sensations, and perceptions forward as your outer awareness ***** ***** open your eyes when you are ready ***** give your partner a hug for what you have just shared with one another."

Can you now begin to comprehend that the process of the outer mind's thinking or trying to understand cannot occur simultaneously with the state of knowing? The most frequently asked questions in this regard always focus on "How will I know whether I am in the space of my inner guidance or my outer mind?" Intellectually you cannot differentiate; however, what you felt and experienced in this exploration, or what you experience in any other exploration when the inner feelings, sensations, and heightened energies are present, allows for the emergence of a different form of communication. Many individuals begin to receive or sense an inner knowing being directly felt or an inner dialogue occurring during this exploration. If one remains within the heightened energetic space while feeling this level of inner knowing, then it is emerging from the depths of one's inner guidance. But if one loses the inner space and moves into an outer awareness, experiencing the energies as contracting, then the dialogue is from the outer mind and intellect. When you are within the inner space you know that you are there, and when you are asking if you are there, that is the clue that no, you are not! These initial subtle differences will become very obvious as you deepen in your exploration and as the awakening energies deepen within your heart and triune brain. You will also notice an ease in both your physical movement (a depth of inner calmness and quiet) and an increase in your ability to remain within this space while performing outer activities. This space of coexistence can be maintained as long as you allow your inner-awareness to continue the process of reeducating your outer mind into a new way of perceiving and interacting with life.

Have you ever felt that you would like to be more knowledgeable about things and to be able to feel into the various directions that your life might be taking prior to the emergence of the reactive process? Have you ever grown tired of feeling that there were no options available to you or that the options you did have were limited and confining? As individuals open into the heart chakra and inner guidance, they begin naturally to perceive and feel the availability of new options. At one point in my own life, however, I became frightened and overwhelmed after three or four months of seeing a multitude of different options; I no longer wanted to be confronted with so many options nor did I want to be responsible for undertaking so many drastic changes in my life. The fun and excitement of my journey quickly disappeared, and I reached the point where I decided: "Enough is enough. No more options. I don't even want to know!" At that point my life literally fell apart and confusion reigned. This created one of the worst dilemmas I had experienced in years. One part of me wanted to know more and felt great excitement at being able to explore life with such fun and adventure; but another part of me was overwhelmed because I was changing so fast that I had no opportunity to even grasp or understand who I was.

Now whenever I reach this point of feeling that I want "no more," I realize that I am ready to change and awaken into a much more vast, much more empowering inner space within me. But if I stop the inner movement and become engrossed in my outer crisis and pain, I then prolong my previous feelings and avoid having to make any immediate change. What a paradox! One would think that I were being asked to give up great levels of success in my life. Even though my life might seem to be going well from an outer perspective, this still would not necessarily mean I had inwardly reached the levels of peace and nurturing that were attainable. I now realize that when I have been shown avenues of change they have always been for the purpose of directing me toward a new level of inner peace and an inner feeling of love. Once I was able to acknowledge the paradox of feeling both excited and frightened by the changes, I was able to move into an inner-awareness and allow this to evolve into other parts of my life. I thus release into the heightened energies of transmutation and the heart chakra and allow myself to once again feel a deep inner sense of love and peace. This provides me the opportunity to keep changing and to continually have yet another option available. Wouldn't it be wonderful to truly believe that inside of you there always exists another option? If you believed this, then why would you ever allow yourself to "get stuck" in a crisis of any sort?

There is a lot of existing confusion concerning what this concept of inner knowing is all about. Some individuals relate that they experience an inner voice or varied forms of visual inner perceptions. Most individuals experience this form of inner knowing only rarely, or perhaps not at all, and resentfully wonder what is wrong. They may feel that they "got into the wrong line at birth" when inner voices or inner perceptions were being passed out. Everyone thinks that their experiences are unsatisfactory because they are not identical to everyone else's. Many think that if they could just experience things like someone else does, or like I do, then life would be better for them. And yet, every human being has his or her own unique inner voice and inner perceptions. What becomes important is to learn how you explore your inner communication and how you can bring the levels of inner guidance into your day-to-day living. The process that we are exploring together in this book will bring you into your own levels of inner-awareness and will allow you to experience the various means of communication that exist within all human beings. They can only emerge from the depths of inner silence and the self-actualizing pulse. For years I grew angrier and angrier, feeling that I was one of those individuals who had definitely gotten into the wrong line at birth; no matter how much I read and studied there was no obvious inner-awareness or communication within me! Once I moved into the inner space of knowing, however, I was shocked to discover that the feelings and inner sensations had always been with me, but I had clouded them over with my primitive human feelings and the fact that I was stuck within my worries and problems. Only through the inner depths of silence and the heightened energies that we are exploring, can we begin to understand the communication that is and always has been with us!

We block our levels of inner communication in our emotional and feeling states more than in any other area of life. Therefore, the emotional quadrant of the expanded inner screen is the most difficult for individuals to experience. In order to explore the process of transmutation and change, we must move through this blockage and into the spaces of being able to "feel." For many individuals being so in tune with such depths of feelings creates a state of panic, and unconsciously they cease allowing themselves to experience the levels of inner guidance and the feeling states from the fourth state of awareness of unconditional love. This is why many individuals who move quickly through the blockage within the emotional levels of inner chatter, panic as the blockage becomes freed and a multitude of feelings and energies are released into their physical body, creating the next level of inner chatter.

In order to really work with change through the process of transmutation, there are a series of feelings through which virtually every human being progresses. I'm not saying that you absolutely must follow this specific sequence of feelings and emotions; I'm merely stating that the majority of people who get stuck do follow a very predictable pattern. Therefore, I would like to explore this progression in greater detail, as it may help you understand some of your own difficulties.

The further removed we are from our own inner guidance (or any level of inner-awareness), the more we are focused within depression. The emotional opposite of depression is anger. Feelings of anger are usually transferred or projected onto other individuals or onto other outer situations. If the anger is not projected outwardly, and the process of transmutation does not occur, we become depressed, which is the result of feelings of anger being turned inward at oneself. But if we cease being angry at either ourselves or at our environment, we suddenly encounter fear. Then, as our fears are removed, we feel overwhelmed. And if we allow the feelings of being overwhelmed to be removed, we automatically move into our feelings of unconditional love. Each one of these feelings holds a particular energy or vibration, and the further each vibration becomes removed from our inner awareness, the more hopeless and limited our outer perceptions become. The feelings of unconditional love are always present, but due to our outer focus and the perceptions we hold, they at times seem impossible to attain. A book I read early in my own journey, called **Love Is Letting Go Of Fear** by Gerald Jampolsky, helped me realize that all emotions and feelings initially stem from a feeling or energy of fear. I also realized in my own life that once this fear was removed, I automatically would begin to feel overwhelmed with various feelings and sensations (which are part of our physical inner chatter), and that this also prevented me from experiencing the inner levels of love.

Often individuals become so frightened with the changes that are forthcoming that they would rather stay in their feeling states than allow themselves to move into the heart center. Thinking about changes can only make the situation worse, because thinking cannot produce the heightened energy that is needed to transmute the perceptions into a vibration of unconditional love. When individuals begin to feel the inner fluidity from the heart, they automatically begin to spiral into their own inner-awareness and the feelings of the fourth level. Through an exploration of the subtle energy bodies, one can sense and experience each distinct and separate energy body and can then understand how it relates to the others. For example, at times you may feel a strong and balanced energy on a physical and emotional level, but suddenly you will notice that on a mental level your energy body is very weak. This indicates that you will encounter very little difficulty with a particular task as long as you are not intellectually thinking about it and its consequences. But if your thoughts begin to focus on what is going to happen to you, and if you continue to ponder about it, you will move into a panic state and will ultimately create nothing. A similar imbalance in the process can occur with any one of the energy bodies. For any level of true inner success, all five levels need to be balanced and synthesized into one cooperative inner system.

Have you ever felt during meditation that you can accomplish a specific thing, knowing that you are going to get it done, no matter what it takes? But when you come out of your meditation and try to take action, you literally freeze? Or, once out of your mediation, you find that you can't even remember what you had known so clearly only moments before? It is as though there is suddenly a distinct separateness between the inner space of knowingness and what you want to act upon in your outer world. This occurs as a result of a breakdown in the process of the living energy body, which makes it difficult to bring the inner energy into the outer world. One's emotions and feelings usually play a critical role in this breakdown. It is of utmost importance, though, for you to realize that experiencing such a breakdown is not necessary. It can be avoided by going directly into the inner self-actualizing pulse, and fully experiencing the feelings of unconditional love. This is precisely what we are exploring through the energy body explorations.

There are no real benefits to be gained from painstakingly exploring each one of the corresponding outer emotional layers. We could spend weeks or even months with any one of them, making perhaps some measure of headway, but most likely losing the focus that we were trying to restructure and slipping back into the former 2% of known awareness. Let's just briefly look at the basic process. When you are depressed, and when your depression finally erupts into anger toward someone or something, you feel as though you have at last accomplished something. When you are extremely angry, it becomes very difficult for you to allow someone to remove that anger and balance you, because you feel as though they are taking away an important part of who you are. The anger is yours, and you want to keep it! After all, you have a great deal invested in that anger, and no matter what anyone says or does, you're going to hold onto it until you feel that you are completely finished with it. If you are overcome with fear, can another person talk you out of that state? No. You cling to the fear, and consider yourself to be perfectly rational and logical. The fear is very real. You can justify it and intellectually prove it. And you most certainly are going to maintain a hold on it until you're ready to say, "I'm going to move through my fear because the fear is not the real issue." When you feel overwhelmed by new feelings and new perceptions that begin to emerge, you will likewise hold onto the feelings of being overwhelmed until you finally say to yourself, "I want balance. I want the new energies. I really want the new perceptions and unity to emerge for me." No human being can ever force themselves or another into unconditional love. I have tried it many times over the years. I have tried it on myself, and I have tried it with other people. It just does not work. It is not possible to force anyone into experiencing the levels of inner love; nor can you force others into feeling overwhelmed. You can push others into fear, anger, and depression only when they are already experiencing these feelings. This feeds directly into their emotional state, and it simultaneously keeps things going for you, since they in turn are "feeding more fuel into your fire." All of these are very real energies, and when we are caught in any one of them, it becomes very real. Thus the cycle is continually perpetuated.

Any feeling you are dealing with at any given time is actually a scapegoat, for at that moment you have the potential for change.

You have the potential to allow a heightened energy to emerge. Usually the level of your fear, overwhelming feelings, anger and depression also indicates the availability of a corresponding level of unconditional love. It is all the same energy. The difference lies only in one's focus. It is a question of whether your outer mind or your inner guiding force channels your focus. Become consciously aware of your behaviors and the behaviors of others. When people are angry, fearful, depressed or overwhelmed, you will begin to see that they are ignoring other potentials. Most people, believe it or not, actually think it is safer to remain overwhelmed or angry than it is to simply move into the energies of unconditional love. Unbelievable as it may seem, many people actually prefer to spend hours caught up in anger, fear, or being overwhelmed rather than changing the emotion by allowing a feeling of love to enter them and thus allowing a new perception of reality to emerge. I have done this in my life, and I must admit that I still do it, although much less today than ever before. I, like anyone else, can get caught into thinking that such feelings and perceptions are more real than anything I've explored from within the inner-awareness states of unconditional love!

In EXPLORATION #18: THE QUADRANTS AND THE SUBTLE ENERGY BODIES, we will explore how different all of the energy bodies are and how they relate to the quadrant process. Sit in a comfortable position for this exploration, and when you are ready, close your eyes.

"Ask your screen to expand and allow yourself within the next minute to find that inner self-actualizing pulse *** *** *** ask to deepen and synchronize your whole triune brain within the color green * blue * violet * and white *** bring your awareness into the body quadrant, the lower right *** ask your physical energy body to emerge in front of you *** have your physical energy body stand, and ask its hand to touch you on the top of your head *** ask your inner screen to expand *** keep asking your inner screen to expand until you have a very clear sensation of being physically touched *** have your physical energy body hand touch you on your cheek *** feel it stroking gently your cheek *** ask the screen to expand if you're not able to fully experience the sensation *** ask to feel and sense that movement deepening *** ask the physical energy body to sit down facing you *** ask its hand to touch your body at the heart chakra *** ask one hand to touch the heart and have the other hand touching the crown at the top of the head, transferring a quality of energy to you *** *** ask the hands to lower *** ask the physical energy body to reenter your physical form through your heart chakra *** become aware of how that feels *** *** bring your awareness to the emotional quadrant and ask the emotional energy body to stand in front of you *** *** ask it to put one hand on the top of your head, and feel the pressure *** ask the other hand to move toward your heart chakra *** ask to feel the heart-crown connection through the emotional energy body with your focus in the emotional quadrant *** become aware of these sensations, the feelings, the movement of energy *** ask your screen to expand until you feel it very clearly *** *** ask your emotional energy body to reenter through your heart chakra *** *** bring your awareness to the mental quadrant *** ask the mental energy body to stand in front of you *** ask to feel one hand touching your head *** and the other hand touching your heart chakra *** *** ask your mental energy body to reenter your physical form through your heart chakra *** *** bring your awareness into the spiritual or potential quadrant, the upper right *** ask that energy body to step forward and stand in front of you *** ask to feel its hand on your head *** the other hand on your heart *** *** ask your spiritual energy body to reenter your heart*** *** ask to bring your awareness into the center point of your screen *** ask this living energy body to step forward *** ask to feel one hand on your head *** the other on your heart chakra *** *** ask this energy body to reenter through your heart chakra *** *** ask to unify spirit, mind, emotion, and body *** ask that level of heightened energy to remain inwardly connected *** ask to bring your inner-awareness forward as your outer reality *** *** open your eyes whenever you're ready."

Go through this exploration until you can fully experience each one of the energy bodies feeling the same as if some actual person were physically touching you. Also let yourself deepen in the experience of allowing each energy body to transfer a level of energy to your heart-crown connection. This connection will aid you in the development of allowing the inner living awareness to become your outer awareness in daily life. After having done this exercise several times, move directly into EXPLORATION #19: ENERGETIC SYNTHESIS. Once again, sit in a comfortable position and close your eyes:

"Ask your screen to expand and allow yourself during the next minute to find that inner self-actualizing pulse *** *** *** ask to deepen and synchronize your whole triune brain within the color green * blue * violet * and white *** bring your awareness into the body quadrant, the lower right *** ask your physical energy body to emerge in front of you *** have your physical energy body stand, and ask its hand to touch you on the top of your head *** ask your inner screen to expand *** keep asking your inner screen to expand until you have a very clear sensation of being physically touched *** have your physical energy body hand touch you on your cheek

*** feel it gently stroking your cheek *** ask the screen to expand if you are not able to experience the full sensation *** ask to feel and sense that movement deepening *** ask that your name be called out to you *** ask to feel the presence, that essence of your inner guidance with you *** ask that the essence begin to merge with you, becoming one *** allow your body to move if it needs to—to sway or to straighten into whatever position it needs *** allow that inner vibration to align your outer physical body into your inner alignment *** start by bringing your awareness into the spiritual quadrant, the upper right *** allow that inner spiritual energy to emerge and blend with you *** allow your awareness to maintain a focus both in the spiritual quadrant and at the connective point or the corpus callosum *** allow this spiritual energy to begin to spiral down from this point moving through each major energy center until it reaches the heart chakra *** *** from the heart chakra allow it to move through each energy center spiraling down until it reaches the bottom of your feet *** *** allow yourself to deepen and open into this deeper essence of who you are *** *** allow your awareness to shift into the mental quadrant, the upper left *** feel the inner rotation through the right and left hemispheres of this column of energy *** ask this to deepen within you, and open to your new perceptions, your new attitudes and beliefs *** *** bring your awareness to the emotional quadrant, the lower left *** feel the column of energy connected into the two soft spots at the back of the head *** allow your emotions to shift into the energies of unconditional love *** *** allow your awareness to shift into the body quadrant, the lower right *** feeling that column of energy turning within the old brain *** moving through the brain stem and spinal column *** merging into your physical form *** bring your awareness into the center point *** ask to feel that deepening in your heart chakra *** bringing your awareness into the crown chakra at the top of your head *** asking the energies to unify in spirit, mind, emotion, body *** ask to feel the crown energy descending in a spiral slowly into the heart chakra *** *** ask it to deepen within the heart *** *** ask it to slowly spiral down to the bottom of your feet *** *** ask it to deepen in the heart *** *** ask to keep the heart-crown connection open to whatever degree is normal *** *** ask the energy to spiral upward from the heart into the crown *** *** ask the waves of this essence to slowly pulsate from the center of your chest throughout your body and beyond, aligning you with the inner forces of unconditional love *** throughout all of time *** throughout all of space *** ask that you remain connected within this inner space *** that this level of inner-awareness becomes your outer awareness *** *** and now open your eyes, when you are ready ***."

I would like to move us directly into EXPLORATION #20: TRANSMUTATION THROUGH THE ENERGY BODIES. The basic purpose of this exploration is to provide feedback on the status of each energy body, even those that may initially seem to be in a flow of balance. As the process of transmutation begins, an energy body which is in balance will also change into a new level of balance or unity. Each energy body will continually experience change because the situation that you are exploring is changing. For example, each time you present a given speech, you are at a different level of inner focus; therefore, your impact will vary accordingly. By exploring each energy body, you will be able to determine your current level of focus and change your level of creation. The goal is to allow each energy body to open into the fourth state of energetic awareness, and then to allow this structure to synthesize into a new unified energy that can be brought forward into the outer world. This completes the cycle of allowing a heightened energy to transmute a lower energy and begins the creation of a new energetic structure. In this particular exercise we will be exploring your ability to feel comfortable with the energies and feelings of unconditional love. This same exercise may be used to explore any particular focus, but for now just focus on the comfort of allowing the energies of unconditional love to be present in your life. Once again, seat yourself in a comfortable position, close your eyes, and we will begin:

"Ask that your screen expand ... and bring your awareness into the center of your chest, the heart chakra *** during the next minute allow yourself to move through the following part of the exploration (ask to deepen and synchronize your whole triune brain within the color green * blue * violet * and white *** ask to bring your awareness into your potential quadrant * mental quadrant * emotional quadrant * physical quadrant * center point of your screen and heart chakra *** now ask your screen to expand again, bring your inner-awareness to the center point, and deepen your awareness at the heart chakra *** feel that inner self-actualizing pulse deepening and merging with your essence *** allow the pulsation at the heart to move in a spiral moving first to the solar plexus, several inches above the navel *** feel it moving all the way up to the upper heart, an inch or two above the heart chakra *** feel it moving down to the spleen, below the rib cage on the left side *** and feeling the movement into the lower abdomen at the sexual center *** feeling that moving up into the throat *** down into the root *** up into the third eye *** to your left elbow *** both knees *** your right elbow *** to the crown, at the top of your head *** the palm of your left hand *** both feet *** the palm of your right hand *** and the transpersonal point *** ask to expand your screen *** bring your awareness into your physical quadrant, the lower right *** and ask your physical energy body to step out in front of you *** ask your physical energy body to sit down in front of you and to represent your physical ability to feel unconditional love in your life *** become aware of how this physical energy body feels and senses, or of its image *** have your physical energy body touch your hands *** begin a hand-to-hand energy exchange with that part of yourself *** begin a heart-to-heart exchange *** allow your physical energy body to continue changing until you experience a flow of energy between you and your physical energy body moving toward a feeling of acceptance of unconditional love in your daily life *** *** after several minutes ask your physical energy body to move into the level that is needed to accept and live from an energetic perspective *** *** ask your physical energy body to slowly merge through your heart back into your physical form, unifying this feeling *** *** ask to expand your screen *** bring your awareness into your emotional quadrant, the lower left *** and ask your emotional energy body to step out in front of you *** ask your emotional energy body to sit down in front of you and to represent your emotional ability to feel and accept unconditional love in your life *** become aware of how this emotional energy body feels and senses, or of its image *** have your emotional energy body touch your hands *** and begin a hand-to-hand energy exchange *** begin a heart-to-heart exchange *** allow your emotional energy body to keep changing until you experience a flowing of energy between you and your emotional energy body moving toward a feeling of acceptance of unconditional love in your daily life *** *** (several minutes) ask your emotional energy body to change into whatever level is needed in order to accept and live from this energetic perspective *** *** ask your emotional energy body to slowly merge through your heart back into your physical form, and unify this feeling *** *** ask to expand your screen *** bring your awareness into your mental quadrant, the upper left *** and ask your mental energy body to step out in front of you *** ask your mental energy body to sit down in front of you and to represent your mental ability to accept and live with the levels of unconditional love in your life *** become aware how this mental energy body feels and senses, or of its image *** have your mental energy body touching your hands *** begin a hand-to-hand exchange *** begin a heart-to-heart *** allow your mental energy body to keep changing until you experience a flowing of energy between you and your mental energy body moving toward a feeling of acceptance of unconditional love in your daily life *** *** (several minutes) ask your mental energy body to move into the level that is needed to accept and live from this energetic perspective *** *** ask your mental energy body to slowly merge through your heart back into your physical form, and ask to unify this feeling *** *** ask to expand your screen *** bring your awareness into your potential quadrant, the upper right *** and ask your potential energy body to step out in front of you *** ask your potential energy body to sit down in front of you and to represent your potential ability to feel and accept unconditional love in your life *** become aware of how this potential energy body feels and senses, or of its image *** have your potential energy body touch your hands *** begin a hand-to-hand exchange *** and a heart-to-heart *** allow your potential energy body to continue changing until you experience a flowing of energy between you and your potential energy body moving toward a feeling of acceptance of unconditional love in your daily life *** *** (several minutes) ask your potential energy body to change to the level that is needed in order to accept and live from this energetic perspective *** *** ask your potential energy body to slowly merge through your heart back into your physical form, and unify this feeling *** *** ask to expand your screen *** bring your awareness to the center point of the screen and at your heart chakra *** ask the energy body of your living unified self to step out in front of you *** ask your unified energy body to sit down in front of you and to represent your abilities to live from and interact with life from the feelings of unconditional love within your life *** become aware of how this unified energy body feels, senses— or become aware of its image *** have your unified energy body touch your hands *** begin a hand-to-hand *** a heart-to-heart *** allow your unified energy body to change until you experience a flowing of energy between you and your unified energy body moving toward a feeling of acceptance of unconditional love in your daily life *** *** (several minutes) ask your unified energy body to change into the level needed in order to accept and live from this energetic perspective *** *** ask your unified energy body to slowly merge through your heart back into your physical form, and unify this feeling spiritually, mentally, emotionally, and physically as your living unified state *** *** ask to expand your screen *** ask your unified energy body to emerge in front of you and to sit down *** do a hand-to-hand and heart-to-heart for one minute *** *** begin to connect with a joint spiral doing a solar plexus-to-solar plexus *** upper heart-to-upper heart *** spleen-to-spleen *** lower abdomen-to-lower abdomen *** throat-to-throat *** root-to-root *** third eye-to-third eye *** left elbow-to-left elbow *** both knees-to-both knees *** right elbow-to-right elbow *** crown-to-crown *** left hand-to-left hand *** both feet-to-both feet *** right hand-to-right hand *** transpersonal point-to-transpersonal point *** *** ask to deepen for several minutes within this space *** feeling totally connected with your unified energy body through each chakra *** open into the potential or spiritual quadrant to deepen your new energetic structure and ask to feel and to experience yourself living from this new perspective *** *** ask that energy of unconditional love to merge with your awareness in the mental quadrant *** *** allowing new perceptions, attitudes, beliefs to emerge, and ask to feel and experience yourself living from this new perspective *** *** ask that energy of unconditional love to merge with your awareness in the emotional quadrant *** *** allowing your new living emotions and feelings to move into this inner-awareness, and ask to feel and experience yourself living from this new perspective *** *** ask that energy of unconditional love to merge with your awareness in the physical quadrant *** *** allowing your body to live at these new inner feelings and energies, and ask to feel and to experience yourself living from this new perspective *** *** ask that energy of unconditional love to merge with your awareness at the center point, unifying the energy into one living vibration that you can directly feel and experience *** and ask each energy center to adjust its vibration to this living energy of unconditional love *** transpersonal point *** right hand *** both feet *** left hand *** crown *** right elbow *** both knees *** left elbow *** third eye *** root center *** throat *** lower abdomen *** spleen *** upper heart *** solar plexus *** heart chakra *** and have this energy slowly enter your physical form through the heart chakra and merge as one living energy *** *** *** ask this inner actualizing pulsation to slowly move through and beyond your physical body *** *** connecting you with all of time and all of space in this livingness ** *** and allow your inner-awareness to emerge as your outer awareness *** and open your eyes when you are ready *** ."

This then becomes the process of transmutation. Were you able to begin to experience the differences among each of your energy bodies? Were you aware of the change from before you began the exchange of heart energy to after the exchange and the shift into the fourth level of inner-awareness? As you become increasingly familiar and comfortable with working with each one of the quadrants as well as the entirety of the process, you will be able to move into a totally new perception and structure within fifteen minutes. You may encounter more difficulty in the transformation of some energy bodies than others. If you find this to be the case, allow yourself more time with those particular areas. If there is a difficulty with a certain body and the exchange of energy just doesn't seem to be occurring, ask your screen to keep expanding, maintaining your focus and energetic connection within that quadrant, and know within your heart that it will change! Sometimes additional time is needed to expand and fine tune a certain perspective before the heightened energies can emerge and bring it into a new awareness. I have never seen this process fail to work. What I have seen, however, and have also experienced in my own life, is that inwardly a part of me is not ready to change, regardless of what my outer thoughts may be shouting. And because of this I neglect to take the time (a mere fifteen minutes) to allow the change to occur, even though I always seem to have sufficient time to ruminate about a problem for hours, days, weeks, months, or even years. Interesting, isn't it?

When individuals are exploring within the inner energetic structures, they sometimes experience flashes of images or feelings moving through their inner screen. If you experience this, just maintain the observer state and you will begin to notice that your perceptions and feelings automatically change in the corresponding areas of your life. If you feel yourself "getting stuck" and stopping within any particular perception, or if the thought stays with you after the exploration, this usually indicates that you need to do some heightened energetic exploration with that particular situation. Many levels of information and experiences are state-bound to various levels of energies that the outer mind does not even know exist. These are the experiences that block us from directly feeling, sensing, and experiencing the inner state of unconditional love. Being at a certain energetic vibration, however, allows one to automatically transmute many structures in life. It makes no difference if you explore only one particular aspect of self through unconditional love, because as a result, other areas of your life will also begin to change. Whatever needs to move will move as long as the inner-awareness has awakened and a heightened energy can emerge to bring your awareness into a new outer perspective.

Sometimes individuals sense a strong vibration that seems to quicken when doing these explorations, or they may even feel it later during the day or that night. I remember numerous instances of having awakened from a deep sleep and feeling that the whole room was shaking from an earthquake. On other occasions I have experienced a brilliance of light in a totally dark room and could perceive things as if it were daylight. These experiences and others like them are quite normal as the energetic structures awaken and shift into new perspectives, thus allowing us to move into the unknown awarenesses of reality. Remember, we perceive our reality as we do because of the energetic and brain structures that are in place, and in order to move into another level of perception or into an artistic level of creation, new energetic and brain structures are needed. The seemingly unexplained and unexpected things that you experience as a result of your shifts are all a part of the normal, nurturing process of change. From this perspective, awakening into your creative potential is a wonderful and exciting experience!

I would like to take you through one additional energy body exploration related to the physical body and sports. In EXPLORATION #21: SIT-UPS THROUGH THE SUBTLE ENERGY BODIES, we will explore utilizing the energy bodies to release any blocks that may be present for us, and then to explore the process of transmutation for creating inner changes prior to actually moving the physical body. Once this process has been mastered, many individuals can use it while training in a sport or even while participating in actual competition. We always bring into play some form or image for ourselves when we are in training and/or are participating in the actual game or competition. Why not allow this form or image to be our inner-awareness of heightened energy? This then becomes an exploration into the heightened order of creative functioning as it relates to sports and exercise.

Please follow my instructions related to the number of movements through which I will be guiding you. Often participants enthusiastically do three or four times the number of movements during this initial exploration and consequently wake up very sore the next morning. Your body will move through even more levels of change in this exploration than you experienced within Exploration #8: Mind-Body Education: Inner-Directed. If for any reason you feel uncomfortable or have physical difficulties with the exploration, please stop the inner movements and rest. Remember, this is a process of nurturance, not of the traditional torturous philosophy of "no pain, no gain." In this instance, pain means that you are pushing, and you will not make as much progress. Either seat yourself with ample empty space in front of you, or lie flat on the floor with an empty area beside you. Close your eyes and let's begin.

"Ask that your screen expand *** bring your awareness into the center of your chest, into the heart chakra *** ask to deepen and synchronize your whole triune brain within the color green * blue * violet * and white *** ask to bring your awareness into your potential quadrant * mental quadrant * emotional quadrant * physical quadrant * center point of your screen and heart chakra *** ask your screen to expand again *** focus your inner-awareness at the center point *** deepen your awareness at the heart chakra *** feel the inner self-actualizing pulse deepening and merging with your essence *** ask to expand your screen *** bring your awareness into the physical quadrant, the lower right *** and ask your physical energy body to step out in front of you *** ask your physical energy body to lie down in front of you and to do three sit-ups— one, two, three *** become aware how the physical energy body feels, senses, or images with these sit-ups *** connect your heart center to your physical energy body's heart center and begin the exchange of heart-to-heart energy *** *** now allow your physical energy body to begin to do ten sit-ups— continue with the energetic exchange — one, two, three, four, five, six, seven, eight, nine, ten *** continue to experience a flowing between you and your physical energy body of this energy involved with doing sit-ups *** *** ask your physical energy body to move into the energetic level that is needed to perform the physical movement of sit-ups *** *** ask your physical energy body to slowly merge through your heart back to your physical form, and unify this feeling *** *** ask your screen to expand again *** bring your awareness into the emotional quadrant, the lower left *** and ask your emotional energy body to step out in front of you *** ask your emotional energy body to lie down in front of you and to do three sit-ups— one, two, three *** become aware of how the emotional energy body feels, senses, or images with the sit-ups *** connect your heart center to your emotional energy body's heart center and begin the exchange of heart-to-heart energy *** *** allow your emotional energy body to begin to do ten sit-ups as you continue with the energetic exchange— one, two, three, four, five, six, seven, eight, nine, ten *** continue to experience a flowing of the energy related to doing sit-ups between you and your emotional energy body *** *** ask your emotional energy body to move into the energetic level that is needed to desire and to complete the physical movement of sit-ups *** *** ask your emotional energy body to slowly merge through your heart back into your physical form, and unify this feeling *** *** ask your screen to expand again *** bring your awareness into your mental quadrant, the upper left *** and ask your mental energy body to step out in front of you *** ask your mental energy body to lie down in front of you and to do three sit-ups— one, two, three *** become aware of how the mental energy body feels, senses, or images with the sit-ups *** connect your heart center to your mental energy body's heart center and begin the exchange of heart-to-heart energy *** *** allow your mental energy body to begin to do ten sit-ups as you continue with the energetic exchange— one, two, three, four, five, six, seven, eight, nine, ten *** continue to experience a flowing of the energy between you and your mental energy body *** *** ask your mental energy body to move into the energetic level that is needed to do the physical movement of sit-ups *** *** ask your mental energy body to slowly merge through your heart back into your physical form, and unify this feeling *** *** ask your screen to expand again *** bring your awareness into your potential quadrant, the upper right *** ask your potential energy body to step out in front of you *** ask your potential energy body to lie down in front of you and to do three sit-ups— one, two, three *** become aware how this potential energy body feels, senses, or images with the sit-ups *** connect your heart center to your potential energy body's heart center and begin the exchange of heart-to-heart energy *** *** allow your potential energy body to begin to do ten sit-ups as you continue with the energetic exchange— one, two, three, four, five, six, seven, eight, nine, ten *** continue to experience a flowing of this energy between you and your potential energy body *** *** ask your potential energy body to shift into the energetic level that is needed to perform the physical movement of sit-ups *** *** ask your potential energy body to slowly merge through your heart back into your physical form, and unify this feeling *** *** ask your screen to expand again *** bring your awareness into the center point of your expanded screen at the heart chakra *** and ask your living unified self energy body to step out in front of you *** ask your unified energy body to lie down in front of you and to do three sit-ups— one, two, three *** become aware of how the unified energy body feels, senses, or images with the sit-ups *** connect your heart center to your unified energy body's heart center and begin the exchange of heart-to-heart energy *** *** allow your unified energy body to begin to do ten sit-ups as you continue with the energetic exchange— one, two, three, four, five, six, seven, eight, nine, ten *** continue to experience a flowing of the energy between you and your unified energy body *** *** ask your unified energy body to shift into the energetic level that is needed to perform the physical movement of sit-ups *** *** ask your unified energy body to slowly merge through your heart back into your physical form and ask to unify this feeling spiritually, mentally, emotionally, and physically as your living unified state *** *** ask to expand your screen *** ask your unified energy body to emerge in front of you and to sit down *** do a hand-to-hand and heart-to-heart exchange for one minute *** *** now begin to connect with a joint spiral doing a solar plexus-to-solar plexus *** upper heart-to-upper heart *** spleen-to-spleen *** lower abdomen-to-lower abdomen *** throat-to-throat *** root-to-root *** third eye-to-third eye *** left elbow-to-left elbow *** both knees-to-both knees *** right elbow-to-right elbow *** crown-to-crown *** left hand-to-left hand *** both feet-to-both feet *** right hand-to-right hand *** transpersonal point-to-transpersonal point *** *** and ask to deepen for several minutes within this space of opening yourself into the process of sit-ups *** feeling totally connected to your unified energy body through each chakra *** open into the potential or spiritual quadrant to deepen your new energetic structure and ask to feel and experience yourself doing the sit-ups *** *** ask that energy to merge with your awareness in the mental quadrant *** *** allowing new perceptions, attitudes, and beliefs to emerge, and ask yourself to feel and to experience yourself doing the sit-ups *** *** ask that energy to merge with your awareness in the emotional quadrant *** *** allowing your new living emotions and feelings to move into this inner-awareness, and ask to feel and to experience yourself doing the sit-ups *** *** ask that energy to merge with your awareness in the physical quadrant *** *** allowing your body to live at these new inner feelings and energies, and ask to feel and experience yourself doing the sit-ups *** *** ask that energy to merge with your awareness at the center point, unifying the energy into one living vibration that you can directly feel and experience *** and ask each energy center to adjust its vibration to this living energy *** transpersonal point *** right hand *** both feet *** left hand *** crown *** right elbow *** both knees *** left elbow *** third eye *** root center *** throat *** lower abdomen *** spleen *** upper heart *** solar plexus *** heart chakra *** ask this unified energy body to do a number of sit-ups easily, effortlessly, and at a movement that extends beyond outer time, and whenever your unified energy body stops, honor this *** *** *** have this energy slowly enter your physical form through the heart chakra and merge as one living energy *** *** *** ask this inner actualizing pulsation to slowly move through and beyond your physical body *** *** connecting you with all of time and all of space in this livingness ** *** and allowing your inner-awareness to emerge as your outer awareness *** open your eyes when you are ready *** and if you desire, physically do the sit-ups, allowing your inner-awareness to actually move your physical body a number of times just as you experienced through this exploration *** ***."

Individuals are surprised, after doing the explorations, that their body feels as if their muscles had actually been worked. They were! What becomes important in this process is the realization that some part of your inner-awareness knows how to move into this level of doing sit-ups, easily and without any great effort. Your outer mind has blocked these awarenesses from emerging. Thus you physically have to push yourself into doing the sit-ups since you do not have the inner energetic structures readily available. With this type of exploration, regardless of the sport or exercise, you will be surprised at how quickly and easily you will be able to accomplish the physical movements and create a new level of mastery. Your body will begin to physically change in order to facilitate moving into the images and feelings that occur through the inner exploration. You might even notice an excitement or a desire to perform the physical exercise or sport that you've never felt before. As the process develops for you, you will no longer physically ache or be exhausted after a workout if you allow the inner guidance to pull you along at the pace of change that is awakening within you. When you are performing the physical movement, just allow yourself to move back into and feel the heightened energetic structures as you did during the exploration; in this way you will move naturally into a new space from which to physically create. You will soon discover how easy it is to maintain and explore your outer activities from your inner-awareness.

CHAPTER ELEVEN

LIVING FULLY AWAKE: THE ODYSSEY BEGINS

As you deepen in your own explorations with the subtle energy bodies, you will directly experience how fluid one's perceptions really are. No matter what we may hold as the outer perception of reality concerning ourselves, other individuals, situations in life, or our environment, every perception holds the potential of an inner-awareness. The first step in moving into one's inner-awareness is to allow the focus of consciousness to shift into the observer state, thereby allowing an inner self-actualizing pulse to emerge and change our outer perceptions. The second step is to allow a heightened energy to emerge through one's inner guidance, which will allow us to perceive and interact in life through the inner perceptions of unity. This then moves us into our fourth state of awareness— the heart chakra awareness. Through this process we can begin to bring the alignment of our inner-directed soul guidance into the physical body, thus allowing the intellectual and emotional self to be reeducated. From this perspective our inner-awareness emerges as our outer reality, and we thereby cease living from the separation of our inner and outer awareness. Through this awakening, we move into our post-biological development, allowing ourselves to live from the heightened states of creative energies. In this way we can experience new levels of artistic and physical abilities in every aspect of life, thus joining the next evolutionary leap into man's human potential!

Through the process of perceptual shifting, we come to realize that every perception is state-bound to a certain energetic vibration and that we continually have the choice to create from any one of the many levels of exciting perceptions. There are several different methods which can be utilized to personally explore this. The first method is through the process of the subtle energy bodies which we experienced in the last chapter. In this way we are able to directly feel or inwardly sense how a particular issue is being experienced and, through awakening the heart energies, can alter our inner experiences into a new level of creation. This new level can then be brought directly into one's outer reality and feedback can be derived from the levels and depths of change that have occurred. I have seen individuals become so startled by the ease and depth of change resulting from this form of exploration, that they initially think they must be tricking their body into believing they can do this, since they have experienced change so quickly and easily! In a way they are correct, because they did trick their body into doing something. But from this same framework of thought, they must then admit to likewise tricking the mind and body whenever they are unable to perform some specific activity.

Another form of perceptual shifting occurs when, in order to allow a new perspective to emerge, you permit your inner guidance to alter your various levels of perceptions. Utilize EXPLORATION #15: AWAKENING YOUR CREATIVE POTENTIAL and, each time that you shift from one color to the next, become aware that you are also shifting into the next level of inner-directed guidance and ask to perceive the situation you are exploring. Once you have perceived it at that given level, ask for any additional clarity to emerge. Then just put aside your question and deepen into the next area of your inner guidance with the next color, asking it to move throughout your triune brain. When this is complete, allow yourself to again view the perception, ask questions, put them aside, and deepen into the next area. By the time you have completed the exploration, you will either no longer be aware of why you perceived this particular situation as a problem in the first place, or you will have difficulty in recalling what the problem or situation was all about. From that point you can shift into EXPLORATION #20: TRANSMUTATION THROUGH THE ENERGY BODIES and allow a new level of energetic inner-awarenesses to emerge.

A third form of perceptual shifting can be explored while watching a television show or listening to a debate or radio talk show. Allow your focus to shift to each of the various energy centers and become aware of the varied feelings, body reactions, sensations, and inner-awarenesses that emerge through each of the different chakras. Do this by focusing first at the level of the third eye and allowing all of your energy to be focused there, similar to the process we explored through the heart chakra. Maintain your focus at this level and allow yourself to listen or even interact with another person while holding these emerging perceptions. Then shift into your solar plexus and interact in the same way. Then focus through the sexual center or lower abdomen. Then focus at the heart chakra using EXPLORATION #10: DIRECT ACCESS INTO YOUR INNER-DIRECTED GUIDANCE. Maintain each one of the designated focuses for at least five to ten minutes, and become aware of what transpires for you. Another means of experiencing this is to tape a specific dialogue or debate between two people. Then listen to it through each of the different energy centers and become aware of the perspective that emerges. Listen to it focused solely through the third eye; play it again and listen through the solar plexus; then through the lower abdomen; and through the heart. You will find this to be very enlightening. In my supervision classes, I teach the students to utilize a process of perceptual shifting (instead of using traditional methods) for practicing their listening and communication skills. They quickly become aware of how changed their verbal communication and listening skills become without having made any effort to affect a form of outer change. Merely by moving into the direct access of their inner guidance, they are able to shift whatever they are saying or hearing into a different perspective, thus changing the outcome of any situation they are exploring.

A fourth method of perceptual shifting is similar to the one just explained, except that in this process you listen to a piece of music while focused within each of the various energy centers. Become aware of how your physical body changes, as well as how the forms of images and memories that are released vary as you move through each one of the chakras.

A fifth method of perceptual shifting involves allowing yourself to connect with another individual or group of individuals using EXPLORATION #11: EXPLORING THE ENERGIES OF UNCONDITIONAL LOVE. However, instead of focusing at the heart chakra, focus from one of the other energy centers. Once you have opened into the inner collective space, listen to a piece of music or a taped dialogue, or even carry on a conversation with someone. Then allow yourself to shift and repeat the process through each of the other energy centers. You will be surprised at how easily one can maintain a certain perspective and how easily some individuals can induct others into a like focus. You will notice that the same potential exists for inducting other individuals into the focus of the heart and the feeling states of unconditional love.

By the time you have moved through these various forms of perceptual shifting, it will hopefully become difficult for you to cling to your old belief that the 2% of reality is all that exists. As some inner part of you awakens, you will have a desire to emerge into and explore other levels of your own unknown awareness. Learning to live in a fully awakened state can be compared to the process athletes explore when competing in the sporting event called a Triathlon. In a triathlon an individual trains and competes in three different competitive sports—swimming, cycling, and running. The Hawaiian Ironman Triathlon requires over nine continuous straight hours of performance in order to complete the 2.4-mile swim, the 112-mile bike ride, and the 26.2-mile run. I know competitive athletes who would have difficulty finishing just one of these areas, let alone all three. Likewise, learning to live in a fully awakened state asks individuals to encompass a totally new kind of mind-set in expanding their capabilities and potentials to live from the heightened energetic states of creative functioning.

Living in a fully awakened state is not just learning how to meditate and maintain an inner silence; nor is it merely learning how to eliminate old habit patterns; nor is it learning to shift into the now moment—it is all of these and more! I believe that "living fully awake" is the triathlon of consciousness whereby one lives and creates within the everyday world. It is, first, learning to explore the depths of inner silence that are achieved in the mental, emotional, physical, and spiritual areas while in a meditative state, and then allowing this inner state to be brought forward and lived as one's normal level of functioning. Secondly, it is allowing the heightened energetic states of one's self-actualizing pulse to be fully present and experienced within all outer activities—from walking, running, shopping, working, studying and making love to the "chopping of wood and the carrying of water." Finally, it is the process of allowing an inner-directed guidance to move through one's physical form, awakening us to perceive, communicate and interact with one another and with everything we do from a totally new and creative way. This constitutes living in the now moment.

The triathlon state of consciousness is not achieved by living within the boundaries of our outer senses; nor is it achieved by viewing our guidance or mind as being contained by new limits and boundaries; nor is it achieved through the exploration of the psychic phenomena of the inner subjective world. It is achieved as we allow an exploration into the 98% of the unknown awareness, where we can directly experience this form of consciousness within our own physical bodies. It makes no difference whether we term this inner-directed consciousness as being a form of one's guidance, soul, spirit, mind, or divine aspect. We know it exists without limits, and that it has the potential to direct us through what we call the boundaries of our physical reality. This awakens us to our inner creative potential while achieving a heightened state of creative energies.

Our final exploration will deal with the process of learning how to live from one's inner-directed guidance. I consider the explorations in this book to be the foundation of awakening to one's inner creative potential. Through my own personal explorations I firmly believe there exists a heightened creative energy within each human being, and that our existence has evolved into the exploration of this inherent creative process. I also sense that a similar mechanism of creative energy exists which allows for a comparable foundation for all of our structures of reality. Since this heightened creative force is an inherent part of our existence, I do not believe that an individual can be taught such a form of creativity. The only thing that I can offer other human beings is a process that will allow them to shift from one level of perceiving reality into another. Whenever the inner timing awakens, an inner guiding force will reach into the heart of that person and begin to guide them through the next phase of creative functioning— their post-biological development. Through the awakened self-actualizing energy, we are then able as human beings to live simultaneously on two levels of existence. One part of our existence maintains an inner-awareness which allows us to perceive and to be guided through a multidimensional nonlinear structure of reality that operates within unrestricted levels of both time and space; and, secondly, we are simultaneously living and creating within a linear structure of our outer world. Learning to coexist within these two levels of our existence is what I believe constitutes the next evolutionary leap in man's awareness. Through the process of coexistence, a new form of human being will develop, one who is fully awakened to the inner essence and who can function by channeling a new order of heightened creative energies into all aspects of living.

Let's now begin EXPLORATION #22: LIVING FULLY AWAKE. "Sit in a comfortable position, but one from which you can easily stand up *** close your eyes for a moment *** ask to expand your screen and simultaneously focus and awaken at the heart *** ask the energies to open within that inner space and ask them to pulsate throughout and beyond your physical body into the room or space around you *** allow your eyes to partially open, seeing through what I call relaxed-eyes *** ask your screen to expand and, except for when otherwise instructed, keep your eyes in the gently relaxed-eyes position *** *** allow your screen to continue expanding until you can feel the inner pulsation moving *** *** now open your eyes very wide *** do you notice how the energy shifts and no longer is as free flowing *** allow your eyes to slowly relax and move into a space where your eyes are open *** but that still allows you to maintain your previous level of inner-awareness *** *** slowly move your hands out in front of you while maintaining this inner flow *** *** you are now coexisting between the two spaces— inner and outer *** *** feel yourself 'turning on' with the colors green * blue * violet * white * first within the old brain *** then in the mid-brain *** the neocortex *** the connective point *** as this deepens within you, notice that your boundaries are becoming more fluid and soft *** ask your eyes to flicker several times and let them shift into a deeper inner focus, still being open and relaxed *** *** ask the heart energies to deepen and connect directly with the old brain *** ask it to expand your hearing *** ask the boundaries to move beyond you and attune to the sounds in the room *** ask your energies to deepen and expand into your eyes *** allowing another inner shift to emerge through your outer perception *** to move into your hands and feet, similar to the process of energy exchange *** into your throat in order that your words are spoken from this inner space *** softly say your name out loud *** ask that your name be called out to you from within this inner space *** ask your brain to adjust and deepen into an inner focus *** ask that inner focus to deepen in its outer awareness *** stand and walk around the room, maintaining the inner feelings and structures *** *** ask your eyes to open wide and notice what happens *** ask to expand and refocus at the heart *** ask that you can create this inner coexistence at any time and in any place that you desire *** *** ask for the energies to adjust to maintain this gentle, loving inner touch *** maintain this as your natural existence."

You will be surprised at how easily this will evolve as your natural state of living if you will regularly allow yourself the time and nuturing to utilize this last exploration. Many individuals report that once they have awakened into the heightened energy, they naturally move into the inner spaces without having to ask. It is at this point that an individual truly has begun to live from the third phase of the Transformational Process, where no separation exists between external and internal reality, for both are felt and experienced as being one and the same. This can occur only at the levels of coexistence and unity that we have been exploring together in this phase of our odyssey.

I have seen thousands of individuals successfully explore these processes since 1983, allowing themselves to move through various levels of personal transformation. Individuals who have experienced a life threatening illness have begun to live very productive lives, and in some cases are free of their illness. Others have found a profound peace in their process of dying. I have observed individuals who previously were physically limited by pain or injuries but who are now living a life in which only a memory of those times exists. I have assisted individuals in exploring these processes to enhance their growth in the areas of music, art, teaching, business, addictions, child birth, parenting, financial structures, relationships, and every other aspect of living. The process of awakening one's creative potential is not a cure, nor an end in itself; rather, it is merely the beginning of a journey into both a personal and planetary transformation where we can be guided on an individual and collective basis into our own inner potentials for living.

If you will explore this entire process as a step-by-step journey, you will immediately realize there are new choices to face at every step along life's way. You will no longer be capable of feeling or thinking that no other choices or options exist; you will automatically realize that you can either maintain your current feelings and perceptions or allow them to shift into an inner-awareness. Initially the awareness of the choices available to you in life creates a vibrant feeling of aliveness and joy. You know that at some point you will get it right! But in time you will begin to realize that every perception that you hold today has the potential to deepen into yet another unified structure. There always exists another level of perception to explore. In some situations these perceptions will be very minor, while others will awaken you into a totally new inner level of awareness. It is at this point that most individuals begin to feel overwhelmed by the number of existing possibilities. Some stop their process at this point and allow the familiar crisis or reactive situation to once again emerge. Many others, however, maintain their excitement and truly learn to allow the inner-directed guiding force of their heart to nurture them and guide them through the inner realms of their outer world.

Once individuals open to the levels of inner-awareness, they begin to understand what is meant by exploring the 98% of unknown reality and why so few individuals ever go beyond the traditional 2 or 3%. Many individuals do journey beyond the 2% at various times during their lives, but they often turn back, due to the fears and apprehensions related to the vast opportunities that lie in wait for them in the levels of the unknown. I believe that if individuals can maintain an inner quiet and allow the self-actualizing pulse to emerge, they will eventually be able to perceive that any given perception is but one level of what reality truly has to offer. These remarkable levels of inner guidance are available for all human beings to explore, regardless of what their outer situation may be bringing forward. We miss much of our inner guidance and information due to the external mental noise, the emotional fears and doubts, the perceptions of our physical limitations, and the very restricted concept of our spiritual self as it relates to all aspects of life. When we can at last allow the inner spiritual emergence to awaken and become the guiding light through our odyssey of life, we will then feel an inner security and love that few human beings have heretofore ever experienced. This is the process of learning to live in a fully awakened state.

Throughout my day I spend time in a process that I call free-falling, whereby I open into EXPLORATION #16: EXPLORING THE ESSENCE OF UNITY or EXPLORATION #15: AWAKENING YOUR CREATIVE POTENTIAL. During this time I refocus my awareness into my inner self-actualizing pulse, and allow my inner guidance to emerge and "pull" me along within the "black-out space" that I earlier described. As I move back into an outer awareness I then allow myself to shift into EXPLORATION #22: LIVING FULLY AWAKE and move into the level of coexistence. Exploring this process several times per day, the first thing in the morning, at mid-day and in the early evening, allows me to feel alert and alive for 18 to 20 hours per day. Whenever I find myself caught in a situation that moves me out of this focus, I allow myself to immediately move into a level of refocusing by utilizing EXPLORATION #22, and later in the day, EXPLORATION #20: TRANSMUTATION THROUGH THE ENERGY BODIES. These various processes truly are effective, if I will just allow myself the time to explore. If I do not, there is a part of me that "falls asleep while I am physically awake," and I begin to create and react to life from the traditional perspective that the 2% is the only reality that exists. The rest of my journey then feels as though it is nothing more than a distant dream. When I finally "awaken to being fully alive" I can perceive very clearly what I need to do. It is so simple, and yet, oh, so very hard!

In bringing forward **Awaken Your Creative Potential**, I have fulfilled a deep and profound dream within the essence of my own being. I now stand at this point of coexistence ready to explore my next levels of unknown awareness. I await with eagerness and excitement the emergence of the next pulse in my continuing phase of human development. As I move from this present phase of my journey I would like to again share my current understanding of my purpose of being human, in the hope that it may in some way also lend meaning and fulfillment to your purpose:

> **"In exploring this odyssey through life,**
> **I am to awaken to my inner heritage of being a creative**
>   **human being;**
> **I am to open to all of life that manifests this Divine**
>   **Essence;**
> **I am to create and live from this union of the Divine**
>   **with my physical body, allowing the focus of my**

awareness to be within the rhythm of my inner
heart, from which each thought, feeling, and
image emerges.
Through this inner awakening of my self-actualizing
energy, my own livingness will emerge into a
heightened order of creativity.
And thus evolves the next evolutionary leap into our
human potential!"

Conrad Satala
April 1988
Fort Wayne, Indiana

EPILOGUE

I would like to introduce you to Joy Heinbaugh. She has greatly assisted me in allowing the information that I have brought forward to move into the final edited version of this book. Through a series of meditations that began in December of 1986, I was given information about a person who would begin the process of editing a book with me which would be called **Awaken Your Creative Potential**. Although I was not shown the physical image of this person, nor his/her name, I was told when the time was right for me to seriously write this book, he/she would come forward. I would know it was the "right" person, as they would consistently share with me their feelings related to the importance of being involved with this project, although not necessarily understanding why.

I first met Joy in the fall of 1986, in a class I was exploring at the center, and subsequently she decided to enroll for a trip I was offering that spring to the Mayan ruins in the Yucatan Peninsula of Mexico. Throughout this time, I was unaware of Joy's dream to write and to be a teacher of consciousness. But during the summer of 1987, she began to experience a series of dreams and information emerging from her meditations indicating that she was to assist me in the editing of this book. At this point, no one knew of my own earlier meditations concerning the emergence of such an individual.

At first this all seemed very strange to Joy, and she pushed aside her feelings and images. But during the next several weeks they became so strong that she decided to share her feelings with several of my associates and with my wife, Ilene. They all encouraged her to share them with me. After several brief meetings, I knew she was the person for whom I was waiting, which also meant that I was in position to begin my "serious" writing.

I had already attempted several books in the past few years, and I was to attempt one other book in early 1987 before I would begin in August of that year to seriously write this book. I was curious about the information I received from my inner guidance dealing with my being "seriously ready to write." How many books did I need to try to create before I moved into the necessary inner space? In each of the previously attempted books I had brought forward clear linear information about transformation. These works focused on the techniques and the end result of transformation. I later realized that they all lacked one small but vital element— my own personal journey and process of transformation through this odyssey. Once I decided to give up the outer structure regarding how I thought this book should evolve, it became clear that none of the previous information would fit into the new book. Thus, I began again, and in less than three weeks time I had written nearly 200 pages, all without ever knowing the exact direction that the book would be taking. Yet, when I later read what I had written, the information and the process of the journey integrated in ways that I would never have been able to structure intellectually. Once again I felt compelled to put my writing aside for another three months. There was a difference, however, between putting this book aside and my putting all of the other ones aside. This time, everything that I felt, saw, touched, and experienced in life seemed to revolve around the information that was emerging for the book, and yet the inner timing did not yet dictate completing the manuscript. Between Christmas and New Year's of 1987, I realized the time was right, and within the next few weeks I rewrote over 60% of what I had previously completed in August, added an additional 100 pages, totally altered the structure and chapter divisions of the book, and was able to add several important points that had previously been missing. This became one of the most creative and productive periods of my life, and yet I felt no stress or tension.

During the following two and one-half months, with the aid of Joy, I was involved in the editing of the manuscript. At the same time, I was exploring the physical creation of the book by working with the typesetting, marketing, cover design and coordination of various other aspects in order to bring the book into its final form by early April of 1988. In addition, I maintained a very active teaching, consulting, and travel schedule. The publication of this book from the inner process is in itself a testimony to the fact that the concepts brought forward in this book do work. I was able to allow myself to move into a heightened level of creativ functioning, and as I allowed the inner self-actualizing energy to emerge, it took me into directions that my outer mind declared were impossible to create. At every moment I had a choice to either spend my time thinking about all that had to be accomplished or to utilize my time being inwardly focused and creating. There was never time to do both!

I realized that the job of editing encompassed a very important and critical role. The editor had to be sensitive to the inner flow of the ideas that emerged from the author, yet allowing some structures to be changed while still maintaining the author's energetic direction. Joy was able to explore this process with me in very deep and profound ways. One morning in my meditation, I envisioned the cover of the book including the phrase "with the assistance of Joy Heinbaugh." I immediately realized the importance of her direct involvement in the timely completion of this project. I realized that direct acknowledgement of this was extremely important for both of us. This resonated on some very deep inner level within my own heart. Thus Joy had become a very important element in the process of editing this book.

Joy describes her ultimate involvement in the process of publication as follows:

"I inwardly know that my involvement with this literary work is far more intricate and complex than outer appearances portray. Although I cannot relate even to myself all of the multifaceted reasons for my participation in editing this book, it is sufficient to know that it is vital to my own growth and life's purpose, as well as to that of many others."

I personally thank Joy for following and acting upon her own level of inner guidance with each step of this odyssey.

In the course of working with many groups, I have explored several hundred different explorations devoted primarily to creating a foundation series for awakening others to the awareness of their own inner-directed soul guidance and unknown inner spaces. I have also developed some one hundred other explorations devoted to awakening the capabilities for us as human beings to coexist within the simultaneous levels of our inner existence. I plan in late 1988 to complete a companion workbook utilizing these explorations in the daily aspects of living, and in early 1989 to complete two other books that will explore specific aspects of the process of coexistence. One will deal with the physical body in allowing the inner self-actualizing energies to emerge into new levels of physical functioning; the other will explore the process of creating transformational organizations, which will include the area of financial awareness.

I am available to conduct seminars throughout the country in exploring the basic foundation material that is presented within this book. I also conduct group explorations in the process of dreams and healing rituals, which play a significant role in personal and planetary transformation. These processes can also be utilized in conjunction with flotation tanks, which provide yet another avenue for exploring one's inner depths.

ACKNOWLEDGMENT

Profound love and appreciation —
John Cottrell — soul support and editing of linear
material
Sharlene Edelstein — soul support and editing of linear
material
Linda Kroells — editing and transcription
Sharon Moore — soul support and confirmation
Ilene Rush-Satala — friend, lover, companion, and
profound soul support
Jeanne Sylvia — soul support
Victoria Wilson — soul support
To my initial friends who began this odyssey with me —
Charles, Jack, Jacqueline, Linda, Michael, Myra,
Norm, Ronn, Robert, Steven, Yvonne
The teaching staff at The Center For Mindbody
Education in Fort Wayne, Indiana — Kathren, David,
Beth, Nicholas, Sharon, Edith, Mary, Henry, Rosalie,
Janine, Jeanne, Lee, Beverly, Diane, Patricia, David,
Lois, Pat, Richard
The staff at The Center For Creative Expression in San
Luis Obispo, California — Carol, Nancy, Anna, Susan,
Lillian, Melissa, Ginny, Marcie, Sandra, Sandra Rose,
Marcy, Sue, Vicki, Jacque, Gail
The seminar participants and friends in Fort Wayne and
San Luis Obispo
Two important outer teachers in my odyssey —
Brugh Joy and Carolyn Conger